Against Immediate Evil

Against Immediate Evil

*American Internationalists
and the Four Freedoms on the Eve
of World War II*

Andrew Johnstone

Cornell University Press
Ithaca and London

First published 2014 by Cornell University Press

Printed in the United States of America

Library of Congress Cataloging-in-Publication Data

Johnstone, Andrew (Andrew E.), author.
   Against immediate evil : American internationalists and the four freedoms on the eve of World War II / Andrew Johnstone.
      pages cm
   Includes bibliographical references and index.
   ISBN 978-0-8014-5325-0 (cloth : alk. paper)
  1. United States—Foreign relations—1933–1945—Public opinion.
2. Internationalism—History—20th century. 3. Neutrality—United States—History—20th century. 4. Public opinion—United States—History—20th century. I. Title.
   E744.J665   2014
   327.73009'04—dc23   2014014717

Cornell University Press strives to use environmentally responsible suppliers and materials to the fullest extent possible in the publishing of its books. Such materials include vegetable-based, low-VOC inks and acid-free papers that are recycled, totally chlorine-free, or partly composed of nonwood fibers. For further information, visit our website at www.cornellpress.cornell.edu.

Cloth printing   10 9 8 7 6 5 4 3 2 1

Contents

Acknowledgments

This book has been many years in the making. The first archival research took place back in 2007, but the project was put on the back burner as other more immediate article writing and book editing projects took priority. Four years passed before I was able to give this book anything like my full attention again, but one advantage of the lengthy development time was that it helped me to clarify exactly what I wanted to do. So what began as a relatively straightforward investigation into three internationalist organizations developed into a more detailed investigation of their motivations. This was inspired by the idea that too many histories of the years immediately before America's entry into World War II adopted an overly narrative approach that saw the United States slowly inch closer to war before war ultimately came to America with the attack on Pearl Harbor. Conversations with colleagues reassured me that I was not alone in feeling that too many works on this period adopted a "war comes to America" approach that failed to sufficiently highlight internationalist impulses in the United States prior to 1941, impulses that subsequently developed dramatically during the war and beyond.

Another result of the book's lengthy development is that there are a lot of people I want and need to thank for their various forms of support, without which this book would not have been completed. First, I must thank the archivists at the National Archives at College Park, the Library of Congress, the Franklin D. Roosevelt Library, the Seeley G. Mudd Library at Princeton University, the Houghton and Baker Libraries at Harvard University, Columbia University, the University of Virginia, and New York Public Library. Their assistance helped me find the vast array of primary sources this book is based upon, most of which were photocopied in 2007 and digitally photographed in 2011 and 2012.

I must also thank a number of bodies for the financial support that made the completion of the book possible. To undertake the first archival research trip in 2007, I received two grants: a grant-in-aid from the Franklin and Eleanor Roosevelt Institute and a Small Research Grant from the British Academy. This enabled me to start working on the broader project in earnest, and early thoughts can be found in my chapter in *The U.S. Public and American Foreign Policy*, a book I co-edited with Helen Laville, published by Routledge in 2010. Subsequent research trips were partially funded by the University of Leicester. To write the book I was freed from teaching duties in 2012. For the first half of the year this was thanks to research leave from the University of Leicester; in the latter part of the year it was thanks to an Arts and Humanities Research Council Early Career Fellowship. Without this assistance, this book would have taken even longer to complete.

I also thank various individuals who have helped me clarify my ideas on this project and provided a wide range of advice on everything from interpretation to research funding. At the University of Leicester these include numerous colleagues from the School of History and the Centre for American Studies, among them James Campbell, Martin Halliwell, Andy Hopper, Norman Housley, Prashant Kidambi, Zoe Knox, George Lewis, and Roey Sweet. From further afield, I thank a number of academics who have provided many different types of support, from suggestions at conferences to references for grant applications. This list includes Brooke Blower, Steven Casey, David Ekbladh, Warren Kimball, Helen Laville, Scott Lucas, Christopher McKnight Nichols, Inderjeet Parmar, Andrew Priest, Katharina Rietzler, Simon Rofe, James C. Schneider, John Thompson, and Carl Watts. I'm sure there are others—you know who you are, even if I have forgotten. Some of these people may not even have realized they were helping me, but I can assure you I am extremely grateful for something.

I must also thank Michael McGandy and everyone at Cornell University Press for helping this project through to publication. I met Michael when the project had barely begun, yet he continued to remember who I was at conferences every year or two, encouraging me to let him know when I started writing. When I finally had something for him to look at, he was extremely supportive, no doubt relieved that the barely published academic he met in 2007 had produced something worthwhile.

Outside academia, I thank my friends and family, who have encouraged me through the last few years and have frequently asked what I was working on and how I was progressing, usually (as far as I could tell) with a sincere and genuine interest. I'd also like to thank them for giving me distractions that had nothing at all to do with the book. These particularly include old friends such as Mat, Jams,

Phil, Muttley, Andy, Stinger, Tim, and Ben, at least one of whom will buy this book purely because my name is on the cover. This group also includes relatives and near relatives on the East Coast of the United States, such as Ruth and Ray, Dick and Pat, Bev and Dan, and Janet and Raymond, whose hospitality made long archival trips much easier to bear. Finally, it includes the many members of the mighty Aylestone Athletic RFC, who show far more genuine interest in my work than I could possibly have expected (especially Dan Hapgood, whose knowledge of Grover Cleveland's nonconsecutive presidential terms is as impressive as it is irrelevant to this book).

On a more personal level, I thank my parents, Bob and June, who have always been a never-ending source of support. Finally, I thank Zoe for her constant love and encouragement. I hope she knows just how much she means to me.

Abbreviations

ACNPJA	American Committee for Non-Participation in Japanese Aggression
AUCPE	American Union for Concerted Peace Efforts
CEIP	Carnegie Endowment for International Peace
CCPE	Committee for Concerted Peace Efforts
CDAAA	Committee to Defend America by Aiding the Allies
CSOP	Commission to Study the Organization of Peace
FFF	Fight for Freedom
LNA	League of Nations Association
NPC	Non-Partisan Committee for Peace through Revision of the Neutrality Law
USSR	Union of Soviet Socialist Republics

Introduction

Four Freedoms

On December 7, 1941, the Japanese attack on Pearl Harbor brought the United States into World War II. Four days later, after both Germany and Italy also declared war on the United States, the United States became involved in ongoing wars in Asia and Europe. In a fireside chat to the nation, President Franklin Roosevelt explained to the American people why the nation was at war. "The sudden criminal attacks perpetrated by the Japanese in the Pacific provide the climax of a decade of international immorality. Powerful and resourceful gangsters have banded together to make war upon the whole human race." In the face of such aggression, despite the setbacks of the previous days, the American people needed to remain strong and determined. The United States would win the war and win the peace that followed, as American force would be directed "toward ultimate good as well as against immediate evil."[1]

Yet while the attack on Pearl Harbor brought home the destructive nature of that evil, the preceding years had seen most Americans want little or nothing to do with the ongoing conflicts in Europe and Asia. The prevailing mood in the United States was one that has been commonly described as isolationist, though it is more accurately characterized as non-interventionist. At the height of non-interventionism in the spring of 1937, 94 percent of Americans favored efforts to keep out of war entirely over efforts to prevent war. As late as November 1941, despite clear evidence of fascist expansionism, opinion polls revealed that barely a quarter of Americans wanted an actual declaration of war against Germany, let alone Japan. This non-interventionist sentiment has been examined in considerable detail by historians who have attempted to understand why the United States seemed so unwilling to stand up to fascist aggression and engage with world affairs more broadly in the 1930s.[2]

Less well examined are those Americans who made the case for greater American involvement in world affairs prior to 1941. This book focuses on those internationalist Americans who worked to influence both the American government and the wider public about the need to stem the growing tide of fascist aggression. In particular, it focuses on three organized groups of American citizens: the American Committee for Non-Participation in Japanese Aggression, the Committee to Defend America by Aiding the Allies, and Fight for Freedom. Though they were initially in the minority, these Americans felt that world affairs—and the looming clouds of war in particular—could not be ignored. As the global situation worsened, they called for steps that moved the United States further from isolation and neutrality and closer and closer to conflict. By urging restrictions on trade with Japan, greater military support for Britain, and ultimately an American declaration of war before the Hawaiian attack, these organizations actively promoted a more global role for the United States between 1938 and 1941, long before war came to America. It is the aim of this book to examine the organization, activity, and ideas of these internationalist citizens' groups in order to understand the nature of internationalism on the eve of World War II.

While it is possible to examine American internationalism in this period through an examination of President Roosevelt, his administration, or other key intellectuals from the time, these organizations (and their organizational predecessors) have been chosen for four reasons. First, these private citizens' organizations were able to speak openly about foreign affairs and America's stake in the world; in contrast, political constraints meant that Roosevelt was rarely so bold, especially prior to 1941. Second, unlike other long-standing citizens' groups such as the Foreign Policy Association and the League of Nations Association, these three organizations were created very specifically to respond to the escalating world crises. Third, they sought to directly influence the political process. Unlike some smaller organizations created during this period that took a more abstract approach to educating the public (such as the Council for Democracy and Friends of Democracy), these three organizations attempted not only to educate but to translate that education into direct political action.

Finally, building on the previous point, these organizations provide an insight into the relationship between politics and public opinion in the United States. All three played a key part in the great debate over the direction of American foreign policy on the eve of World War II. As war approached, and especially following the outbreak of war in Europe in 1939, foreign affairs dominated the political agenda. Throughout this period, Roosevelt made numerous references to the power of public opinion. After the passage of the Lend-Lease Act in 1941, Roosevelt stated that "we have just now engaged in a great debate. It was not limited to the halls of Congress. It was argued in every newspaper, on every wave length, over every cracker barrel in all the land; and it was finally settled and decided by the American people themselves." Such references to "public opinion" and the "American people" were not simply lip service to a democratic ideal; Roosevelt was all too sensitive to the power of the people. The new social science of opinion polling brought the views of the nation to Washington on a regular basis. But that mass opinion was also represented through citizens' organizations that sprang up to symbolize the public mood, mobilize the American people, and influence the government.[3]

This project began with the aim of addressing a number of related issues with both broad and specific implications, but the underlying question was this: Why did many Americans want their country to play a more active world role prior to December 1941? This book examines the combination of political, economic, cultural, and security considerations that led them to such a position. More simply, it highlights the global aspirations of many Americans not just prior to the Cold War but before the nation joined the fight against fascism in 1941. The United States did not simply go from isolationism in 1941 to superpower status in 1945, and this book tells the story of the organizations that first made the case for that transition.

To examine this underlying question, a number of more specific issues are addressed. The significance of the key internationalist organizations of this period is assessed in detail. The aims, structures, and leadership of the organizations are examined in depth, as are their views on key policy debates. Links between the different organizations are evaluated, and the tensions and divisions between them are highlighted. To address these issues, this analysis has undertaken a detailed examination of the activity, writing, and rhetoric—both public and private—of all three organizations and of those individuals who led them.

Yet this is more than a bureaucratic history.[4] It also looks to situate these organizations within the wider body politic. It does this by considering how these internationalist organizations sought to mobilize and represent the wider American public opinion around them. In addition, it examines the role they played in the creation of American foreign policy and how effective they were at influencing the Roosevelt administration. This analysis brings us closer to an understanding of American internationalism—what it stood for, who represented it, and how it functioned—in the crucial years immediately prior to American entry into World War II.

The Organizations

The first and least well known organization under consideration is the American Committee for Non-Participation in Japanese Aggression (ACNPJA). It was established in August 1938, just over a year after the Japanese invasion of China. The organization's title successfully—if not succinctly—outlined its aim: to limit the ways in which the United States directly and indirectly assisted the aggressive Japanese war effort. In terms of personnel, the initial driving force was the missionary Harry Price. Of great significance as the committee developed was its president, the former Foreign Service member Roger Greene. From January 1939, its honorary chairman was former secretary of state and future secretary of war Henry Stimson. (The ACNPJA was occasionally referred to as the Price Committee but also as the Stimson Committee.) Other big names adding prestige to the group included former Harvard president A. Lawrence Lowell, *Emporia (Kansas) Gazette* editor William Allen White, and retired commander in chief of the U.S. Asiatic Fleet, H. E. Yarnell.

The ACNPJA kept a very tight focus on urging Congress to limit credit and the sale of war material to Japan. Their narrow focus reflected a concern for the victims of aggression and a feeling of guilt regarding American complicity in that aggression. This in turn reflected the missionary tendency in the organization's origins. The group admitted that "doctrinal isms, domestic issues, and the European situation, however important, are beyond its scope." This approach recognized the strength of wider non-interventionist trends in American public opinion at the time. While the Japanese were clearly the aggressor in Asia, even internationalist leaders were reluctant to promote wider embargoes on material to Japan, let alone policies that might draw the United States closer to conflict, such as aid to China. After the outbreak of war in Europe, however, the focus of the American people shifted to Europe, and the ACNPJA's single-issue approach saw its influence fade as 1940 progressed. Nevertheless, the work of the American Committee for Non-Participation in Japanese Aggression reveals the first steps of internationalist organization on the eve of war. Just as important, it reveals that American internationalism had an Asian dimension.[5]

The largest and most well-known internationalist organization to develop between the outbreak of war in Europe and Pearl Harbor was the Committee to Defend America by Aiding the Allies (CDAAA). Created in May 1940 in response to the dramatic German advances in Europe, the committee had more than eight hundred chapters by December 1941. Its origins lay in the conservative wing of the peace movement and can be traced through 1939 and 1940 in the work of two predecessor organizations, the American Union for Concerted Peace Efforts (AUCPE) and the Non-Partisan Committee for Peace through Revision of the Neutrality Law (NPC). Based in New York out of the offices of the League of Nations Association (LNA), the CDAAA included a number of ACNPJA members and was initially chaired by William Allen White. As a midwesterner and lifelong Republican, White provided geographical and political cover for an organization wary of being seen as part of a liberal eastern elite, and White was so closely associated with the CDAAA that it was frequently referred to as the White Committee (though this was also due to the cumbersome nature of the committee's full title). However, the CDAAA was far more than simply William Allen White's committee. Behind the scenes, the driving force of the organization was Clark Eichelberger, director of the LNA, and the CDAAA continued to grow after White's resignation in January 1941.

The committee's title may not have been elegant, but it was accurate, as its purpose was to urge the United States to provide all possible aid to Britain after the fall of France. The committee's opening statement of purpose argued that the war in Europe represented "a life and death struggle for every principle we cherish in America" and that it was time for the United States to "throw its economic and moral weight on the side of the nations of western Europe, great and small, that are struggling in battle for a civilized way of life." Unlike the ACNPJA, the CDAAA was focused largely on European matters, reflecting the greater public interest in the aggression of Nazi Germany. It was also far more willing to provide aid to those opposing aggression, rather than simply wishing to avoid assisting aggression. As a result, the CDAAA played a significant role in the debates through 1940 and 1941 over the destroyer-bases exchange, the Lend-Lease Act, and Atlantic convoying. It did not, however, go so far as to call for war.[6]

That final step was left to Fight for Freedom (FFF). This new group evolved out of a more informal collective that had been created the previous summer, known either as the Century Group (after the exclusive Century Club location where it met) or as the Miller Group (after one of its leaders, Francis Pickens Miller). Many were also CDAAA members but had become impatient with the CDAAA's unwillingness to take the final step to call for war. Once the Lend-Lease Act was passed in March 1941 enabling maximum aid to the Allies, the CDAAA was seen by some to have reached its natural conclusion, and with no significant new policy from the CDAAA, Fight for Freedom was announced to the public in April 1941. Like the ACNPJA and the CDAAA, it had a prominent figurehead in its honorary chairman, Senator Carter Glass, and its chairman was the Reverend Henry Hobson of Ohio. Like the other organizations, however, FFF was driven largely by one of its less well-known members, in this case Ulric Bell, formerly of the *Louisville Courier Journal,* who served as chairman of the executive committee.

The more militant FFF agitated for full American involvement in the war. It argued that the world conflicts represented an "irreconcilable struggle between dictatorship and freedom, and that if dictatorship wins in the present area of conflict, there will be little hope for freedom anywhere. We therefore represent all citizens who share our convictions that this is our fight for freedom in which we must play our full part." Bell admitted that the organization was in the propaganda business—for "propagation of the truth." As the government was "not equipped to mobilize and channelize public opinion," FFF filled a need, representing a "real and insistent demand from thousands of citizens, high and low, for a medium through which to express their views."[7]

From its creation, FFF fought alongside the CDAAA to educate public opinion about the need to get material aid to Britain, China, and—from June onward—the USSR. Yet despite overlapping memberships and similar worldviews, the relationship between the organizations was not always easy. Each saw the other as competition, and many FFF members became increasingly frustrated with the CDAAA's unwillingness to dissolve and make way for the more belligerent group. On a more personal level, there was animosity between some of the group leaders, most notably Eichelberger and Bell. On the whole, FFF policy was half a step in advance of the CDAAA.

Despite their policy differences, the leaderships of all three organizations had a great deal in common. While they sought to represent the American people, none of them had leaderships that reflected a cross section of American society (though they did reflect the social structures of the time). Many of the leaders were drawn from the eastern establishment elite—white male Anglo-Saxon and Anglophile Protestant figures educated at East Coast preparatory schools and Ivy League universities. This was especially true in FFF, which evolved from the socially exclusive Century Club. The CDAAA tried to be more representative of the public, or at the very least it sought to bring in people who could be seen to represent the wider public. Yet on the whole, the groups' similarities outweighed their differences.

Understanding Internationalism

In addition to examining who the internationalists were and what they did, the larger and more important question is, why did they do it? By examining the longer-term geopolitical, economic, and cultural assumptions supporting American internationalism and considering how internationalist organizations perceived the threats posed by Germany, Italy, Japan, and even the Soviet Union, we can develop a more detailed understanding of American internationalism and how it evolved in the crucial years immediately prior to American entry into World War II. This movement was not just of significance on the eve of war but would dominate American foreign relations for years to come.

A brief consideration of the term "internationalism" is required here. The phrase is frequently used by historians of American foreign relations, but it is rarely clearly defined. The historians Warren Kuehl and Gary Ostrower have highlighted that the term "has had different meanings for nearly every generation of citizens and diplomats." It has also had different meanings for different historians, international relations theorists, and politicians, to the point where it has almost no meaning left at all. A 1986 article by Kuehl represents one of the few attempts to analyze the term. He expressed surprise at how little had been done to analyze internationalism as a concept, and little more has been done since.[8]

At its most basic, internationalism has been used to describe any American involvement overseas—whether it is action undertaken multilaterally or unilaterally, whether it is for the good of the world or in America's narrow self-interest—simply because it is international in a geographic sense. This understanding of internationalism has little analytical value, as it is so broad that it includes almost every aspect of American foreign relations. It is also limited, as it is often posed in opposition to the supposed isolationism that runs through American foreign relations—a term that is equally flawed. The history of American foreign relations in the 1930s and 1940s is far more complex than claiming that the United States was isolationist until Pearl Harbor and internationalist after.

However, attempting to create a universal definition is arguably a Sisyphean task in the face of such a wide variety of internationalisms. Instead, given the diverse array of meanings, it is more effective to analyze the term in a particular historical context. The very fact that the meaning of internationalism has changed through the years reveals a great deal about evolving American attitudes regarding the nation's place in the world. This book therefore gives detailed consideration to the internationalist ideas that existed immediately prior to Pearl Harbor. More than that, it considers the different factors and motives that lay behind those ideas. In examining why internationalists sought a greater role for the United States in world affairs, it is necessary to look at the particular ideas, convictions, and assumptions that underpinned their arguments and their worldview. As they saw a potential—if not immediate—threat to these convictions, they felt compelled to respond.

Ultimately, there is much more to internationalism on the eve of World War II than a simple desire to defeat isolationism for its own sake. The internationalism that resulted was complicated, but any simple definition would be misleading. What the history of the movement proves is that a purely narrative approach to this period is insufficient. A history that sees the United States as following a seemingly inevitable step-by-step series of events that led to the Pearl Harbor attack overlooks the Americans who recognized—for whatever reason—that the United States needed to engage more comprehensively with global affairs. Emily Rosenberg has highlighted the "infamy framework" of remembering the war that "builds upon a tradition of national history in which World War II makes its appearance on December 7, 1941." Yet it is not sufficient to simply say that "war came to America." Many Americans were already looking for it. And they were looking for four main reasons.[9]

Four Freedoms Foretold

In his annual message to Congress on January 6, 1941, Franklin Roosevelt outlined his future vision of a world founded on four essential human freedoms.

> The first is freedom of speech and expression—everywhere in the world. The second is freedom of every person to worship God in his own way—everywhere in the world. The third is freedom from want—which, translated into world terms, means economic understandings which will secure to every nation a healthy peacetime life for its inhabitants—everywhere in the world. The fourth is freedom from fear—which, translated into world terms, means a world-wide reduction of armaments to such a point and in such a thorough fashion that no nation will be in a position to commit an act of physical aggression against any neighbour—anywhere in the world.

The passage went on to be one of Roosevelt's most memorable, helped by Norman Rockwell's 1943 paintings of the four freedoms.[10]

Although Roosevelt's message was an important one, it was not entirely original. The arguments of the internationalist movement for the previous two and half years had been based on largely the same themes. For the movement, internationalism was defined by a combination of the four freedoms. The desire to be free from fear was seen in concerns regarding America's national security. The desire to be free from want was expressed in anxieties over the nation's future economic prosperity. The need for freedom of speech was represented in concerns over the potential loss of political freedoms. Finally, the need for freedom of worship was seen in the emphasis on religious freedoms.

National security was at the forefront of internationalist concerns, especially after the fall of France in June 1940. This was in part due to a genuine fear of an existential threat to the continental United States. While an outright attack might not have been imminent in 1941, internationalists believed that the nation's future security was ultimately threatened by the rise of fascism (and Nazi Germany in particular). The prospect of a "Battle for America" (in the name of one CDAAA pamphlet) was not entirely beyond the realm of possibility. One result of this fear was an expanded conception of American national security interests that extended beyond U.S. borders to the wider Western Hemisphere and beyond into Europe and Asia. Even if a direct attack remained a distant prospect, the fear and emotional reaction conjured by such an idea was a powerful force to mobilize. You did not have to believe in the prospect of an attack on the United States to recognize that the best way to appeal to the public was on the most basic grounds of self-defense and survival. Americans wanted freedom from fear, and given the growing evidence of the strength of fascist forces, it appeared that the United States was no longer safe behind two oceans.[11]

While national security concerns may have been the most prominent aspect of prewar internationalism, they were by no means the only aspect. Other ideas were often more prominent than national security considerations, especially in the two years prior to the fall of France, as events overseas represented a broader threat to the American way of life. Three other less concrete but significant ideas were promoted as part of the internationalist worldview.

Perhaps the most surprising in the context of the 1930s was the internationalist emphasis on economics. The desire to be free from want was clearly displayed in the emphasis on the potential economic impact on the United States of success-ful fascist aggression, even if it did not penetrate the Western Hemisphere. As a popular book promoted by FFF argued, "You can't do business with Hitler." The economic implications of a fascist victory were an openly stated concern for the internationalists. The need to promote global free trade was at the heart of such thinking, and the inability of the United States to prosper in a world driven by slave labor was a theme that came up again and again. The implications were clear to the internationalists: the spread of global fascism represented a direct threat to American standards of living, which were still struggling to improve in the after-math of the Great Depression.[12]

Of course, these were just the explicitly stated economic concerns. There is no doubt that the Anglo-American business connections of many internationalists benefited from a world of free trade and international commerce. Such connec-tions went unmentioned, as no one wanted to appear eager to profit from war. They were particularly controversial in the context of the 1930s, when debates about the nature of America's entry into World War I were still very much alive, and there was a strong sense that the United States had been drawn into war in 1917 to line the pockets of international financiers and munitions manufacturers. However, it is clear that many internationalist businessmen on the eve of World War II did not want war, preferring the ease of international trade, limited gov-ernmental regulation, and controlled production levels that came with peace.[13]

Because many internationalists believed that a sustained international peace could exist only in a world of democratic nations, it was no surprise that they fully supported democratic political systems. The need for a world with freedom of speech was reflected in the internationalist promotion of political freedoms and democracy in particular. The developing wars in Asia and Europe were depicted as ideological ones by which totalitarian aggression was inflicted upon innocent democracies. To simplify this picture, the worst excesses of the British Empire and the limited nature of democracy in China were hastily glossed over. What remained was a story of right and wrong, and of conflict between two worlds. With the nation's deep historical commitment to democracy and political freedom, there was no question where American internationalist sympathies lay.

The fear of undemocratic totalitarian regimes was largely a result of fascist aggression, but there was also a pronounced fear of Soviet communism. This was certainly the case until the German invasion of the USSR in June 1941, though the situation became less clear after the American decision to aid the Soviets in the shared fight against fascism. But even after the decision to provide Lend-Lease aid to the USSR, both main internationalist groups continued to keep their distance from American organizations (or international ones) that were sympathetic to communism, especially those whose stance on American involvement reversed in the immediate aftermath of Operation Barbarossa. The exception to this general anticommunist stance was a limited amount of support for Chinese communism in the ACNPJA, though this Marxist interpretation of internationalism was never more than a minority view. This was largely because of the incompatibility of communism with the main driving force of the ACNPJA: religion.

Religion was in fact a key issue for all three main internationalist organizations, and freedom of worship was a core element of the internationalist worldview, though it was particularly prominent in the ACNPJA and in a broader sense for FFF and its predecessor, the Century Group. In both cases, the connection between organizational leadership and religion is clear. The ACNPJA leadership had a tradition of missionary service, and religious language and views were prevalent in the organization's thinking and its literature. Not only did it make arguments on explicitly religious grounds, but it targeted its materials at religious audiences who were perceived to be at the heart of the non-interventionist movement. After Nazi advances across Europe, however, there was the perception of a broader, longer-term threat to Christianity in the United States. FFF subsequently argued that Hitler sought to "destroy Christianity."[14]

However, the internationalist desire for freedom of religion did not exist simply in the sense of freedom of worship. It can also be seen in the broader sense of concern for the future of Western or Anglo-American Christian civilization. The internationalist view of history was one in which modern civilization had developed in a particular teleological fashion that reached its zenith in the American experience. The wars in Europe and Asia represented a threat to that very civilization—"a world revolution," in fact. Arguably the most significant and lasting part of that civilization was religion. The leadership of FFF in particular promoted ideas about the relationship between the United States and Europe—and Britain in particular—in the development of Western civilization. Their activist view of Christianity, informed by the Social Gospel movement, was also clearly visible in their internationalist activity.[15]

Despite the overlapping memberships of the internationalist organizations, there was of course diversity within the movement, and emphasis on the four freedoms varied between organizations. Internationalists differed in their geographic concerns, with emphasis on Europe and Asia but not always both. While they shared an interest in immediate events, they differed in their level of concern with long-term interests. The combination of sympathy for victims of aggression, international responsibility, and national interest that drew them into international affairs also varied. They shared the view, however, that an internationalist vision based on the four freedoms led to an acceptance of the need for the United States to play a greater world role.

Of course, one main area in which internationalists disagreed was on the issue of a declaration of war. Some were far more openly interventionist in that sense than others, and the issue proved to be a significant area of contention for the Committee to Defend America by Aiding the Allies in particular. Yet unlike some works that examine this period, this book makes no attempt to distinguish between internationalists and interventionists. This is because the line between the two was not as clear as might be expected, even well into 1941, and especially on an organizational level. On the face of it, Fight for Freedom was openly interventionist, yet it did not call for a formal declaration of war until October 1941, almost six months after its creation. Meanwhile, the Committee to Defend America by Aiding the Allies never called for a declaration of war because even though a number of its leaders quietly supported war prior to Pearl Harbor, they held back for fear of alienating their domestic audience.

Admittedly, the internationalist version of the four freedoms focused on their importance for that domestic audience and did not immediately share the president's concern with ensuring freedoms "everywhere in the world." Indeed, largely missing from the internationalist worldview expressed by these organizations was a sense of the wider world itself. With so much emphasis placed upon convincing the forces of non-interventionism within the United States to play a greater role in the world, there was little detail on what that role would be—beyond the not insignificant immediate task of helping to defeat the global forces of totalitarian fascism. It seemed obvious that the freedoms promoted by the internationalists would need to be sustained in the long term. Yet questions about exactly *what* role the United States should play in the world, or *how* the United States should play a greater role in world affairs beyond the war went largely unanswered, if they were even asked to begin with. The exception here is the emphasis placed by the CDAAA on winning the peace through a belief in international cooperation and multilateral institutions such as the League of Nations. This provided a particular understanding of how the United States would remain free from fear into the future. Beyond this, though, the future of American foreign relations remained a somewhat cloudy vision in the distant future.

The internationalism that developed also represented a very particular understanding of the four freedoms and their significance. That understanding was based on a belief in global free trade, the need to make the world safe for democracy, a fear of attack on religion and the end of Western civilization, and a genuine fear of attack. As a result, despite the universal-sounding language of Roosevelt's address, non-interventionist Americans did not necessarily agree with the president's speech, let alone the broader internationalist worldview. They countered that the four freedoms did not currently exist in the United States, let alone in the world; that any future conflict would betray those freedoms rather than promote them; and that the broad scope of such aims was unrealistic, if not a blueprint for perpetual war.[16]

Indeed, the biggest ideological division during these years was between the three internationalist groups and the Chicago based non-interventionist America First Committee. The CDAAA and FFF spent much of 1941 working to oppose and undermine the America First argument. Yet this was far more than a fight between citizens' organizations. Ulric Bell argued that America First held the ear of Congress, which was disproportionately non-interventionist. As a result, the role of internationalist organizations was "to play a modest part in persuading our great representative body to be representative" and to inform not only Congress but also the Roosevelt administration of a growing internationalist mood in the country. Examined below are how the internationalist organizations mobilized public opinion around them and how they influenced the development of American foreign policy through connections to the U.S. government.[17]

Mobilizing the Public

The role of the internationalist organizations in representing and mobilizing public opinion is a complicated and multilayered one. Public opinion has always been of great significance in the United States. The nation has always been known as a country of "joiners" who have regularly come together in organizations and associations to express a political opinion or outlook. As Alexis de Tocqueville wrote in 1835, "Better use has been made of association and this powerful instrument of action has been applied to more varied aims in America than anywhere in the world." These internationalist organizations came together to mobilize wider public opinion, and in representing that opinion they aimed to influence the government.[18]

While their leaderships were drawn from a relatively narrow elite, the organizations sought to mobilize the support of millions of Americans from diverse geographic, social, and economic backgrounds. Not only did they work individually to mobilize public opinion, but they occasionally worked with each other to maximize internationalist support against non-interventionist sentiment. This *horizontal* interaction with other citizens' organizations also included working with other, smaller groups concerned with foreign affairs. Finally, they worked with existing citizens' organizations that did not traditionally focus on foreign affairs, such as women's, labor, and religious groups. These interconnected and overlapping networks of activity aimed to reach not only the maximum number but also the widest range of Americans.

The first thing that should be emphasized is that these organizations did indeed represent a substantial part of the American public. The CDAAA and FFF in particular cultivated mass memberships. Yet the fact that these groups represented the *American* public needs emphasizing as it has been suggested that they represented something more conspiratorial and non-American. It was suggested at the time, and has been subsequently repeated by historians, that the ACNPJA was a Chinese lobbying organization and that FFF was a front for the British government. Yet while the organizations certainly had connections to foreign governments, they were by no means their puppets. The fact that the internationalists were aware of such accusations was one reason why it was so essential for them to prove they had support among the wider American public.[19]

While the ACNPJA was focused primarily on lobbying Congress through influential connections, the dramatic growth in interest that followed the outbreak of war in Europe saw both the CDAAA and FFF develop mass memberships with hundreds of local chapters. Chapters were developed across the United States in order to prove that the growing interest in global affairs reached from sea to shining sea—and beyond, in the case of the CDAAA outpost in London. The two organizations had more than one thousand branches by the time of the Pearl Harbor attack.[20]

Expanding local chapters was important in proving that the internationalists had popular support, but the organizations sought to demonstrate not only numerical clout and geographic reach but also sociological breadth. In developing those mass memberships, they deliberately worked with different sectors of American society so they could claim to represent the broadest possible range of the public; more than a male Anglophone Atlantic elite and certainly a broader range than the non-interventionists of America First. In outlining its brief history, FFF highlighted the wide array of different social groups involved, including actors, architects, artists, military personnel, government officials, authors, dramatists, businessmen, bankers, clergy, directors, educators, journalists, labor officials, lawyers, musicians, publishers, scientists . . . and women.[21]

Both the CDAAA and FFF leaderships knew they were open to the charge that they were led largely by men, and particularly white men who were privileged and too old to fight. Both organizations created special divisions to counter this accusation, adopting a "qualitative approach . . . to develop support in these 'weak spot' areas in which opposition is most likely to take root." Three sections of society specifically targeted because of their divided nature were young Americans (especially students), women, and organized labor. The CDAAA developed four national divisions: youth, college, women's, and labor. FFF also created four special divisions: youth, women's, labor, and African American.[22]

In addition to these internal connections, the internationalists made links to organizations representing rural and urban America, business and labor, women's groups, veterans, and a range of religions and religious denominations. The vast number of these organizations helped to develop public opinion for greater involvement in world affairs. The diverse interest created by their widely spreading message also helped to legitimize and strengthen their cause when appealing to Congress and the White House.

Influencing the Government

The ultimate aim of the internationalist movement was to change the direction of American foreign policy by influencing the U.S. government. In addition to interacting horizontally with other citizens' groups, they utilized a number of methods to achieve *vertical* interaction with the government. In attempting to influence Congress, the organizations gained credibility through their mass memberships, who were encouraged to flood the legislative branch with letters in support of internationalist policies. The American Committee for Non-Participation in Japanese Aggression was particularly interested in congressional politics because any embargo on war material to Japan would have to pass through Congress. The Committee to Defend America by Aiding the Allies and Fight for Freedom also strongly encouraged their memberships to target the legislative branch, both with regard to specific bills such as Lend-Lease and more generally in the hope of altering what was perceived to be an excessively non-interventionist congressional mood.

However, while Congress was to be the target for the rank and file, the leadership of all three organizations focused on cultivating relationships with the executive branch. Here the nature of the internationalist leadership was crucial, as it gave the organizations access and enabled them to develop close personal links to the State Department and the White House. The political experience of organization leaders became advantageous to both the internationalists and the

Roosevelt administration as they worked together for shared goals. The public reputation of William Allen White, the governmental experience of Lewis W. Douglas, the personal relationship with Franklin Roosevelt of Thomas Lamont, and the State Department connections of Clark Eichelberger and Ulric Bell were increasingly important. Indeed, what makes these internationalist organizations truly significant is the extent of their interaction with the administration.

Although it is incorrect to describe the organizations as administration fronts, there is no doubt that they were clearly sympathetic to the administration. Despite the nonpartisan nature of all three organizations, they often went out of their way to act as informal propaganda agencies for the administration and its policies. Despite being a prominent Republican, William Allen White worked hard to harmonize CDAAA policy with that of the government. Admittedly, White's relationship with Roosevelt was close enough for the president to comment that White was "a very good friend of mine for three and a half years out of every four years." Regarding CDAAA activity, White later confirmed that "I never did anything the President didn't ask for, and I always conferred with him on our program."[23]

What this reveals is that the line between "public" governmental action and "private" organizational activity was frequently blurred during this period. As will be seen, a notable example of this vertical interaction came with the destroyer-bases agreement of 1940, when the CDAAA and the Century Group cooperated to ensure that Republican candidate Wendell Willkie did not make a political issue of the gift of fifty destroyers from the United States to Britain in exchange for leases on naval bases in the Western Hemisphere. Internationalists also worked hard to convince Roosevelt that the exchange was constitutional.[24]

While the internationalists looked to influence government policy, they were also willing to be influenced by the Roosevelt administration. As war approached, both the CDAAA and FFF looked to the White House for advice. For example, in April 1941 FFF was asked to limit its calls for Atlantic convoying of Lend-Lease aid to Britain because of the strength of congressional opposition and fear of a backlash. A further request from the White House in September delayed a proposed push for a congressional declaration of war. Although Roosevelt himself frequently used trial-balloon speeches to test the winds of public opinion, it is telling that he thought that even some private actions could do more harm than good. On the whole, when FFF and the CDAAA received advice from the White House, they acted upon it.

Nevertheless, it was clear that Roosevelt valued the role of the internationalists. His feelings on the matter were revealed to actor Douglas Fairbanks Jr., a prominent CDAAA member, who recalled Roosevelt's discussing the techniques of leadership at the White House. A democratic leader must never let himself get too far ahead of his constituents, or else he loses contact with them. Like a military leader, he can't get so far in front of those he leads that they can no longer hear him. What you and your committee—or anyone urging governmental action—must do is to first build up huge public support for a particular bill or law, and that will "push" the leader. He then advances a little until his followers catch up. After that, with more support, he advances a bit again, until once more his followers join him. So that's what you've got to do. Because even a President of the United States can only go so far without the majority of the whole nation—not just his own party—supporting him. Now go out and get the public to push me!

In a letter to Ulric Bell a few weeks after Pearl Harbor, the president argued that the work of FFF "made a contribution to the national defense and to the national security which is incalculable," and that the government "appreciates everything you did to arouse the nation to impending peril."[25]

Between 1938 and 1941 the internationalist movement attempted to arouse the nation in order to defeat non-interventionism at home and fascism overseas but also to promote a new vision of internationalism. As conflict grew closer, the ideological nature of both the war and American internationalism became more pronounced. Faced with the possibility of a world of totalitarian fascism, internationalists emphasized what were perceived to be America's strongest values, glossing over more troublesome issues in the process and minimizing political divisions at home to focus on what was perceived to be the greater enemy overseas. They also emphasized the common ideals shared by the United States and its allies and downplayed the differences (which was easier with Britain than with China, let alone with the Soviet Union). More broadly, internationalists increasingly characterized the growing global conflict as one between two distinct worlds. In doing so, they set the tone for decades to come.

Chapter 1

The Sino-Japanese War and the American Committee for Non-Participation in Japanese Aggression

The outbreak of war between China and Japan in July 1937 initiated a period of global conflict that ultimately led to the Japanese attack on Pearl Harbor. Yet at the time, the impact of the Sino-Japanese War on the American people was limited. The American response to the war was in line with the non–interventionist outlook that had characterized American opinion since the rejection of the League of Nations in 1920. When polled in September 1937 on their sympathies in the conflict, 43 percent of Americans favored China and just 2 percent Japan. Yet American attitudes were most clearly represented by the 55 percent who sympathized with neither side. Most Americans simply wanted to stay out of any conflict. In addition, 54 percent of those polled supported the withdrawal of all U.S. troops in China in order to avoid becoming involved in the conflict. To further insulate the United States, 95 percent said American banks should not lend money to either Japan or China during the conflict.[1]

Polls from the time offer further insights into the non-interventionist nature of American popular opinion in the late summer of 1937. The desire to avoid any conflict, not just an Asian one, was confirmed by the fact that 73 percent wanted a national referendum before any congressional declaration of war. In fact, even after the outbreak of war in China, more Americans thought that any future world war would be started in Europe, with either Germany or Italy responsible. This reflected a concern with the rise of fascism in Europe but also the fact that Asia was seen by most Americans to be a secondary threat and one that would not affect them.[2]

President Roosevelt was clearly concerned by Japanese aggression and attempted to influence American public opinion away from non-interventionism.

At an October address in Chicago, he spoke out against acts of aggression with what became known as his quarantine speech. While reiterating his determination to "pursue a policy of peace," he suggested that "when an epidemic of physical disease starts to spread, the community approves and joins in a quarantine of the patients in order to protect the health of the community against the spread of the disease." His speech was clearly aimed at the Japanese, but despite the lack of specific detail or any machinery to enforce a quarantine, the response was mixed. While general reaction was not as bad as Roosevelt had feared, the speech achieved little. At best it helped mobilize moral opinion against acts of aggression, but no quarantine was forthcoming.[3]

This remained the case even after the sinking of the USS *Panay* near Nanjing on the Yangtze River. The gunboat was bombed and sunk by Japanese aircraft in December 1937, with the loss of two American lives. Yet neither the attack nor the destruction of Nanjing that followed inspired widespread calls in the United States for retaliation or vengeance. In fact, it had the opposite effect. The number of Americans who supported the withdrawal of troops from China increased to 70 percent in the aftermath of the attack. By February 1938, the percentage sympathetic to China had risen to 59 percent, but 40 percent still favored neither country. And despite that rise, 64 percent of Americans felt that the United States should not allow shipment of arms or ammunition to China.[4]

The only reason arms shipments were allowed was that the president had not invoked the Neutrality Act. This law, which built on previous Neutrality Acts from 1935 and 1936, was passed by Congress in May 1937. It banned the sale of arms and munitions to belligerents, and other material could be sold only if nations paid cash and carried the material away in their own ships. This "cash and carry" clause enabled the United States to keep trading with belligerents while keeping the country at arm's length from conflict, but it applied only if the president invoked it. In this case, Roosevelt chose not to, as China was heavily reliant on arms imports, and it lacked both the cash and the ships to transport other goods across the Pacific. His decision was made easier by the undeclared nature of the Sino-Japanese War. Nevertheless, Roosevelt was still clearly ahead of mainstream public opinion.

Despite the general trend of opinion, a minority of Americans were increasingly concerned with events in China. Displaying a clear sympathy with China, they felt the United States was not doing enough to help the victim of aggression. Frustrated with the lack of a quarantine or economic sanctions against Japan, those who were sympathetic to China felt not only that aid to China must continue but also that the United States needed to stop providing material to Japan. In doing so, it was arguably supporting Japanese aggression. In the spring of 1938, a number of articles and trade statistics revealed the amount of war material flowing from the United States to Japan. In the June edition of *Harper's Magazine*, economist Eliot Janeway stated that "we are selling Japan the means of mass production of war." Former secretary of state Henry Stimson argued that "China's principal need is not that something should be done by outside nations to help her but that outside nations should stop helping her enemy." It was in response to these calls that the American Committee for Non-Participation in Japanese Aggression was formed.[5]

The American Committee for Non-Participation in Japanese Aggression

The initial driving force behind the ACNPJA was Harry B. Price. The son of a southern Presbyterian missionary, Price had spent much of his life as an educational missionary in China, most recently at Yenching University in Beijing. He would play such a significant role in the group that it was sometimes referred to as the Price Committee. At the end of May 1938, he and his brother Frank W. Price (also an educational missionary in China) arranged a meeting in New York for a select group sympathetic to the Chinese cause. It included two additional missionaries, B. A. Garside and Edward Hume; *Amerasia* editor Philip Jaffe; Thomas Arthur Bisson of the Foreign Policy Association; and Earl H. Leaf, a writer employed by the Chinese government to undertake public relations—or propaganda—work. The group's general aim from the outset was to develop a program of political action, and it soon focused on the aims of mobilizing domestic support behind an arms embargo, targeting Congress in particular.[6]

The political focus led Harry Price to Washington in early June to "sound out sentiment" about a possible campaign to mobilize support for an embargo on the sale of war materials to Japan. While it is possible that the committee would not have gone any further without positive feedback, Price really spoke only to sympathetic ears. Stanley Hornbeck, chief adviser on Far Eastern affairs in the Department of State, urged "a general strengthening of sentiment and morale and more moral courage on the part of the American people." Senator Key Pittman, chairman of the Senate Foreign Relations Committee, was also in support of a boycott, arguing that if the American public would not support "the slight sacrifices involved, how can it be expected to support more serious and stern measures?" Democratic congressmen David Lewis of Maryland, Jerry O'Connell of Montana, and Byron Scott of California all expressed an interest and offered to help in any way possible. Despite the words of encouragement, Hornbeck and Pittman cautioned that an embargo might not be enough. The most downbeat assessment came from the State Department China specialist John Carter Vincent, who argued that the outlook for an embargo was "discouraging," with no likelihood of European cooperation and he suggested that it was too little too late.[7]

Price returned from Washington with a positive outlook. There were significant obstacles in the way of any embargo legislation: most notably a lack of public support, fear of the consequences of any such legislation (in the worst case, war with Japan), and the existing neutrality legislation. Yet Price returned convinced that the State Department was sympathetic and that if public support could be mobilized, then an embargo could be a genuine possibility. He also returned with a list of significant public names that might be asked to support the committee in order to add weight to its fledgling operation.[8]

Prominent names were required because of the committee's approach to organization. Following the advice of the public relations firm Perry and Wise, the group decided at the very beginning to avoid becoming a mass membership organization. Instead, the plan was to create a group of between fifty and one hundred people who were significant "either because of themselves or the organizations with which they are connected." The committee, based in New York, was to utilize every possible method of promotion available to build support for an embargo on the sale of war materials to Japan. Methods included mass meetings, direct mail, radio, publications, posters, and newsletters. Any individuals mobilized by the committee would direct their opinions to Washington in a personal, spontaneous manner that avoided the appearance of a deliberate and calculated campaign.[9]

A further piece of advice Price received from *Washington Post* editorial writer Barnet Nover was that any appeal to the public must be based on American interests—ideally defense. Nover highlighted that an appeal based on purely humanitarian grounds or in China's interest would be less likely to succeed. In part this was a recognition that American business would resent any interference in what it saw as legitimate trade with its biggest Asian trading partner, especially in the context of the Roosevelt recession.[10]

More significant, however, was the suggestion that the committee was being set up for specifically Chinese interests. There is no doubt that there were connections to the Chinese government at the outset, most notably through Earl Leaf, and that the creation of the committee was supported by that government. On his June visit to Washington, Harry Price also visited the Chinese embassy, speaking directly to the ambassador, C. T. Wang (Wang Zhengting). He also stopped in New York to speak with P. C. Chang (Zhang Pengchun), a Chinese public diplomacy agent who, like Leaf, had provided money to help support the new committee. Indeed, certain connections and communication channels remained in place throughout the committee's existence. To refer to it as a "Chinese lobbying organization," however, is to exaggerate the nature of those connections.[11]

The committee member who most clearly recognized the potential danger of Chinese influence on the ACNPJA was Roger Greene. Greene joined the group in July, and in December 1938 he became chairman. He was the son of missionaries to Japan, where he spent most of his childhood before being educated at Harvard alongside Franklin Roosevelt. He then entered the consular service, working in Brazil, Japan, Russia, and China. In 1914, he joined the Rockefeller Foundation's China Medical Board, where he remained until 1935. The connections he made and sustained in those years proved invaluable for the new Committee. As Warren Cohen has argued regarding American policy on China and Japan in the interwar years, "No one outside the government was in a better position to exercise influence than Roger Greene." In his role as chairman, Greene focused on political connections to Washington, while Price focused on administrative matters. Despite references to the Price Committee, it was ultimately Greene who turned the ACNPJA into an organization of significance.[12]

Concerned that the group might be seen as a puppet of foreign propagandists, Greene wrote to Price in mid-August urging that the committee "refund as soon as possible the advance made to our committee by Mr. P. C. Chang, and that all future funds be from Americans only." He also constantly sought to downplay (though not hide) links between the ACNPJA and Chinese agencies. A week later, Greene argued that an appeal letter from the committee should be signed by individuals with more "American connections" than "China hands" such as himself and Price: the embargo question "concerns the interests of Americans here, and for such a discussion we might well be prejudiced by our Chinese connections." The need to eliminate all such connections immediately led to the resignation of Earl Leaf on September 1.[13]

The need for the committee to be truly American became more pressing the week after Leaf's resignation as the State Department began registering agents of foreign principals. Had the ACNPJA been funded from overseas or had it still directly involved Earl Leaf, it would have been required to register. The day after the registration program was announced, Greene wrote to Price urging that the committee get advice from a lawyer regarding the status and obligations of the ACNPJA and that it "make every effort to refund Mr. P. C. Chang and any other official or semi-official Chinese, or any Chinese not a resident of this country, such sums as they may have advanced to our Committee."[14]

This would continue as ACNPJA policy for the remainder of its existence. When sending promotional material to, or when offered financial support from, Chinese citizens in the United States, Price stated that the ANCPJA was not able to accept financial support from "our Chinese friends, unless they are American citizens by birth," so that the committee could legitimately claim to be wholly sponsored and supported by Americans. Price also informed the committee's bank of any potentially suspicious deposits, such as those from the China War Relief Association in San Francisco, which Price claimed was composed of first-generation American citizens born to Chinese parents. Price even went so far as to consult with the State Department to ensure that such contributions did not violate any existing laws.[15]

However, the line was not always quite as rigid as Greene wanted, largely because of the committee's limited finances. Connections were maintained with Earl Leaf, who encouraged contributions. Chinese groups such as the China Society were encouraged to contribute through members who were American citizens rather than as an organization. In the final active weeks of the committee in December 1940, Price even appealed to the new Chinese ambassador, Hu Shih (Hu Shi), for assistance in finding further financial support: "Once or twice before you have been so thoughtful as to suggest to American friends who wanted to help China that they make their gifts to this committee, and this has seemed in no way inconsistent with the necessity for maintaining our position as an independent American-initiated and American-supported organization." The committee also accepted a number of large anonymous donations, including one from a "friend of the China Information Service," which had also been set up by Frank Price and other missionaries in the autumn of 1938. Price even conceded to the State Department that the ACNPJA occasionally received small contributions from Chinese citizens, yet the department reassured him that it was not necessary for the committee to register as an agent of foreign principals.[16]

This does not detract from the fact that the ACNPJA was, on the whole, an American organization led and run by Americans and funded almost entirely by Americans. It is not at all surprising that Americans such as Roger Greene and Harry Price were sympathetic to China, given their personal histories and connections to it. Connections to China were to be expected in an organization that sought to assist China through an arms embargo on Japan. These were seen in correspondence between Price and Chinese leader Chiang Kai-shek (Jiang Jieshi), who thanked the committee for "working so staunchly and valorously for China in her hour of need." Yet most of the committee members agreed with Greene that non-participation in Japanese aggression was in America's interest as much as in China's.[17]

The committee's public campaign began on August 1, 1938, with the publication of an eighty-page pamphlet entitled *America's Share in Japan's War Guilt*, and the group became even more "American" as it gained influential national figures over the following months. The quest for prominent names led to the appointment of Henry Stimson as honorary chairman. Having already spoken out against Japanese aggression, and as a prominent and experienced national politician, Stimson was seen as the ideal choice. Yet he did not agree until three other significant names were brought on board as honorary vice chairmen: Dr. A. Lawrence Lowell, president emeritus of Harvard University; Dr. Robert E. Speer, former president of the Federal Council of Churches of Christ in America; and William Allen White, editor of the *Emporia Gazette*. Just as the ACNPJA was sometimes referred to as the Price Committee, it was also occasionally known as the Stimson Committee after its honorary leader. Stimson's role, however, was as a significant figurehead but little more. He was not involved in the day-to-day running of the organization, which was left to Chairman Greene and Executive Secretary Price.[18]

The ACNPJA announced its new leadership lineup with a press release on January 19, 1939. Greene's statement underlined the ACNPJA's aims of high-lighting to both the public at large and the government the extent to which American material was contributing to Japan's war effort. "The Committee will endeavor to help in crystallizing public demand and support for governmental executive action designed to check the flow of American credits and war materials to Japan. The Committee will also work toward obtaining the enactment of a measure at the present session of Congress prohibiting the extension of economic aid for war purposes to a country which is in process of violating a solemn treaty of peace to which the United States is a party."[19]

The committee's leadership was augmented later the same day with a fourth honorary vice chairman in Jonathan W. Daniels, editor of the *Raleigh News-Observer*, who had been suggested to Greene by (soon to be Supreme Court Justice) Felix Frankfurter. As well as adding geographical balance to the letterhead, Daniels was a Democrat, which helped to assuage Greene's concerns about the preponderance of Republicans in the committee. This completed the formative stage of the ANCPJA, though two further honorary vice chairmen would be added in November 1939: Henry I. Harriman, former president of the United States Chamber of Commerce, and Admiral Harry E. Yarnell, retired commander in chief of the Asiatic Fleet. At a lower level, the committee's national board would ultimately comprise twenty-nine members, and the total number of sponsors reached eighty-six. With a solid organizational structure in place, the committee could focus on its broader aims.[20]

Persuading the Public, Persuading Washington

In outlining ACNPJA strategy, Harry Price argued that it was the "proper function of a democracy to encourage free mutual interchange of opinions and convictions between citizens and the official representatives in Washington." He added that the ACNPJA was certainly not a group that was trying to "force its wishes upon the President." Yet the committee openly conceded that it was in the propaganda business and that its ultimate aim was to persuade the president and Congress that its opinions and convictions were the right ones. The aim was achieved by two methods. First, the ACNPJA worked to educate and mobilize public opinion, which in turn would place pressure on political leaders in Washington. Second, it would target politicians directly through the personal connections of its elite leaders.[21]

In mobilizing the public directly, the committee worked in a number of different ways. Press publicity had the advantage of reaching the widest possible general audience. Unsurprisingly, the committee utilized the print media in a variety of ways, including the distribution of formal press releases. It also employed the rapidly expanding medium of radio, providing information and scripts to commentators and arranging programs and debates at both local and national levels. The group also responded to requests for speakers on the Far Eastern situation, though it did not sustain a formal speakers' bureau.[22]

Despite the potential reach of these methods in getting its message across, the ACNPJA in fact put most of its effort into the production of literature. It distributed hundreds of thousands of booklets, leaflets, flyers, reprints, and letters to educate Americans about the role American material played in the Japanese war effort. The literature was disseminated at meetings and through the mail, but the distribution was by no means scattershot. As the committee was being organized, seventy select organizations were contacted to provide potentially interested names. The response led to the creation of a master file of twenty-two thousand citizens who were sent *America's Share in Japan's War Guilt* in August 1938. The master list grew to more than one hundred thousand by 1940; twelve thousand of those showed sufficient interest in ACNPJA activity to be placed in the "active file" of friends and supporters.[23]

Some of those active supporters felt strongly enough to create local committees of their own. Despite the ACNPJA's decision to reject a mass membership approach to organization, it was happy to accept the development of local committees to help spread the message. Although the local groups utilized ACNPJA material, information, and advice, they were largely autonomous in their activity. Committee literature nevertheless boasted about their influence in setting up meetings, creating publicity, and distributing literature in cities as geographically diverse as Boston, Richmond, Durham, Toledo, Chicago, Kansas City, Denver, Seattle, and Los Angeles.[24]

Rather than developing its own network of cooperating committees, the ACNPJA took a different approach, focusing on working with existing organizations and committees with shared interests. One key advantage to this was that it was much cheaper than setting up a network of local organizations. Instead, the ACNPJA used existing organizations to distribute its literature and to garner support;

the vast majority of these were not usually or primarily interested in foreign policy issues. The committee boasted of connections to national, regional, and local organizations as diverse as the Southern Baptist Convention, the American Association of University Women, the Young Women's Christian Association, the Convention of United Auto Workers, and the American Student Union.[25]

In a quantitative sense, these connections immediately provided an audience of more than forty million Americans. The vast majority of those came from religious organizations, with more than half from Robert Speer's Federal Council of Churches of Christ in America. Yet the diverse array of organizations gave ACNPJA a vast qualitative reach, as well as the opportunity to appeal to Americans of all kinds. Christian and Jewish organizations, labor and business, young Americans, women's groups, and peace organizations were all represented. This was not a conscious drive for breadth, and the priority for the ACNPJA appeared to be on quantity, but it did allow the committee to claim support from a more diverse sociological range than its more elite leadership.[26]

The ACNPJA also created links with other organizations interested in American foreign relations more generally. The two main examples were both connected to the conservative wing of the peace movement, and both held close ties to the ACNPJA. The first was the American Union for Concerted Peace Efforts, whose chairman, Clark Eichelberger, was also a sponsor of the ACNPJA. Like the American Union, the ACNPJA was located at 8 W. Fortieth Street in New York in the offices of the Woodrow Wilson Foundation. The second was the National Committee on the Cause and Cure of War, a coordinating committee of women's organizations headed by the ACNPJA vice chairman Josephine Schain. The memberships of these organizations overlapped, but the ACNPJA repeatedly emphasized its more specific focus on the issue of Japanese aggression by contrast with the broader concerns of the other internationalist bodies.[27]

One advantage with such a specific focus was that it was easier to create and mobilize support for a clear political message. Yet even with this message, the ACNPJA was not above asking for professional assistance in maximizing its effectiveness from the rapidly developing field of public relations. In January 1939, it sought the assistance of the John Price Jones Corporation, a public relations and fund-raising corporation based in New York. Though this was done primarily to capitalize on that month's leadership announcement, the corporation provided advice for the committee's future. In particular, it noted that the committee's leadership needed strengthening to include "at least one man or woman from each of the social, economic, racial, religious, political or geographic groups" to be asked for support, and that local committees should be arranged. While the ACNPJA largely chose to ignore this advice, it agreed with the corporation that publicity counsel was needed "urgently."[28]

The following month saw the ACNPJA approach two companies for public relations advice. For five weeks between February and April, the committee utilized the services of the Phoenix News Publicity Bureau. The bureau arranged radio time for the group and attempted to secure magazine and newsreel publicity, in addition to providing a clipping service. The contract was canceled for lack of funds, but not before the bureau's president informed the committee that despite its tight focus on Japanese aggression, the lack of a specific legislative program hampered its effectiveness. The contract with the firm of Hartwell, Jobson and Kibbee lasted considerably longer, through to April 1940, though it too began with a critical appraisal of the ACNPJA organization. In particular, the firm suggested that the ACNPJA lacked any "persons of broad influence with the general public," which was "a severe handicap." It recommended that committees of prominent industrialists, educators, actors, clergymen, and columnists be created in order to provide a higher publicity profile.[29]

With the help of public relations professionals, the ACNPJA worked tirelessly to spread the message about Japanese aggression across America. The message was directed through individual citizens, domestic-oriented citizens' organizations, and foreign affairs–related organizations. It was then reflected back from the public to politicians in Washington, DC. Yet mobilizing the general public was not sufficient for the ACNPJA leaders. From Harry Price's discussions in the group's formative weeks, the committee sought to develop connections to key members of both the Roosevelt administration and Congress. As Roger Greene wrote in February 1939, though the ACNPJA could not let up on the campaign throughout the country, "Washington is now the most important place in which to work." It was in the nation's capital that much of the committee's activity took place.[30]

In its own literature, the ACNPJA did not describe itself as a "special interest" group but instead as an organization that represented the broader public interest in order to bring the "greatest benefit to all concerned, including the Japanese people themselves." Despite this rather disingenuous distinction, the committee conceded that it was indeed a pressure group, working to bring public opinion to bear on Congress to stop the provision of war materials to Japan. Yet given its limited resources, the approach was often a targeted one. Roger Greene in particular was keen to focus on a limited number of influential senators and congressmen. This approach was reinforced by supporters such as former missionary and commentator Upton Close. Close argued not only that the committee needed to target key strategic congressmen, such as those on Foreign Relations Committees, but that key constituents—"the right people"—who could not be ignored should be urged to contact those politicians. In addition to targeting particular individuals, the ACNPJA also kept very friendly relations with important and sympathetic senators such as Senate Foreign Relations Committee chairman Key Pittman, Lewis Schwellenbach, and Elbert Thomas.[31]

The closest relationships with Washington figures were reserved not for Congress but for the State Department. ANCPJA members utilized their connections to the Roosevelt administration in order to place pressure on the State Department but also to coordinate with the department on how best to move forward. On the whole, the strategy of the committee was to work in cooperation with the Roosevelt administration wherever possible. From the very beginning, Price argued that the committee existed to support the State Department's desire for a strong and united public opinion. Although the ACNPJA was no puppet of the department, it occasionally held fire on criticizing an administration that in its eyes was not moving fast enough toward an embargo. Despite the risk of being seen as an arm of the State Department, the committee was openly proud of its friendly relations with the government. The connection between them was strengthened by the establishment of a Washington office in January 1940, manned by Roger Greene, who most clearly followed the strategy of constructive support.[32]

The organization's key contact in the State Department was Stanley Hornbeck. Previously chief of the department's Division of Far Eastern Affairs, from 1937 Hornbeck was special adviser to Secretary of State Cordell Hull. Hornbeck was generally supportive of ACNPJA activities insofar as they helped to mobilize wider public opinion behind a more critical view of Japan and greater global awareness. Yet while he was happy to engage in regular correspondence with the committee, he kept a certain distance when it came to policy decisions. Similarly, he was truly interested in the group only as long as it served and supported the administration's needs. Nevertheless, the ACNPJA's cooperative stance ensured that their relationship remained close.[33]

With the State Department viewing the committee as useful, both Greene and Price had occasional access to the secretary of state himself. This was particularly important to them, not simply because of Cordell Hull's position but because of Greene's view that a strong statement from the department on the embargo issue would be extremely influential in Congress. As a result, even Greene became frustrated with the department's inaction on the issue, but he refused to criticize the administration in public. For his part, Hull encouraged the committee to continue by congratulating it on its work, which had been "exceedingly valuable." Like Hornbeck, he recognized the value of the ACNPJA in educating public opinion on the issue, as it provided an informal propaganda service that stayed on message. He also knew that the ACNPJA had no real alternative but to work with the administration.[34]

The State Department remained the committee's primary point of access to the administration. Contact with the president himself was much more limited in nature, even with Greene's personal connection. Greene informed the president of the new committee's activities when they met in the autumn of 1938, but while he occasionally received a signed response from Roosevelt to his letters, the correspondence was almost entirely one-way. The odd telegram from Price—mostly to commend the president on action already taken—had no discernible impact.[35]

Beyond Doctrinal "Isms"?

Despite the limited influence of the ACNPJA in Washington, it continued to argue for an embargo and to educate the public about the nature of America's role in aiding Japan until 1941. This was no small task given the public's relative lack of interest in events in Asia. Yet, regardless of its claims, there was more to the group's worldview than this narrow aim of limiting the sale of material to Japan. In its initial booklet, the ACNPJA described its aim as the one indicated in the organization's title: non-participation in Japanese aggression. It was noted that "doctrinal isms, domestic issues, and the European situation, however important, are beyond its scope."[36]

While that may have been true in a very narrow sense, ideas about the embargo did not exist in isolation from a wider worldview or sense of internationalism. The internationalism of the ACNPJA cannot be easily defined, partly because of the differing views within the organization. Yet it consisted of a number of elements that reflected the personal histories and background of the organization's key leaders, in addition to core elements of American history and the nation's relationship with China. In particular, those elements were closely related to concerns about the four freedoms: religious freedoms, national security, economic prosperity, and political freedoms.

The driving force behind the ACNPJA was a series of close personal and institutional connections between organization leaders and China. The limited public interest in the Sino-Japanese War (at least compared with interest in the subsequent outbreak of war in Europe in 1939) showed that American interest in Asia was a minority issue. The war offered no immediate threat to the United States at a time when the nation was still primarily concerned with domestic matters and sought to avoid foreign entanglements. Yet those who initiated the ACNPJA— most notably the Price brothers, Leaf, and Greene—had a deeper connection to China that inspired their efforts. That connection was shaped in large part by the long American missionary tradition in China and the role of religion.

While other religious leaders remained at the pacifist end of the peace movement, ACNPJA leaders put religion at the heart of their internationalism. With China's vast size and population, it was, in the words of historian Andrew Preston, "the missionary movement's ultimate prize." Given the personal (and indeed family) histories of the ACNPJA founders in that movement, it was no surprise that the organization sought to mobilize indirect support for China through an embargo. Yet the justification it used in promoting an embargo was closely related to religious themes, as it utilized moral arguments about foreign relations. The ACNPJA frequently made its case on the grounds of right and wrong.[37]

Sometimes the connections to religion were overt, such as in ACNPJA literature. The committee's opening statement of purpose to the public, *America's Share in Japan's War Guilt*, contained six pages of quotes from religious leaders. The Right Reverend Alexander Mann, bishop of Pittsburgh, noted American acknowledgment of the "unprovoked and brutal war of aggression on the part of Japan," but that "our moral judgement which condemns Japan for this war is practically nullified by our trade with her." A statement from the Catholic Association for International Peace argued that the American people could not stand by in the face of acts of international aggression, even if they were not directed at the United States. Instead the nation must "join with other nations in making some distinction in the treatment accorded to the guilty and the innocent."[38]

Crucial to this morality-based outlook was a criticism of the failure of neutrality in existing foreign policy. As the Sino-Japanese War was undeclared, the United States had not invoked the Neutrality Acts that had been passed between 1935 and 1937. The result of this was a situation favorable to Japan as it could keep purchasing war materials. But if Franklin Roosevelt had invoked the acts, the situation would have become even worse for China. It would not have been able to purchase any munitions itself, and it had neither the industrial capability to turn raw materials into war materials nor the merchant marine to ship such materials to China. The acts had been designed with the European situation in mind and were primarily concerned with keeping the United States out of war. Ultimately, whether the acts were applied or not, the United States made no distinction between aggressor and victim in international conflicts, or between right and wrong. Whatever the United States did in this case favored Japan. While secular organizations could clearly also take issue here on the grounds of natural sympathy toward victims of aggression, the religion-infused ACNPJA seized on this issue to strengthen its argument for an embargo.

Such arguments could be seen in *Christian Hands of America*, a brief pamphlet directly targeted at churches, which with an estimated circulation of two hundred thousand was the ACNPJA's most widely distributed publication. It emphasized America's historic ties to China, the vast scope of the Christian movement there, and the Christian leadership of the Chinese government, including Chiang Kai-shek, his wife, and many of his advisers. More immediately, it highlighted how the issue of guilt in the Sino-Japanese War was so clear that "the American people and above all Christians of America can no longer escape making a decision one way or the other" about the need to take a stand. This particularly Christian sense of moral responsibility also ran through the organization's direct appeals to missionaries in China.[39]

At other times, the religious language and audience targeting was less explicit, but the moral argument remained strong. The 1940 pamphlet *Shall America Stop Arming Japan?* argued that the United States was not responsible for policing the world but that it was responsible for "her own conduct and influence in the world." The language dripped with guilt. Though it was conceded that friendly relations should be maintained with Japan if possible, that did not justify "complicity in crime." One particularly vivid passage claimed that "millions of Americans can think only with shame and dismay of American-motored aeroplanes, fuelled with American gasoline, dropping American metals to be blown into the bodies of Chinese men, women, and children who have traditionally regarded America as their best friend." These emotionally manipulative passages were clearly designed to provoke support for the Chinese cause, and for the cause of the ACNPJA. While this moralistic approach would subsequently be criticized by realist scholars such as George Kennan, it clearly permeated the internationalism of the ACNPJA. And though it could be dismissed as mere rhetoric, the deep background of the ACNPJA leadership revealed a genuine missionary tendency at work.[40]

Of course, Japanese aggression was seen not just as morally wrong but as legally wrong, and this legal angle was also emphasized by the ACNPJA. In particular, the committee highlighted how Japanese aggression undermined the Nine Power Treaty of 1922, which it saw as the cornerstone of American policy in Asia. The treaty affirmed that all parties, including the United States and Japan, would respect the sovereignty, independence, and integrity of China. With Japan ignoring the treaty, the committee argued that the United States could legitimately enact a boycott as "a logical and reasonable consequence of such treaty violation." While its legal argument focused on the Nine Power Treaty, the ACNPJA also emphasized that Japan's actions went against the Kellogg-Briand Pact of 1928, in which the contracting parties renounced war as an instrument of policy.[41]

The emphasis on legal issues reflected the growing interest in the interwar years in matters of international law. Although they were more abstract than moral appeals, legal appeals highlighted the wider Japanese threat to international order and were likely to bring support from other internationally minded Americans (though here the committee was arguably preaching to the converted). Nevertheless, behind the ACNPJA's efforts lay "the conviction that the great and inevitable influence of the United States . . . should be placed on the side of justice and fair play, not on the side of wanton and ruthless aggression."[42]

More important, the legalistic focus on Japanese aggression meant that the ACNPJA could argue that Japan represented a national security threat to the United States. From its beginnings, the committee had argued that a Japanese victory would lead to long-term international instability. Japanese success would consolidate the military's position in government and lead to an expanded imperial presence through Asia. A militaristic Japan would be "capable of threatening the peace and security of the world for years—possibly generations to come." Given that Japan would still not be self-sufficient, its success would lead to further expansion in areas "where American interests are deeply involved," such as the Philippines. The language used by the ACNPJA was vague but alarming and hinted at threats beyond Asia. It noted that a victory for Japan was a victory for force and aggression. The success of such aggressive nationalist forces in Asia had the potential to unleash or encourage similar forces elsewhere.[43]

Subsequent ACNPJA literature placed Japan's expansionist activity into a wider historical context. Beginning with the first Sino-Japanese War of 1894–95, Japan's recent history was explained as one of constant expansion. Through war with Russia in 1904–5, the annexation of Korea in 1910, the acquisition of League of Nations Pacific mandates in 1919, and the invasion of Manchuria in 1931, Japan was portrayed as opportunistic and aggressive. This military mentality was explained by reference to Japan's feudal past, which was still seen to influence Japanese political culture. The modern-day warlords and samurai sought to build up military and economic strength, expanding through Asia and threatening American territories such as the Philippines and Guam, with the ultimate aim of "the rise of Japan to world dominance."[44]

Of course, it was quite a leap from dominance of China to world dominance, but the portrayal of Japan as a direct threat to Pacific territories of the United States, if not the continental United States itself, was a key part of ACNPJA rhetoric. The moral appeals went only so far. A wider audience could be mobilized by playing to more basic national security fears, assuming that the claims of the Japanese threat were credible and supported by evidence. Initial advice to the committee suggested that any appeal to the American public must be based on American interests, ideally in the area of national defense. At the top of Harry Price's list of reasons for supporting the stoppage of war materials to Japan was "ultimate American security."[45]

The national security argument was at the same time the most dramatic and least convincing reason for supporting an embargo on war materials to Japan. It was dramatic to the point of scaremongering, as there was little genuine belief in an immediate Japanese threat to the United States. Tellingly, at no point were the Hawaiian Islands mentioned in ACNPJA literature as an area under specific threat. Yet the use of fear was very deliberate, as it was seen as the most effective way to mobilize Americans behind the embargo issue. Even then, though, there was a clear awareness that the fear issue could not be overplayed. The national security threat was best represented as part of a longer-term threat to international law and order that came with Japanese expansionism.

The other two main areas of the ACNPJA's argument were more slightly more convincing but ultimately less dramatic in appealing to the public: politics and economics. Regarding politics, there were two sides to the committee's view of the conflict: concerns over the political culture of Japan and overly positive judgments about China. Assessments of Japan were closely related to concerns over national security in that they emphasized the militarist nature of the Japanese political leadership. Japanese society was shown as a totalitarian state—undemocratic and led by a dominant military elite. While the country had seen considerable industrialization, this had not come with liberal reforms to provide individual freedoms. The emphasis on the Japanese leadership enabled the ACNPJA to blame the government without dismissing the Japanese people in general, offering hope for the future. It also revealed the limits to ACNPJA rhetoric, and it was easy to imagine a more strident line of attack. Nevertheless, these views were not especially controversial, but neither were they necessarily enough to engender sympathy for an embargo or a wider internationalist worldview.[46]

The more controversial aspect of the committee's political outlook was its portrayal of China as the "world's greatest open market for freedom." Efforts to gain sympathy for China on political grounds were more challenging, as it was not exactly a bastion of freedom. While it was clearly the victim of aggression, the conflict hardly represented a clear-cut case of good versus evil. Yet the committee tried, partly through comparison with totalitarian Japan and partly on its own merits, to portray China as an ally of freedom. Such arguments were based partly on the limited progress the Republic of China had made toward becoming a modern democratic state and partly on existing sympathies with the Chinese cause. China was seen to be "making a magnificent struggle for liberty." Again recognizing that exaggeration would undermine their arguments, committee literature made reference to the "democratic trend" in China. While acknowledging that there was still some way to go for the developing republic, the ACNPJA was able to argue that China was on the side of democracy in a world increasingly divided between democratic and totalitarian states.[47]

There was one potential flaw in the political argument: communism. This political system was feared by most of the internationalists of the ACNPJA—even more than Japanese fascism. The idea that China was a promising democracy appeared to be undermined by the existence and strength of the Chinese Communist Party. This was a point that the ACNPJA needed to counter not only for political reasons but also for religious ones, as an atheist communist China was anathema to the committee's considerable religious support. Even the number of prominent Republicans on the committee and its desire to "keep to the Right" failed to shield it from accusations of supporting communism. Harry Price even felt it necessary to contact Representative Martin Dies of the House Committee on Un-American Activities to refute suggestions that the ACNPJA was a "communist front."[48]

Regardless of such rebuttals, the accusations kept coming. Letters to the committee accused it of "backing up the communists," suggesting that helping China was providing "help to a communistic cause." The group's response was to argue that China was in no way dominated by communists and to emphasize the Christianity of Chiang Kai-shek and his wife. It acknowledged that there were communists in China but claimed that they were limited in number and concerned primarily with agrarian reform and the Three People's Principles of Sun Yat-sen. They could therefore be dismissed as they were not "communists in the Marxian sense." ACNPJA's corresponding secretary, Mrs. Grover Clark, was simply wrong rather than conspiratorial when she argued in 1940 that "there is not the remotest possibility, we believe, of the Communist armies overcoming the Government forces and in making China into a Communistic nation."[49]

Of course, not all ACNPJA members were equally hostile to the possibilities of communism in China. Both Philip Jaffe and Thomas Arthur Bisson were subsequently linked to Soviet military intelligence during World War II. Even so, while it is likely that Bisson influenced the ACNPJA's view of Chinese communism as being limited and distinct from a strict Marxist interpretation, there is no evidence to suggest that Jaffe or Bisson had any significant influence over the ANCPJA's overall direction. It should also be noted that Frederick V. Field, executive secretary of the communist-leaning antiwar American Peace Mobilization group, followed the ACNPJA's support for China until late 1940. However, at that point the committee's growing support for Britain and lack of support for a cooperative arrangement between the United States and the Soviet Union caused him to register his disappointment with Price and the ACNPJA's direction.[50]

Despite denying the significance of Chinese communists, the ACNPJA used the fear of communism to support its own cause. The group argued that an embargo on war materials to Japan was the best way to stop any further communist infiltration of China. Price argued that Japanese aggression had been the greatest single impetus to the development and expansion of communism in China, as the few communist leaders had been the most determined in their opposition to Japanese aggression (though this did contain implied criticism about Chiang Kai-shek's leadership). He also suggested that if the United States continued to arm Japan, then China might be forced to turn increasingly "albeit reluctantly" to the Soviet Union, where it would be forced to accept assistance on Soviet terms.[51]

If the political argument for non-participation in Japanese aggression was con-tested, so too was the economic argument. The idea that the United States would undertake any foreign policy for economic reasons was highly unpopular in the 1930s. The claim that the country had entered World War I to support financial interests and munitions manufacturers in particular was popularized by books such as *Merchants of Death*. The idea was investigated between 1934 and 1936 by North Dakota senator Gerald Nye's Special Committee on Investigation of the Munitions Industry, which concluded that economic pressures had played a part in bringing the United States into a war that was supposedly for the noble cause of democracy.[52]

To an extent, the ACNPJA built its arguments upon these very concerns. It argued that the trade in war materials was destructive, short-term, and bound to lead to a depression. However, there was also a clear sense of national self-interest. In the short term, the effect of an embargo on American industry was believed to be small and was estimated at no more than a week's work. The committee noted that the profits of trade in war materials were more than offset by the losses in peacetime trade of other goods to both sides; therefore, if the embargo was effec-tive, the United States would benefit in terms of trade. The group further argued that Americans would also benefit from a reduction in taxes that were being spent to build up naval defenses in the Pacific.[53]

The potential for trade with China was strongly emphasized and was described as incalculable given the size of China's population and the perceived good-will of the Chinese toward the United States. On the other hand, the ACNPJA highlighted the potential trade threat from imperial Japan to future American interests. With its designs on an Asian monopoly, supported by a vast supply of raw materials and a subservient labor force, a Japanese empire would benefit from closed markets and greater profits. This would leave fewer markets for American goods, and cheaper manufactured goods had the potential to flood the domestic American market.[54]

The economic arguments promoted by the ACNPJA were surprisingly overt. They were prominently placed in committee literature. One pamphlet, *The Far Eastern Conflict and American Cotton*, focused entirely on the impact of Japanese aggression on the American cotton market. The thirty-page booklet began by asking, "Must America Lose Her No. 1 Cotton Market?" In one respect this eco-nomic emphasis was no surprise, as the very nature of the committee's aim—an embargo on war materials to Japan—was an economic one. Yet in the political climate of the 1930s, to make such arguments was to risk accusations of greedy self-interest and to open the committee to charges that it was willing to risk American lives for profits.[55]

As previously noted, the internationalism of the ACNPJA ultimately built upon four freedoms: religious concerns, political and economic factors, and a long-term concern for American security in a world where international law and order was disappearing. The ACNPJA attempted to convince Americans who were indifferent to the Sino-Japanese conflict or more concerned about domestic affairs that international affairs could not be ignored. In response to a non-interventionist query, Harry Price wrote that though America's internal problems were significant, he did not believe they would "be solved apart from a clear recognition of our place in an interdependent family of nations. . . . I do not think we can escape our share of responsibility for the influence that we do actually exert in other parts of the world."[56]

The ACNPJA was clearly part of a growing movement of internationally minded Americans who recognized that the country might be forced to choose between two goals that had previously seemed to go together: peace and freedom. Increasingly, the two concepts appeared to be mutually exclusive. As the peace movement fractured in 1937 and 1938, many Americans felt it was time to make a choice. On the one hand, pacifists and those who looked to a strict conception of neutrality had no desire for an embargo that might provoke Japan over an issue that did not appear to threaten the United States. On the other hand, internationalists who emphasized collective security highlighted the failure of neutrality policy to distinguish victims from aggressors. They argued it was time to take a stand, and the ACNPJA fell firmly into the latter camp.[57]

The action supported by the ACNPJA represented what it saw as a middle course between aimless policy drift and military intervention. In many respects, especially in light of what would follow, this position was surprisingly moderate. While the group's members sought international responsibility, they were not aggressive interventionists. Based on obvious sympathy for China, their actions aimed to restore Chinese integrity and independence. Yet they did not seek to crush Japan or even overthrow the Japanese government. They did not even seek a ban on imports from Japan, remaining firmly focused on the issue of American exports to Japan. Finally, their geographic focus was solely on Asia and the Sino-Japanese War.[58]

The narrow focus on an embargo was both an advantage and a disadvantage for the ACNPJA. On the one hand, such a clear and specific focus was relatively uncontroversial among internationalists, as there was no real opportunity to disagree on wider "isms." On the other hand, the committee's tight focus was somewhat technical, and the concept of an embargo lacked significant emotional appeal. As the ACNPJA looked to implement its policy in 1939, it had clear direction, but risked being overshadowed by events in Europe.

Chapter 2

The Coming of War and the American Union for Concerted Peace Efforts

As the American Committee for Non-Participation in Japanese Aggression worked to focus political attention on Asia at the beginning of 1939, it found itself struggling to stay ahead of affairs elsewhere. In the six months between the ACNPJA's founding and the announcement of its honorary leadership, the political stability of Europe had been shaken considerably. In September 1938, the Munich agreement saw the United Kingdom and France concede to Hitler's demands and agree to Germany's annexation of the Czechoslovakian Sudetenland. While the agreement averted an immediate conflict, many internationalists believed it merely postponed the inevitable. A majority of Americans (59%) agreed that Britain and France had done the right thing, but a bigger majority (60%) felt it would lead to a greater possibility of war, and an even larger majority (77%) felt the annexation was unjustified. Ninety-two percent of Americans polled in November 1938 did not believe Hitler's statement that he had no further territorial ambitions in Europe. When polled in February 1939, almost two-thirds of Americans believed that in the event of war in Europe, the United States should do everything possible short of entering the war to aid Britain and France.[1]

It was in this context that internationalists began a sustained push for revision of the Neutrality Acts. Whereas the focus on Asia was led by the ACNPJA, the broader campaign for neutrality revision was led by the American Union for Concerted Peace Efforts. In the first eight months of 1939, the activity of the two organizations quickly became entangled as they fought to educate the American public about the need to reject neutrality. Of greater necessity was the need to convince Congress to reject non-interventionism, as congressional support for neutrality was even stronger than popular support. However, the difference in geographical focus and scope meant that the two campaigns for Neutrality Act revision did not always pull in the same direction.

Neutrality Revision in Two Oceans

After its January relaunch, the ACNPJA stepped up its efforts to implement neutrality revision that would lead to an embargo on war materials to Japan. Its focus was on passing some form of legislation through Congress, and its activity was supported by the fact that the Roosevelt administration was looking to achieve a similar goal. Because the president was reluctant to be seen as a warmonger or add to domestic political criticisms that he was a "dictator," he let the push for neutrality revision come from his State Department and from allies within Congress itself. Key Pittman, chairman of the Senate Foreign Relations Committee, was placed in charge of the congressional revision efforts.[2]

Efforts for neutrality revision were given added momentum on March 15, 1939, when Germany occupied Bohemia and Moravia, destroying what was left of Czechoslovakia. Within days, Pittman and the State Department had drafted the Pittman bill, also known as the Peace Act of 1939. The bill repealed the arms embargo aspect of existing neutrality legislation and replaced it with a cash-and-carry provision for all goods. This would have enabled the United States to sell arms to Britain and France without risk of losing American lives or goods at sea. As with the existing Neutrality Act, it prohibited loans to belligerents; unlike the existing act, it would apply to both declared and undeclared wars. Unsurprisingly, noninterventionists in Congress were unhappy, especially with the idea of lifting the arms embargo.[3]

Just as unhappy with the proposed bill were the members of the ACNPJA. Despite pushing for neutrality revision, this was not the revision they had been working for. They wanted it to be harder for Japan to access war materials; this legislation would have made it no more difficult, and it would also have given Japan the ability to purchase arms from the United States. Harry Price wrote to Pittman, Hull, and Undersecretary of State Sumner Welles to emphasize that this new legislation did nothing to help America's ally in Asia. Not only did the proposed repeal of the arms embargo assist Japan, but the bill would also have been detrimental to China's war effort. As Japan dominated the western Pacific, China would have struggled to take advantage of the cash-and-carry clause even if it had been able to afford American goods; as it was, restrictions on credit gave Japan a huge advantage. Unsurprisingly, the formal response from the Chinese government was also one of criticism and frustration.[4]

The difficulty quickly became clear of crafting a neutrality policy that supported America's allies in both Europe and Asia while at the same time keeping the United States away from war. Even the president recognized the challenge. On March 28, Roosevelt wrote to both Hull and Welles pointing out that "while the cash and carry plan works all right in the Atlantic, it works all wrong in the Pacific. The more I think the problem through, the more I am convinced that the existing Neutrality Act should be repealed in toto without any substitute." However, there was no likelihood of full repeal in the spring of 1939. Instead, other congressional suggestions were put forward. Some were on similar lines to Pittman's bill, while others took a more non-interventionist approach, but almost all sought to find an approach that would apply to all nations.[5]

The exception to this rule came from a proposal that had actually been put forward more than a month prior to the German seizure of Bohemia and Moravia. On February 13, Utah senator Elbert Thomas introduced Senate Joint Resolution 67, which would grant the president the authority to prohibit the sale of war material—raw materials as well as arms—to belligerents. In addition, subject to congressional approval, embargoes would be lifted on victims of aggression. It was a clear attempt to distinguish between aggressors and victims. In doing so it had the advantage of allowing the United States to discriminate between democracies and fascist states, between America's allies and its potential enemies.[6]

Although the Thomas resolution offered a solution to the different problems faced in Europe and Asia, it was not enthusiastically supported by the ACNPJA. At a national board meeting on March 15, the ACNPJA decided to "continue its educational program urging action to end America's aid to Japan rather than to sponsor a particular legislative program at this juncture." The committee's relative lack of interest at this stage reflected the Thomas resolution's lack of specificity on the war in Asia, as well as the group's knowledge that other proposals were forthcoming. Two weeks later, after events in both Europe and Washington, the committee decided it was advisable to seek a special resolution dealing with the Far Eastern situation.[7]

As the negative consequences of Pittman's Peace Act for China became clear, the ACNPJA increasingly fell behind the Thomas resolution, though without great enthusiasm. Despite a decision to support the amendment, it stuck to its focus on the war in Asia and continued to push for specific legislation urging an embargo on Japan. In sticking to its original aim, the committee lost the opportunity to play a role in wider debates about America's place in the world. It continued to mobilize public opinion behind an embargo on Japan. Yet at the same time it failed to recognize that while public opinion was increasingly interested in foreign affairs, it was Europe that dominated public concern. Much of the debate over neutrality revision focused on the looming crisis in Europe rather than the existing one in Asia. With such a narrow focus on the embargo issue—largely as a result of the committee's overriding concern for China—the organization risked losing sight of the larger global picture.[8]

The American Union for Concerted Peace Efforts

That picture was being seized by a different organization, the American Union for Concerted Peace Efforts. The AUCPE was formed on March 15, coincidentally on the day of the German advance into Czechoslovakia. The group was organized to campaign for international cooperation and collective security, and it had three stated aims: "to oppose aggression, to promote justice between nations, to develop adequate peace machinery." Its chairman was Clark Eichelberger, who announced that the new organization would promote Senator Thomas's plan for neutrality revision. The union argued that "world cooperation alone can protect American interests. Consequently we support the leadership of the United States in the cooperative use of its moral, diplomatic and economic power to find ways short of war to let the aggressor know that he can go no further."[9]

While this approach appeared to be influenced by the Thomas resolution, in fact the reverse was true. The American Union for Concerted Peace Efforts had evolved out of the existing and similarly named Committee for Concerted Peace Efforts. The CCPE was formed in December 1937 in the aftermath of Franklin Roosevelt's quarantine speech, and it reflected a growing divide within the peace movement. Many of those involved in it were members of the League of Nations Association and also the National Peace Conference. Set up in 1932, the National Peace Conference was a coordinating group created to promote peace and international affairs, but by late 1937 it was increasingly dominated by its pacifist, noninterventionist wing. Those who supported the idea of collective security and the League of Nations became increasingly dissatisfied with the direction of the peace movement. They joined the new CCPE believing that a distinction was needed between aggressors and victims of aggression and that the concept of peace was increasingly problematic. The organization's name was inspired by a line in the quarantine speech that argued that "peace-loving nations must make a concerted effort to uphold laws and principles on which alone peace can rest secure."[10]

In December 1938, the CCPE issued a statement calling upon Americans to contact their congressmen and urge "an amendment which will distinguish between aggressor and victim." The statement went so far as to call the existing Neutrality Act "un-American," emphasizing that it was not neutral and that it encouraged aggression. The statement was quick to highlight the impact that such an amendment would have on the war in Asia, as Japan would not be able to secure much of the war material necessary to support its war in China. However, unlike the ACNPJA, the CCPE was not concerned simply with Asia. The subsequent Thomas resolution followed very similar lines to the group's December statement.[11]

In February 1939, it was decided that the CCPE would evolve and expand into the American Union for Concerted Peace Efforts for the purpose of providing leadership and coordination for all those individuals and organizations that supported the collective security focus of the union's three stated aims. It was hoped that the union would therefore become "a more potent mobilizing force for public opinion." The CCPE board was to become the board of the AUCPE, with some additional members from the League of Nations Association. The relationship between the AUCPE and the LNA was extremely close. Like the CCPE, the AUCPE had the full support of the LNA, whose director, Clark Eichelberger, also happened to be the chairman of the AUCPE. It was agreed that the objectives of both organizations were "identical" but that the AUCPE would focus primarily on "immediate political steps" to win the peace, while the LNA looked at the long-range problem of organizing international society. The LNA's national offices provided a ready-made infrastructure for the new union, which, like the ACNPJA and the LNA, was to be based at the offices of the Woodrow Wilson Foundation at 8 W. Fortieth Street in New York. The overlap in memberships between the two organizations was considerable, and in addition to housing it, the LNA partially funded the AUCPE.[12]

The initial list of executive committee members was a who's who of the collective security-oriented, conservative wing of the peace movement. Included were Esther Caukin Brunauer and Mary E. Woolley of the American Association of University Women, Josephine Schain of the National Committee on the Cause and Cure of War, Bryn Mawr international law Professor Charles G. Fenwick, and Columbia University professor and League of Nations Association president James T. Shotwell. Henry Atkinson of the Church Peace Union was the first AUCPE president, with Edgar Fisher of the Institute of International Education as treasurer and William W. Hinckley of the American Youth Congress as secretary.[13]

Yet it was Eichelberger who provided much of the drive for the AUCPE. Born in Freeport, Illinois, Eichelberger devoted his adult life to the promotion of internationalism. A supporter of progressive politics, he became interested in the League of Nations as a soldier during World War I. He began speaking on behalf of the League of Nations in 1923, and he became director of the LNA in 1934. Through the 1930s, Eichelberger was one of a few individuals (along with Shotwell and Raymond Fosdick of the Rockefeller Foundation) who kept fighting for the League of Nations and for a more engaged—and indeed multilateral—American foreign policy. It was Eichelberger who recognized that the League of Nations Association was not the correct vehicle to fight for neutrality revision, and that the CCPE and the AUCPE were required. He would go on to create further organizations as the international situation deteriorated, most notably the Committee to Defend America by Aiding the Allies.[14]

His assessment of the need to act was partly inspired by a meeting with President Roosevelt on July 8, 1937, when they discussed the possibility of a "dramatic statement" from the president on collective security that would "lead the world on the upward path." Roosevelt was clearly testing his ideas on Eichelberger, and the quarantine speech followed three months later. Just as significant was the effect of the meeting on Eichelberger's plans. Roosevelt concluded their meeting by saying that anything the internationalist leader could do to develop public opinion along similar lines would be helpful. Five months later, following Roosevelt's quarantine speech, the CCPE was born. In a similar vein, its subsequent evolution into AUCPE was also largely inspired by a presidential address. In Roosevelt's annual message to Congress on January 4, 1939, he openly suggested that the Neutrality Acts were operating "unevenly and unfairly," aiding aggressors and denying aid to victims of aggression. Despite the lack of detail, comments such as this from Roosevelt encouraged the development of the new union.[15]

Protecting American Interests

From the outset, the internationalism of the AUCPE was much more global in scope than that of the ACNPJA. This was hardly surprising given its connections to and support for the League of Nations. The group's focus was not specific to any one continent or area of conflict. Yet there is no doubt that its members, unlike the Sinophiles of the ACNPJA, had closer connections to Europe than to Asia and prioritized the Atlantic over the Pacific. Theirs was an outlook that emphasized a Western—and particularly Anglo-American—conception of civilization. This was partly a result of their focus on the league, but it also reflected their close connection to organizations such as the Carnegie Endowment for International Peace (CEIP), which provided financial support.

While this global outlook enabled the AUCPE to engage with larger questions, it also meant the group's arguments were more abstract. At the heart of its case was the idea of collective security. The emphasis on collective security was not unexpected from an organization that had such close ties to the League of Nations Association. The LNA leadership believed in a version of Wilsonianism that had a multilateral international organization at its heart. Perhaps more important, they believed in American involvement in such an organization and that the American rejection of the League of Nations had been a terrible mistake, the implications of which were becoming more and more apparent as the 1930s progressed. However, they acknowledged that the league was not a viable solution to global problems. James Shotwell admitted that both the League of Nations and the League of Nations Association were "marking time in the face of a world of dangers." As a result, a new organization was necessary, one untainted by the league's failings.[16]

A new collective security policy was necessary because technological progress had "united the world." That progress, it was argued, produced enough goods to enable the whole world to "enjoy a good life." In addition, machinery for global cooperation had been created and principles of international morality established. Yet despite all that progress, the world was slipping toward war. The aggressive policies of dictators and militarists were threatening the forces of peace and democracy. One option for the United States was to do nothing in the face of the "new savagery," except perhaps rearm in the event of war. Yet this policy of "isolation" was a mistake. It did nothing to prevent war or build a more orderly world, and the United States could not be "an island of sanity and safety in a sea of madness and war." Not only was such a policy deemed wrong, it was "a betrayal of American interests." Only a policy of world cooperation and universal collective security could protect those interests.[17]

Exactly what those American interests were, however, was less clear. Embedded in AUCPE rhetoric were allusions to being part of a global community, whose values of peace, democracy, and economic justice were under threat. If it was accepted that those values corresponded with American values, then the ACUPE's argument was understandable, but that argument was rarely if ever made in an explicit manner. Nevertheless, the AUCPE's internationalism contained a number of key elements, including three of the four freedoms: concern for America's immediate national security and also its political and economic systems. In addition, it contained a much longer-term vision for the nation's foreign policy than the ACNPJA was prepared to outline, one based on international organization.

The main thrust of AUCPE arguments was along national security lines: a failure to act made war more likely to come to America. This countered the argument of many non-interventionists, who claimed that a more active foreign policy would draw the United States into war, as it done in World War I. This case was consistent with CCPE literature arguing that the Neutrality Act was neither a defense nor a peace policy. Instead, the existing legislation made "certain the further spread of lawlessness and war to South America and to the United States itself." This line of argument could have been dismissed as scaremongering, and the exact nature of the physical threat to the United States was not outlined explicitly. Yet it clearly targeted not only the general public but also the more pacifist elements of the peace movement by suggesting that the ultimate aim was still peace for the United States.[18]

In political terms, the AUCPE emphasized the challenge posed to democracy, highlighting that aggressors were dictators and militarists. Yet while democracy was a key phrase in AUCPE literature, the group did not go so far as to portray the growing world crisis as a battle between democracy and fascism or totalitarianism. Instead it focused on the immorality of aggression. However, it portrayed the moral issue less in the emotional (and religious) terms used by the ACNPJA and more in the mechanical terms of international law and order. Unsurprisingly, the AUCPE sought judicial settlement of international disputes through machinery such as the League of Nations and the World Court and greater emphasis on treaty obligations such as the Nine Power Treaty and the Kellogg-Briand Pact. It repeatedly emphasized the themes of international organization and law. The world had just two alternatives: "one, to organize itself efficiently as a single community of nations; the other, to effect its own ruin by continuing to live in international anarchy."[19]

The AUCPE also strongly emphasized the concept of economic justice. The phrase "economic justice" was a particularly slippery one, but in the context of the AUCPE it related more to a capitalist equality of opportunity than to a socialist equality of outcome. The economic worldview of the AUCPE built on the view of the LNA, which in turn was closely related to the economic principles of the Carnegie Endowment for International Peace. There were a number of links between the Carnegie Endowment, the LNA, and the AUCPE. The endowment funded both internationalist organizations. James Shotwell was a key member of all three: director of the endowment's Division of Economics and History, president of the LNA, and honorary vice president and national board member of the AUCPE. Eichelberger had also previously worked for the endowment.[20]

The most specific statement of the endowment's economic principles came in March 1935, following a CEIP conference held at Chatham House in London. The conference made four recommendations, one of which urged the "restoration of political confidence and security" through a number of policies that utilized "the organs of international organisation." The remaining three, however, focused explicitly on economic issues. The first economic recommendation urged that key creditor nations of the United States and Great Britain consult with other nations with the aim of enabling "debtor nations to meet their obligations"; it also argued for low tariff or free trade unions. The second urged the establishment of "a stable world gold standard." A third urged that the CEIP work with the International Chamber of Commerce to establish a commission "to make a comprehensive and exhaustive survey and study of international economic relations in all their aspects."[21]

The LNA built upon these economic principles in its own work. In addition to promoting the league's own economic activities, the LNA strongly promoted the free-trade ideas of Secretary of State Cordell Hull. It strongly supported his efforts to introduce reciprocal trade agreements, lower tariffs, and increase trade cooperation across the globe in order to pull both the United States and the wider world out of depression. Like its concerns over the Neutrality Act, the economic policies of the LNA and the AUCPE were therefore closely aligned with those of the Roosevelt administration.[22]

Unlike those who claimed that World War I had brought profits to the "merchants of death," the AUCPE argued that war was not good for business. In appealing to the business community, it went as far as to create a businessmen's committee. This was led by Hugh Moore of the Dixie-Vortex Company and Frederick McKee of the West Pennsylvania Cement Company, both of whom would go on to play a significant part organizing and funding the internationalist movement. The businessmen's committee argued that war was not good for business. It would bring a higher tax burden, throw markets into disarray, and ruin thousands of American businesses. It was therefore time for American businessmen to devote some of their "practical brains" and money to the prevention of war.[23]

The emphasis on codified international organizations, liberal free trade, and democracy revealed a neo–Wilsonian vision for the world along American lines (with the primary legacy of Wilson being seen as international organization). While the creation of the AUCPE was inspired by the extent of the growing world crisis, the group's internationalism was one that went beyond both the war in Asia and events in Europe. With its emphasis on justice between nations (in terms of international law and economics), the AUCPE was working not just for immediate peace but for a long-term vision of peace and for the international machinery to enforce and support that peace. Whereas the ACNPJA had a narrow and immediate focus on one policy in one part of the world, the AUCPE's broad vision of the future with its long-term international collective security organization was at the other end of the spectrum.

In a more immediate sense, the ultimate function of the AUCPE was to push for a more active American foreign policy rather than to continue drifting to war. As "incomparably the strongest power," only the United States could provide the necessary leadership required to stop the world from drifting into global conflict. However, the organization took for granted that its fellow Americans would agree the nation was genuinely threatened by global aggressors. As it stood, for those who felt secure in the Western Hemisphere, the union's policy of opposing aggression could appear risky and more likely to lead the country to war, not less. In the absence of a truly threatening war in Europe, the rather abstract pleas of the AUCPE for collective security limited its appeal. Yet for now, the organization sought to continue educating the American public in a broad sense and was unwilling to focus its efforts solely on the political job of neutrality revision.[24]

Cooperating with the Administration

Like the ACNPJA, the AUCPE worked in two ways. First, it worked to educate and mobilize public opinion behind the immediate concern of neutrality revision and the broader need for a more active foreign policy. It did this through traditional channels of the media, mass meetings, and literature. In this area, the AUCPE had a limited amount of success in establishing itself as a group of national prominence, despite its methodical approach to organization. Second, it cultivated close connections in Washington in an attempt to influence the Roosevelt administration. In this respect it was rather more successful, if only because the connections made and its willingness to work with the administration laid the groundwork for future cooperation.

In order to reach the public as effectively as possible, the AUCPE placed a great deal of focus on making its organization and leadership as representative as possible. It recognized that any big names brought on board as honorary chairmen or vice chairmen must be bipartisan and appeal to the greater number of people from all over the geographical United States. However, the failure of the AUCPE to secure a prominent national leader before the outbreak of war in Europe was one of the main factors that limited its appeal. Making connections with representatives of existing public organizations was also deemed essential, especially those organized along professional lines, including artists, scientists, lawyers, business, youth, and labor.[25]

In order to develop the AUCPE, numerous national leaders were invited to take part in the Conference of One Hundred. The event, held at the Shoreham Hotel in Washington, D.C., on April 16, was aimed specifically at leaders of public opinion to persuade them to wield their public influence "boldly and unhesitatingly in the interests of peace." To develop the union further, Peace and Security Week was planned for the week of April 26–May 3 to promote the idea that American national security would be strengthened, not put at risk, by ending aid to aggressors. The week had some effect on expanding interest in the union, most notably through the interest of the Hollywood Committee of Fifty-six, which included celebrities such as Bette Davis, Melvyn Douglas, Groucho Marx, and Edward G. Robinson.[26]

In terms of specific details, the week was used to promote the Thomas amendment to the Neutrality Act, to support Senator Pittman's bill to promote economic restrictions against nations violating the Nine Power Treaty, and to show support for Roosevelt's recent appeals to Hitler and Mussolini to make ten-year nonaggression pledges. The week's statement of purpose declared that "peace for the world and security for the United States depend upon the awakened conscience of the American people and its powerful expression." The AUCPE leaders were so encouraged by the success of Peace and Security Week that they set about organizing local committees. These were to reflect popular opinion "from the roots" in order to mobilize the "spontaneous and enthusiastic" will of the people. To reflect the broadest possible public, local committees were again encouraged to contact local organizations representing churches, labor, businessmen, youth, the legal profession, and women's groups.[27]

Yet while the week may have contributed to awakening the wider public conscience, there were few clear examples of ways in which the public could act on that awakening. The primary message of Peace and Security Week remained the broader and more abstract one of "peace." Neutrality revision was important, but the union still focused on peace as an end without describing the specific means necessary to achieve it. Although its profile and educational value were slowly growing, the union's origins in the broader peace movement still limited its effectiveness in a practical political sense.

Despite this, the Roosevelt administration was both aware of and happy with the work of the AUCPE. With the president unwilling to speak out beyond his annual message to Congress, and with neutrality revision left in the hands of Congress, the administration needed all the allies it could find to get public support for action against international aggression. One obvious reason why the administration was sympathetic to the AUCPE was that they shared the same goals. The union's support for Roosevelt was publicly reflected in its statement supporting his message to Congress and in the group's efforts to promote neutrality revision—such as the Thomas amendment—that would allow the president to distinguish between aggressors and victims.[28]

Another reason why the administration made time for the AUCPE was the group's cooperative approach. The union opted to work alongside the administration because such cooperation represented the best chance of success for neutrality revision. This meant they did not criticize the administration or make any additional proposals for neutrality revision, which would only have added to popular confusion. Even before the expanded union was formed, Undersecretary of State Sumner Welles had informed Roosevelt's secretary, Marvin McIntyre, that the CCPE "has always cooperated and is now cooperating with the Administration and with the Department of State and the members of the Committee have upon many occasions been very helpful."[29]

This cooperative approach was influenced by the attitudes of the AUCPE leadership. Both Clark Eichelberger and James Shotwell had ties to establishment figures in the administration. Shotwell's establishment links were more historic, though still significant. He played a part in the 1917 Inquiry set up by Woodrow Wilson to plan for peace at the end of World War I and in the creation of the 1928 Kellogg-Briand Pact, and he was prominent in the CEIP. Eichelberger was less prominent but more eager for influence and even less critical of the administration as a result. He met with Roosevelt at least once a year from 1936 until the outbreak of war in 1941, and he always looked to assist the president in any way possible. It was with a clear eye on the administration's plans that the AUCPE set about promoting neutrality revision.[30]

Neutrality Revision Failure

One question remained: What kind of Neutrality Act revision was the Roosevelt administration promoting? Much to the administration's frustration, Key Pittman had been unable to secure Senate support for his Peace Act through April and May. Support for revision was divided between those who supported the Peace Act and those who supported the Thomas resolution. Yet a majority in the Senate was against either form of revision and argued to retain to an arms embargo. Roosevelt had been cautious since his January address to Congress, and the result was a state of uncertainty and drift. It appeared that the neutrality issue would have to wait until the next session in 1940.[31]

Yet Roosevelt's growing frustration with Pittman's failure led to one last attempt at revision in May 1939. As the quest for neutrality revision in the Senate ground to a halt, Roosevelt looked instead to the House of Representatives. Sol Bloom, acting chairman of the House Foreign Relations Committee, convinced Roosevelt that reform was possible in the House. Eager to drop the arms embargo from neutrality legislation, Roosevelt arranged for Cordell Hull to send a letter to both Pittman and Bloom. The May 26 letter argued against rigid neutrality legislation that applied equally in all cases. Americans were still to be prohibited from combat areas, and existing restrictions on loans and credits were retained, but Hull urged that the arms embargo must be repealed.[32]

On May 29, Bloom introduced a new neutrality bill in the House. Like Pittman's Peace Act, it did not provide for an arms embargo. Unlike the Peace Act, it included no provision for cash-and-carry, and there was no provision against arming American merchant ships. It gave the President discretion to decide where the bill applied. Noting how quickly the bill came after Hull's letter, the *New York*

Times astutely noted that the administration was pinning its hopes on the Bloom bill rather than the Peace Act. It also noted that the repeal of the arms embargo was its "first and highest hurdle."[33]

The new bill provided momentum for the AUCPE. Previously the union had been reluctant to move too far ahead of the administration, whereas this bill had the administration's full support. Although the group was disappointed that the Bloom bill did not fully embrace the moral distinctions of the Thomas amendment, the bill represented a genuine commitment to neutrality revision from a White House that had, aside from the occasional pro-revision statement, adopted an approach of political caution. More than before, the AUCPE put aside its general calls for peace and focused directly on the legislative specifics of neutrality revision.

In supporting neutrality revision through the spring and summer of 1939, the AUCPE became close allies with the ANCPJA. Despite the difference in emphasis between the two internationalist organizations, they now worked together on a shared goal. This was facilitated by overlapping memberships, most notably through Harry Price's inclusion on the AUCPE national board. Price ensured that all AUCPE board members received ACNPJA literature on neutrality revision, if only to emphasize the distinct nature of the issue in Asia.[34]

The approach of the AUPCE was to support the Bloom bill, as it was superior to the existing legislation. The AUCPE highlighted two key elements of the bill: the flexibility given to the president, which meant the law would not always be invoked, and the repeal of the arms embargo. The former provision ensured that the United States would be able to distinguish between friends and potential enemies, and it would apply only when it was "necessary to promote the security or preserve the peace of the United States or protect the citizens of the United States." It would not, for example, have been invoked with respect to the Sino-Japanese War.[35]

More important, the Bloom bill promised to lift the arms embargo. While the AUCPE conceded that this made no distinction between "nations at war in violation of international law and the nations resisting aggression," the group openly acknowledged that it would give an advantage to the United Kingdom and France by virtue of their Atlantic coastlines and control of the seas. Though it was a line of argument that the Roosevelt administration was unable to make, the AUCPE emphasized that the bill worked against the aggressive tendencies of both Germany and Italy.[36]

The complication of war in Asia, however, meant that the Bloom bill was insufficient on its own. In addition, the AUCPE urged the adoption of an amendment that provided for an embargo against any nation in violation of the Nine Power Treaty. Two amendments were proposed along these lines, one by Key Pittman and one by Democratic senator Lewis B. Schwellenbach of Washington.

Successful passage of either amendment would apply the broad principle of discriminating against aggressors to the specific case of the war in the China. This emphasized the AUCPE's lingering dissatisfaction with the failure of the Thomas amendment and its desire for even more substantial neutrality revision than was actually proposed.[37]

Yet the AUCPE still believed that a strong stand from the United States—in the form of neutrality revision—might be enough to salvage world peace. Thus the group became increasingly frustrated with the lack of progress as the United States continued to provide Japan with more than half of its war materials and as Europe teetered on the verge of further aggression. On the eve of the vote on the bill, the organization's rhetoric hardened. Previous legislation passed in the name of peace was dismissed as "a tragic betrayal of peace." The United States could no longer rely on the niceties of international law: "No longer can the American people expect international justice and law observance and at the same time blindly follow a neutrality policy which gives maximum encouragement to the aggressor."[38]

The ANCPJA also fell in behind the Bloom bill but with even greater emphasis on supplementary legislation that would support China. Hoping that the Tientsin incident in June—when the Japanese navy blockaded the treaty port's British concession—had focused attention on China, Harry Price sought advice on strategy from officials in Washington. They encouraged him to work toward the general principle of neutrality revision rather than specific proposals, either on revisions or on the long-standing issue of an embargo on war materials to Japan. However, this was an unsatisfactory response, as the risk of neutrality revision that took no account of the Sino-Japanese War was too great. The ACNPJA continued to focus its efforts on building support for the Pittman and Schwellenbach amendments, both within Congress and among the general public.[39]

On June 29, the Bloom bill passed, but not before Representative John Vorys of Ohio inserted a crucial amendment that added a partial arms embargo on weapons and ammunition. Much to the frustration of the bill's supporters inside and outside the administration, the amendment largely undermined the bill's intentions, and all efforts to remove it failed. Bitterly disappointed, the administration and the AUCPE quickly shifted their focus back to the Senate, where the Foreign Relations Committee was yet to vote on Peace Act, and where the Pittman and Schwellenbach amendments were still a remote possibility. With its narrower focus on the Far East, the ACNPJA showed less interest in the Peace Act's cash-and-carry plans and refocused on its plans for an embargo of war material to Japan.[40]

Unfortunately, resistance to neutrality revision was even stronger in the Senate than the House. On July 11 the Senate Foreign Relations Committee voted to postpone consideration of neutrality legislation until 1940. On July 14 Roosevelt made a desperate appeal to Congress for action. This was strongly supported by the AUCPE in an emergency letter to its membership, in which Eichelberger argued that the forthcoming week was as important as Peace and Security Week. Yet despite a personal meeting with Senate leaders at the White House on July 18, it was clear that there was no chance of revision in 1939. As Vice President John Nance Garner frankly explained to the president, "You haven't got the votes, and that's all there is to it."[41]

The AUCPE's response was one of disappointment and frustration. Eichelberger's anger was clear as he directed the blame squarely at the congressmen accountable for the decision. He argued they would bear a heavy responsibility: "Will the decision encourage another Munich or encourage the dictators to make war? How many thousand more Chinese will die as the result of scrap iron sold to the Japanese army?" He promised that the union's efforts would continue until the very last day of Congress. Beyond that, an increase in local committees was necessary to get the message through to Washington that "a clear majority of the American people" wished to revise the neutrality law. Polls suggested there was no clear majority. When asked in August whether Congress should revise the law, those who gave an opinion were split exactly fifty-fifty. But it was clear that congressional sentiment—especially in the Senate—was disproportionately non-interventionist.[42]

As well as venting his frustration with Congress, Eichelberger contacted Roosevelt directly to express the AUCPE's dissatisfaction with congressional resistance. While doing so, he effectively promised the full support of the union for the president's foreign policy. Eichelberger offered to support neutrality revision "to the fullest extent of our ability" whether it took place before Congress adjourned or after a recess. He described the AUCPE as a part of a majority of Americans ready to "loyally follow your leadership along the only path which can lead to peace and security for the United States." A reply came from the State Department rather than the Oval Office, but it acknowledged the endorsement of the administration's proposals and made reference to cooperation with the union. It would take two more months, but that cooperation would soon be very real.[43]

An Important First Step in Asia

Despite being increasingly overshadowed by events in Europe, there was by the summer of 1939 a majority of public support for action against Japan. A Gallup poll in July suggested that only a quarter of Americans would do nothing to protect (admittedly ill-defined) American interests in China. Fifty-one percent wanted to stop shipments of war materials, 18 percent supported an official government protest, and 6 percent were willing to go to war. Frustrated over the failure of broader neutrality revision, increasingly frustrated with Japanese aggression in China, and with a clear sense of popular support for action, the Roosevelt administration decided to take what little action it could.[44]

On July 26, 1939, the United States gave six months' notice that it was abrogating the 1911 Treaty of Commerce and Navigation with Japan. It had been suggested that economic sanctions against Japan would be in violation of the treaty, so the administration decided to give the required notice to end it. The decision signaled American dissatisfaction with Japan and that a reduction of trade with Japan was likely in the future. It also raised Chinese morale and proved—despite revision failure—that the United States was not completely uninterested in world affairs. It was not as dramatic as an embargo, but it was a step forward, and one that was not likely to lead to an immediate confrontation. For the administration, it was a victory, albeit a small one.[45]

For the ACNPJA, it was much more than that, though still only "an important first step." Given the focus of the previous months on Europe, the ACNPJA board members were extremely pleased and relieved that action was being taking. They were also somewhat surprised, as this was not an approach they had promoted; in addition, the issue had not been mentioned when Price met with Hull on July 25. Nevertheless, the board offered Cordell Hull its "strongest and most wholehearted support" for providing action in the face of congressional apathy. The decision meant that the executive branch was clearly behind legislation, such as the Pittman resolution, that provided for an embargo against nations who violated the Nine Power Treaty. Hull's action marked a "turning of the tide" that changed the whole picture.[46]

Of course, there was still much to do. Supporters were urged to contact Hull and Roosevelt to push for further action in limiting the trade of war material with Japan. But in addition to pressurizing the administration, supporters were urged to work closely with it. The committee's next objective was to support "whatever may be done further by the Administration towards ending our partnership with Japanese militarism." Supporters were urged to watch the news—especially the actions of Hull, Secretary of the Treasury Henry Morgenthau, and Secretary of Commerce Harry Hopkins—for new proposals to support with telegrams and letters. The committee urged its supporters not to rest but to push ahead and "see this thing through."[47]

The AUCPE was also happy with the treaty abrogation while still disappointed with the larger failure of neutrality revision. Eichelberger acknowledged that Hull's decision was a "magnificent step." However, he conceded that nothing short of war would persuade Congress to reconvene to reconsider neutrality legislation. After discussions with Harry Price in Washington, it was decided that no further efforts would be made to work toward specific legislation "for fear of an anti-climax." Putting direct political appeals aside for the immediate future, the union was to concentrate on expanding its organizational base and a broad program of public education in preparation for the next congressional session.[48]

The communication with Price reflected how cooperative the two organizations had become in the summer of 1939. They shared information, worked together on general strategy, and even jointly prepared a dramatic skit on the issue of supplying war supplies to Japan, which was distributed to radio stations across the country. More significantly, though, their relationship had become sufficiently close for the AUCPE to suggest a merger. They recognized that although the peace movement as a whole had divided over the past year, the pacifist wing had retained a degree of unity. In comparison, the AUCPE and ACNPJA were working separately toward very similar goals. What was needed was a unified movement for peace through an active foreign policy and collective security.[49]

As the ACNPJA leader with the most global vision, Roger Greene brought the suggestion to the committee, noting that the AUCPE was impressed with the work of the ACNPJA and was "anxious to annex some of the talent and leadership." Greene supported the proposal, arguing that his group should work with the AUCPE to support a global policy of discriminating against aggressors, or at the very least a general law that would include the Sino-Japanese War. If the ACNPJA stuck to its narrow focus on China, it took the risk of being overtaken by events in Europe and watching the Roosevelt administration support a cash-and-carry policy that worked against aggressors in Europe but not in Asia. Greene also argued that the committee's financial worries would be eased and that there would be additional efficiencies in administrative and running costs.[50]

However, despite having the case put to them by Eichelberger and Hugh Moore, the ACNPJA board rejected the proposal. Harry Price, who had some sympathy toward the proposal, reminded Greene that there were still no sanctions in place against Japan, but that the abrogation of the Treaty of Commerce and Navigation offered a clear path to embargo legislation in 1940. In contrast, the recent debates over neutrality revision were filled with "complications" that came with a broader vision, and no clear solution was yet in sight. The "beautifully clear-cut" embargo issue had no such complications, and far more obvious public support. Just as important, the majority of the ACNPJA board members were unwilling to relinquish their focus on the Far East. It had been the primary focus of the ACNPJA and was the reason why many Americans had joined it. The committee could not abandon "the responsibilities of an increasingly recognized leadership" on the embargo question.[51]

The ACNPJA thanked the AUCPE for its offer, and despite the majority verdict against a merger, it was unanimous in wanting to continue "the closest possible cooperation." But behind the scenes, it was clear that the ACNPJA felt any further cooperation was bound to limit the emphasis on China. In addition, there were no obvious organizational benefits. The committee had already profited from a close relationship but had no desire to take responsibility for the development, expansion, and promotion of the AUCPE. Price claimed that a merger was still a possibility for the future, but it was a realistic possibility only after the committee had achieved its goal of an embargo.[52]

Ultimately the ACNPJA chose to keep its separate identity and its focus on Asia. Given its priorities, it was an understandable decision. Its concept of internationalism was one that argued for a more active American foreign policy but applied only to Asia—even on the eve of war in Europe. In contrast, the broader internationalist vision of Eichelberger and the AUCPE included the Sino-Japanese War, but concern with Japanese aggression and the future of China was just one part of a vision that was increasingly shifting to focus on European affairs.

In August 1939, organized American internationalists had a number of common concerns. Most significantly, they wanted a more active foreign policy from the United States. Ideally, such a policy would reject the notion that America's priority was to keep as far away from war as possible, which had been the basis of the Neutrality Acts. Instead, they wanted a foreign policy that distinguished between aggressors and victims of aggression, which would enable them to support victims who in many cases were also nations friendly to the United States.

There was disagreement over just how active that policy should be, however. Even within the ACNPJA and the AUCPE, there was disagreement over the scope of American internationalism. For some, American interests were global; for others they were regional. The internationalist strategy varied depending on the geographic priorities of those involved. Those such as the ACNPJA who emphasized the war in Asia were the most enthusiastic about the recent treaty abrogation, but they recognized the need to maintain a tight focus on the Sino-Japanese War. This was not just because of their personal ties and interest in the conflict. They knew that in the event of war in Europe, the American public would become preoccupied with events across the Atlantic.[53]

In the aftermath of the neutrality debates, it was clear that organized internationalists recognized their growing political significance. It was also clear that both the ACNPJA and the AUCPE were increasingly aligned with the administration. Both organizations recognized that their priorities were similar to those of the White House, and both looked more and more to the administration for guidance and direction. After a decade in the political wilderness with the peace movement, a more practical and applied internationalism promised genuine change. They moved into the fall ready to prepare the public for legislation in early 1940. They would not have to wait that long.

Chapter 3

The Phony War and the Non-Partisan Committee for Peace through Revision of the Neutrality Law

On August 23, 1939, Germany and the Soviet Union signed a nonaggression pact that all but guaranteed war in Europe. On September 1, Germany invaded Poland, with Britain and France declaring war on Germany two days later. The long-anticipated European war had arrived. Since the final occupation of Czechoslo-vakia in March, American internationalists had worked to convince the wider public of the threat to peace in Europe and the need for the United States to play a more active role in opposing aggression. Their efforts had been largely unsuc-cessful, in part because Americans were not convinced that war was imminent or that it would affect them even if it was. It took war in Europe for attitudes to really begin to change.

Admittedly, the change was hardly dramatic, in large part due to the "phony" nature of the war which saw almost no military action in Europe until April 1940. In fact, in the short term public attitudes about U.S. military involvement did not change at all. Polls taken in the week war broke out revealed that 84 per-cent of the public did not want Americans to be sent overseas to fight Germany. By the beginning of October, that number had risen to 95 percent. However, this was partly a result of the belief that Britain and France would win the war—a belief held by 82 percent of Americans. In the event that the war went badly for Britain and France, the number against sending American troops to Europe dropped to 71 percent. The biggest shift was in how Americans viewed Neutral-ity Act revision. Although a vast majority of Americans still supported a ban on both keeping American ships out of war zones and allowing American citizens to travel on belligerent ships, a small majority now believed the neutrality law should be changed so that Britain and France could buy war material from the United States (even though over 90% still insisted this be under a cash-and-carry system). By mid-September, 62 percent of those expressing an opinion supported neutrality revision.[1]

The biggest problem facing American internationalists was the gap between the outcome the United States wanted from the war and what the nation was willing to do to make that outcome a reality. In October 1939, 62 percent of Americans wanted to do everything possible to help Britain and France win the war except actually go to war. Yet if the question was rephrased slightly, with the risk of war inserted, then 66 percent of Americans were not willing to do everything possible to help win the war if there was a risk of American involvement. By promoting a more active foreign policy, organized internationalists were among the minority accepting that risk. Between September 1939 and December 1941 they fought to bring the majority around to their way of thinking.[2]

Protecting Vital National Interests

Unsurprisingly, most internationalists began with neutrality revision. They did so in the knowledge that the focus of American interest was now on Europe and that the war in Asia was a secondary concern. The outbreak of war in Europe now attracted the majority of governmental and public attention. For the Western-thinking, Atlantic-facing, Anglophile members of the AUCPE, the focus on Europe was not just understandable but urgent and essential. Their campaign for neutrality revision would pick up where it had left off just months before, underpinned by the belief that American national and economic security—and indeed, the future of world peace—was threatened by another European war. They took no pleasure in the outbreak of war, but it certainly gave them momentum.

In contrast, the ACNPJA lost what little momentum it had gained in the summer of 1939. The new focus on Europe left those Americans who were more concerned with China with a challenge. Given the growing interest and concern in European affairs, how could internationalists maintain any level of interest in the Sino-Japanese War? In response to concerns that the Asian war would slip into the background, Harry Price prepared a memorandum for the ACNPJA entitled "War in Europe—What about Asia?" The primary implication for Price was that Japan was more reliant on the United States than ever before, as European markets for war materials were lost. What he did not publicly acknowledge was his concern that despite a growing popular majority for an embargo on war materials to Japan, the issue was being overshadowed. By October, Price reluctantly conceded that the embargo push had to wait and that neutrality revision was the immediate priority.[3]

Neutrality revision was the priority not only of organized internationalists but also of the Roosevelt administration. After a reluctance to speak out earlier in the year, the president finally committed himself to repealing the arms embargo. After publicly hinting at the issue in a September 8 press conference, he urged Congress to repeal the embargo provisions in a speech on September 21. In highlighting how the Neutrality Acts deviated from international law, Roosevelt asked for repeal on the basis that the provisions were "vitally dangerous to American neutrality, American security and, above all, American peace." He repeatedly emphasized the need to keep the United States at peace, arguing that neutrality revision was the best way of ensuring peace by allowing the sale of all goods through a cash-and-carry system.[4]

This was exactly the leadership the AUCPE had been looking for. With polls suggesting a change in public attitudes on the issue, the prospect of congressional neutrality reform was promising. While retaining its original three aims, the AUCPE placed its immediate focus on neutrality revision, arguing that the failure of Congress to revise the law sooner had in fact encouraged the present round of German aggression. The AUCPE agreed with Roosevelt's claim that revision was the best way to ensure peace for America. In urging "methods other than war and stronger than words," the group distinguished itself from the pacifist wing of the peace movement and "isolationists." Yet this was no call for war either. At this point the AUCPE agreed with Roosevelt's unstated hope that revision was the best way to defeat Germany without American involvement.[5]

With the outbreak of war, Clark Eichelberger immediately sought to align the union's policy with that of the administration. As early as September 3, Eichelberger sent a telegram to the White House asking for an appointment on behalf of the AUCPE which "supports revision neutrality law and administrations [sic] foreign policy." He made it clear that he wanted to know from the president what the AUCPE could do to ensure the passage of revised neutrality legislation. Just four days later, thanks to a positive reference from Roosevelt's adviser Benjamin Cohen, Eichelberger met with Roosevelt at the White House. The internationalist leader outlined the divisions within the peace movement, noting that his group supported revision as it was the best way possible to keep the country out of war, but that if the British and French lost, "the struggle for civilization would be a lone battle for the United States."[6]

For the remainder of the meeting, Eichelberger asked how he could help the president. In doing so, he set a pattern for the next two years (and indeed, beyond) by offering the support of his private organizations to the administration.

Through the great debate of 1939–41 over the direction of American foreign policy, Eichelberger's organizations supported the administration's policy fully. They did so not because of any conspiracy but because their interests aligned almost completely. This had rarely been the case through the 1930s as the League of Nations Association had tried to mobilize public opinion, but here, at a time of greater urgency, the administration and the internationalists were united. In addition, Eichelberger in particular recognized that the best way to achieve results was to work closely with the government rather than wholly independently.

The immediate priority was finding out what the AUCPE could do to ensure neutrality revision. Eichelberger wanted to know what type of revision the president had in mind. Roosevelt's response was to focus on eliminating the arms embargo rather than looking for wholesale repeal at this stage. When asked what types of arguments the AUCPE should make for revision, Roosevelt stated that the AUCPE could make a much more forceful case than he could. In particular, it could make the case that revision would enable Britain and France to win the war without the need for American involvement.[7]

One of the best things Roosevelt believed the private internationalist movement could do was to highlight the uncertainty of an Allied victory. Anecdotal and polling evidence suggested an overwhelming majority of Americans thought Britain and France would win the war (82% in the case of one Gallup poll). Roosevelt argued that the warring sides were in fact evenly matched. The AUCPE could help inform Americans of the different visions of the future the United States could face depending on which side was victorious. If Europe and Asia were dominated by Germany, Japan, and the Soviet Union, there would be a clear threat to American interests, even in the Western Hemisphere. While the president could not make such strong statements for fear of being seen as a warmonger, the AUCPE could.[8]

Eichelberger came away from the meeting with the knowledge that the president wanted the support of the private internationalist movement in order to secure neutrality revision. The administration was also satisfied that it had an ally with the potential to mobilize public opinion behind specific legislation and its broader foreign policy aims. Less than two weeks later, the State Department contacted Eichelberger to see if his organization had taken any steps to encourage support of the administration's proposal. At an AUCPE board meeting the following day, he emphasized the need for Congress to receive correspondence supporting neutrality revision and for the union to coordinate with senators in Washington on future strategy.[9]

What was not clear at that meeting was just how significant the following ten days would be. The AUCPE continued drafting a statement on neutrality revision, with more vivid language than ever before. The statement argued that the current embargo gave an advantage to aggression that was deliberately planned, as was the case with Germany. But it then went much further than previous AUCPE language in specifically highlighting the American interests at stake in the new European war. In violating the Kellogg-Briand Pact, Germany was deemed to have "done a grave wrong" to the United States and to have set in motion forces that "dissipated our national peace and prosperity." The United States had a "vital national interest in the restoration of law and order," and that interest had to be defended. The statement then went further still, arguing that to defend American interests was not to "take sides," but if Germany was to emerge victorious, the Americas would be next.[10]

For the first time, the statement raised the threat of a challenge to the Monroe Doctrine. If the navies of Britain and France were defeated, then nothing stood in the way of German infiltration of Latin America. While this threat was a worst-case scenario, it was not beyond the realm of possibility. As evidence, the statement emphasized German efforts to dominate trade in Latin America, along with the growing influence of Nazi bunds in the United States supported by German agents. While it was somewhat exaggerated, the threat to the continental United States and "Fortress America" was a theme that internationalists would return to again and again in the years immediately prior to Pearl Harbor.[11]

The Non-Partisan Committee for Peace through Revision of the Neutrality Law

Yet even while the statement was being drafted, the decision was made that the AUCPE was not the most appropriate vehicle for promoting neutrality revision. Inspired by his conversations with the president and the State Department, Eichelberger decided to take bold political action. After a week of meetings in Washington, he and his AUCPE colleagues created a new ad hoc organization to focus solely on the immediate neutrality debate. By the end of September they were searching for prominent national names to add weight to the new (and cumbersomely titled) Non-Partisan Committee for Peace through Revision of the Neutrality Law. The new committee was created in just two weeks.[12]

To maximize the publicity of the new organization, it needed a prominent chairman. After consulting with the State Department and congressional allies, the decision was taken to ask the editor of the *Emporia Gazette,* William Allen White. As editor of the *Gazette* since 1895, White was a logical choice for several reasons. As a Republican who was sympathetic to Roosevelt's New Deal, he shored up the new committee's bipartisan credentials. It helped that White and Roosevelt were on good terms; Roosevelt had once said that White was a very good friend for three and a half years out of every four. White had already displayed his support for a more active foreign policy by acting as an honorary vice chairman for the ACNPJA. Perhaps most important, he represented "middle America" in a committee dominated by eastern elites. Given the strength of non-interventionist sentiment in the Midwest, the "Sage of Emporia" provided a certain geographical balance (it was also noted that both Kansas senators were against neutrality revision).[13]

Despite initial reservations, White was sufficiently impressed with the quality of names supporting the new organization that he agreed to join on the condition that he be consulted daily. Wary of the accusations of warmongering, he also insisted that there be no financial assistance from international bankers of munitions manufacturers. However, while he would take much of the internationalist limelight over the following year, much of the work was done for White back in New York. White would later describe his role in the NPC as "pretty much of a stuffed shirt," fronting an organization led by Eichelberger and Shotwell. This underestimated his role, as his own personal prominence brought the NPC (and its successor, the Committee to Defend America by Aiding the Allies) a considerable amount of publicity. But it is just as misleading to look back at the NPC as White's committee. Although it may have been known as such to the public, his role was more limited than subsequent histories have suggested. Most decisions were approved by White, but few were taken by him alone.[14]

The NPC was announced to the public on October 2, 1939. Its lengthy list of members consisted predominantly of religious leaders, academics, and journalists, including *Chicago Daily News* editor Frank Knox, suffrage leader and peace activist Carrie Chapman Catt, *The Nation* editor Freda Kirchwey, and columnist Dorothy Thompson. Initial press releases emphasized that the AUCPE was the NPC's secretariat, and key AUCPE members such as James Shotwell, Hugh Moore, Frederick McKee, Edgar Fisher, and Henry Atkinson were also prominent in the new committee.[15]

Preserving Peace for America

NPC strategy was not unlike that of the parent AUCPE, though with a much more specific focus. For credibility, the NPC sought to make itself as representative as possible by including leaders from all walks of life. Then, through all possible channels of promotion—civic organizations, radio addresses, promotional literature, newspapers, etc.—the NPC aimed to inform and rally public opinion across the nation behind the cause of neutrality revision. Finally, that support was to be reflected back to Washington to ensure prompt legislative action. Like the ACNPJA before it, the NPC used the John Price Jones Corporation for public relations advice.[16]

Despite the growing support for neutrality revision, William Allen White's initial appeal for support reflected the challenge that faced the internationalists. It tried to stay true to the group's roots in the peace movement while at the same time showing a clear desire for a German defeat. Revision of the neutrality laws would go "as far as human ingenuity can" to lessen the possibility of American involvement, but at the same time it would no longer disadvantage the democracies fighting against the spread of dictatorship. By making it clear where their sympathies lay, the internationalists opened themselves up to criticism from non-interventionists. Such sympathies led to criticisms that neutrality revision was not really for peace at all, but the first step on a slippery slope to war. Where arms would flow, armies would follow. Other criticisms built on historical parallels with the Great War, claiming that cash-and-carry would quickly lead to loans, and that losses at sea would draw the nation into war.[17]

Anticipating such criticisms, and with genuine hope for peace still in mind, initial NPC literature emphasized that the sole purpose of the committee was to preserve peace for America. In a list of reasons for revision, the need to stem aggression was played down and placed fifth on a list of six, behind the limits of existing legislation for preserving peace and the reasons why new legislation would be more effective. However, building on Roosevelt's suggestion that the NPC could make stronger arguments than the administration could, this cautious strategy did not last long.[18]

Nowhere was this clearer than in White's October 15 radio address. Describing the current embargo law as "foolish," White began with a strong argument that a cash-and-carry system would offer the best protection from war for the United States. It kept all trade out of American ships, unlike the existing legislation, which saw American ships at risk transporting goods other than war materials. In the second half of his speech, however, White focused on the nature of the war, describing it as "a clash of ideologies." The clash was not just with Germany however, but also with Russia, which had recently completed its invasion of Poland and whose aggressive diplomacy threatened war with Finland. The totalitarian ideals of Russia and Germany were described as identical, and they were "inexorably welded as joint defenders of tyranny." In fighting this tyranny, White argued that the European democracies were "carrying our banner" and "digging our first-line trenches."[19]

Yet despite White's bold ideological vision of the war and his appeals to the "rights of freedom and the justice that symbolizes liberty," he concluded his address by highlighting the peaceful and self-interested nature of neutrality revision. Revision enabled the United States to build up its own defenses, defend its own homes, and secure its own liberties. The jarring nature of his final comments revealed the problem that many internationalists faced: the need to portray the European war as threatening enough to justify legislation to help democracies but not so threatening as to necessitate war (the war in Asia was almost entirely absent from NPC speeches and literature). For some this was a purely tactical decision about the best way to win support, but for others—including White—it was a genuine issue that reflected the increasingly conflicting desires of democratic victory and peace for the United States.[20]

The NPC achieved a tremendous amount of publicity in its first two weeks, by which time much of the congressional battle had been won. While the NPC played its part, there is little doubt that the main factor in winning over Congress was the outbreak of war in Europe. However, Roosevelt's tactic of settling for cash-and-carry legislation—rather than the authority to discriminate against aggressors—was a wise one, as it settled congressional nerves over the growing amount of presidential power. Just as wise was the NPC's decision to loyally follow the president's leadership on the issue and focus on the legislation on offer. On October 27 the Senate voted 63–30 in favor of neutrality revision. The House of Representatives followed on November 2 with a vote of 243–181. All efforts to add amendments failed, and Roosevelt signed the new Neutrality Act on November 4.[21]

A letter from White on November 14 brought the NPC to a close with the assessment that the committee had made a "constructive contribution to the cause of peace." Privately, White's assessment was that the organization had done a good job "but Lord I had nothing much to do with it except to stand around and look wise." Eichelberger was much more upbeat about the "very great part" the committee had played in winning the fight for revision. He too argued that it was in the cause of peace and that revision had lessened the likelihood of war, allowing American sympathies for Britain and France to be expressed through cash-and-carry legislation, rather than "being frustrated until it burst in a war movement." Overall the NPC had done "a great service to our country."[22]

It had certainly done a great service to the administration, and Roosevelt was quick to thank White for his support. "You did a grand job. It was effective and most helpful." While it is almost impossible to evaluate just how effective the NPC was in securing neutrality revision, it is clear that Roosevelt believed their contribution had been valuable. This was particularly true of White's involvement, and the president contacted him again for advice on foreign affairs in December. He was particularly concerned about the public's reliance on the Atlantic and Pacific Oceans for safety. The problem, he wrote, was how to get the American people to think of "conceivable consequences," or worst-case scenarios, without scaring them or being accused of dragging the nation to war. White's response reflected his own ambivalence about the current state of world affairs and his desire to stay at peace while ensuring the defeat of Germany. "I fear our involvement before the peace, and yet I fear to remain uninvolved letting the danger of a peace of tyranny approach too near." After much deliberation, White concluded, "If we can help the Allies surreptitiously, illicitly and down the alley by night, we ought to do it."[23]

Roosevelt's correspondence was prompted by the domestic response to the Winter War between the Soviet Union and Finland. Despite the relative ease with which neutrality revision passed through Congress, and a great deal of sympathy for Finland, there was a widespread sense that to go any further than neutrality revision in aiding the Finns might drag the nation into war. The persistent yet understandable fear of military involvement again restrained the United States from providing aid to victims of aggression and led at least one member of the NPC to suggest that the group's work was not yet done. New York state senator Frederic Coudert argued the committee should remain in place, as global uncertainty meant more congressional legislation was likely in order "to protect the peace, honor and dignity of the United States." In such an event, it was argued that a committee such as the NPC could again prove extremely useful. Within a few months, Coudert would be proved right.[24]

The Commission to Study the Organization of Peace

Yet at the same time that the AUCPE set up the NPC to oppose aggression through neutrality revision, several of its leaders were also organizing behind the union's other two aims: to promote justice between nations and to develop adequate global peace machinery. Even before war broke out in Europe, Clark Eichelberger was developing yet another organization, this time to consider the shape of the future world peace. This group was modeled on the Inquiry set up by Woodrow Wilson in 1917 and first met on November 5, 1939, before even the State Department had begun its postwar deliberations. It possessed another earnest and cumbersome though accurate title: the Commission to Study the Organization of Peace (CSOP).[25]

The CSOP had deep roots in the American peace movement. It was based on the belief that a lasting peace required a well-organized international society. The failures of the League of Nations reinforced rather than erased the belief that some form of world organization was essential. The CSOP quickly became the research arm of the League of Nations Association, but it was sponsored by a number of other like-minded organizations including the AUCPE, the Church Peace Union, the World Citizens Association, and the American Association of University Women. It also had a close relationship with the Carnegie Endowment for International Peace, as its chairman, James Shotwell—who had participated in the original inquiry—was also director of the endowment's Division of Economics and History. Like the AUCPE, the endowment provided financial support for the CSOP, and the lines between the CEIP and CSOP were never entirely clear. Shotwell later described the relationship between the CSOP and the Division of Economics and History as "a personal union" like "the union of Austria and Hungary."[26]

In addition to Shotwell, the new commission shared a similar roster of internationalists with the AUCPE, with Eichelberger as director. Other familiar internationalist names included Roger Greene, Charles Fenwick, Hugh Moore, and Frederick McKee. Within a month there were more than fifty members. Notable names included academics such as Virginia Gildersleeve, William Allen Neilson, Clyde Eagleton, and Quincy Wright; businessmen, lawyers, and bankers such as Henry I. Harriman, John Foster Dulles, and Thomas W. Lamont; and government officials including Katharine F. Lenroot and Marshall Dimock.[27]

While the new inquiry was not formally connected to the White House, Eichelberger had personally raised the concept with Roosevelt in September. The president approved of the idea, with the suggestion that the study should not be done in the name of the League of Nations Association for fear of raising opposition before it even began. That approval ensured the creation of the CSOP, and the short- and long-term goals of the collective security internationalists were in place. At the same time as they were increasingly concerned about the possibility of war and the challenges of American neutrality, they were also looking ahead to analyze the principles of the future peace.[28]

Those principles built on the work of the AUCPE and the program of the League of Nations Association in particular. That LNA program was based to a large degree on the Carnegie Endowment principles outlined at the 1935 Chatham House meeting. Politically, collective security was unsurprisingly at the heart of CSOP planning, based on a revitalized League of Nations with full American participation. Economically, the idea of a new international organization to ensure free trade and minimize economic nationalism was promoted. In terms of social justice, the CSOP also sought to build on the work of the International Labor Organization and develop greater intellectual cooperation between nations.[29]

Even more clearly than the AUCPE's, the CSOP's planning revealed a progressive internationalist vision for the world that was Wilsonian in its emphasis on international organization and aimed to reshape the world on a largely American design. There were a great many discussions to be held and studies to be undertaken, but the initial outline of the CSOP clearly revealed its future direction. Eichelberger explained his thoughts on the commission to Eleanor Roosevelt, hoping for a formal endorsement from the president. He insisted that even in times of war nations needed to prepare for peace and that it was "the task of people in democratic countries" to build a warless world and to improve standards of living through "international social justice."[30]

Unlike the other internationalist organizations stimulated by the outbreak of war, the CSOP took a more elite and research-oriented approach to its activity. While other organizations mobilized public opinion, the CSOP focused on research, detailed planning and creating reports. Shotwell described it as an attempt to study problems rather than to create another organization. It only met monthly, and its public profile was relatively limited; its first ten-page preliminary report was issued after almost a year, in November 1940. Though it was also set up to encourage popular discussion from the outset, only after the United States entered the war in 1941 did the CSOP take on a wider educational role among the general public.[31]

Underpinning the CSOP was a sense of international responsibility. It strongly rejected non-interventionism and fought against "isolationism." It was the same sense of responsibility that had supported the League of Nations Association through the interwar years, and it went beyond specific concerns about the fate of a particular nation such as China or Britain. It even went beyond the emergency concerns of the AUCPE and NPC. It signaled a desire for a more active American foreign policy not simply in the short term but in the long term; not simply in times of danger but in times of peace and stability. Indeed, it was firmly believed that American involvement in good times would help limit future insecurity.

In the autumn of 1939, the CSOP signified an attempt by one particular group of internationalists to consider the long-term issues facing global society. Its lack of public profile reflected its research-led approach but also the fact that most Americans were still conflicted about engaging with world affairs in the short term. They were reluctant to be drawn closer to wars in Europe or Asia, let alone willing to consider postwar issues. The collective-security internationalists led by Eichelberger and Shotwell recognized this and operated along two separate but related paths. The CSOP worked behind the scenes to think about the future, whereas the AUCPE (and its offshoots) focused on the immediate present. Even as organizations such as the NPC focused narrowly on pressing matters, their broader vision of the future could be seen through the CSOP.

Post-Revision Frustration

The more urgent question facing internationalists in the aftermath of neutrality revision was, what next? The revision issue had provided clear direction for the

AUCPE throughout 1939, and even those focused on Asia had deferred to the issue in September and October. The success of the NPC showed what impact the organized internationalist movement could have given a practical political focus and a convergence of interests with the Roosevelt administration. Even before the new legislation was signed, internationalist leaders were planning ahead for the next battle against the forces of pacifism, non-interventionism, and isolation. Unfortunately, the next key political issue was not immediately apparent.

In late November, AUCPE directors met to congratulate themselves on the success of the NPC (which they referred to as the William Allen White Committee) and to add their support to the CSOP. They then recognized the need to clarify their own program, in response to requests from field offices for direction and clarification. A week later, the AUCPE announced its winter program, in which it struggled to find a shrinking middle ground between warmongering and isolationism. It reiterated the need for a more active foreign policy, acknowledging that the United States could not "live its own life of peace in a world of lawlessness and anarchy." However, the union also supported the policy of avoiding military involvement in any conflict. In a war that was deemed increasingly essential to America's broadly defined interests, the AUCPE went no further than supporting the sale of war material to victims of aggression and denying it to aggressors.[32]

The union's specific policy suggestions for the winter were based on its three-point program of opposing aggression, promoting economic justice between nations, and developing adequate peace machinery. On the final point, looking far ahead with the CSOP in mind, the union promised to cooperate with other organizations in a campaign of public education on the future organization of peace. The two other proposals were more concrete. To promote economic justice, the AUCPE sought economic cooperation and lower trade barriers. It therefore supported the renewal of the government's authority to arrange reciprocal trade agreements. Finally, to oppose aggression, it stood for "some form" of embargo on war materials to Japan in order to respect the territorial integrity of China.[33]

By early January, with a new congressional session beginning, the AUCPE recognized the need for a more direct call to action. It emphasized to its members the need to support the secretary of state in extending the Reciprocal Trade Agreements Act, which was up for renewal early in 1940, and the need for an embargo on war materials to Japan. The AUCPE informed members that they must confront the opposition to both issues by writing to their congressmen, arranging local study groups, and informing their community about the relationship between trade treaties, the embargo, and world peace. The fact that this last point was deemed necessary reflected the lack of immediacy facing both issues. While these policies tackled pressing concerns, there was no doubt they lacked the popular attention and emotional appeal of neutrality revision.[34]

Just as the ACNPJA had deferred to the AUCPE during the neutrality revision debates, the AUCPE now allowed the ACNPJA to retake the lead on the embargo issue. Despite his involvement with the AUCPE, Harry Price had never fully taken his eye off that issue. His planning for the New Year began in October, when he began persuading Roger Greene to relocate from Chicago to Washington in time for the new congressional session. The idea was to follow the example of the NPC and meet with congressmen on a one-to-one basis. The committee would then be strongly placed to advocate for an embargo on Japan to begin on or after January 26 when the Treaty of Commerce and Navigation lapsed. After initially declining, Greene eventually agreed to set up a Washington office in early January. Attempts to bring William Allen White to Washington to repeat his NPC successes were unsuccessful.[35]

Immediately after neutrality revision on November 9, Price and Greene were both present at a luncheon given by ACNPJA honorary chairman, Henry Stimson. Also present were Thomas Arthur Bisson, former Foreign Policy Association president Raymond Leslie Buell, and publisher Henry Luce. Senator Key Pittman was unable to attend but sent a telegram that both gave and asked the meeting for direction. Stimson outlined the collective view of the Far East, which aligned perfectly with that of the ACNPJA. Chinese civilization was "pacific, clumsy, tenacious"; the Japanese were feudal and militaristic. With its great investment in China—missionary, educational, and philanthropic—the United States needed a new policy that enabled the Chinese to decide their own future. With no disagreement on the need for action, it was decided that any embargo must be justified solely by Japan's violation of the Nine Power Treaty and not tied to any further neutrality revision. With a specific focus, congressional action appeared to be a possibility.[36]

Yet Congress was only one part of the government. One of the key lessons of the NPC campaign had been the ad hoc committee's close alignment with the Roosevelt administration. While Price was focused on the possibility of legislation in Congress, Greene raised the question of the president's attitude on the issue. He recognized that Roosevelt's involvement would be crucial. Presciently, he told Price that it would prove very difficult to get any embargo legislation through Congress unless Roosevelt let it be known he was behind it. Greene's efforts to meet with Roosevelt to uncover his views firsthand were unsuccessful.[37]

Unfortunately, it rapidly became clear that the administration had no plans to push ahead with an embargo on Japan. Price and the ACNPJA argued that the primary significance of war in Europe was that it increased American influence in the Pacific. Unfortunately, this interpretation was not shared by the administration. For the president, the significance of war in Europe was that it was now the main foreign policy priority. As a result, the United States could ill afford to antagonize

Japan and risk a conflict in the Pacific. Price's interpretation was not shared by the rest of the nation either. In the eyes of the wider public, the European war now dominated popular discourse. It overshadowed the conflict in Asia, making it increasingly difficult to mobilize public support for action against Japan. Public attitudes had not moved against an embargo; it was simply no longer a major issue (it had not been a priority even before September 1939).[38]

As early as mid-December, Greene warned Price that they would receive little support from the Department of State for the embargo proposal. The State Department was considering restrictions on imports, not exports, as they were deemed to be less provocative and would not require new legislation. It was clear that administration support for an embargo had cooled dramatically. Administration officials were unwilling to support any of the four proposed congressional bills to impose an embargo unless they were certain of its passage. However, without their full support and backing, the passage of any bill was unlikely. A lengthy public letter to the *New York Times* from Henry Stimson urging prohibition of the sale of war materials to Japan had no discernible effect at all.[39]

As expected, when the Treaty of Commerce and Navigation lapsed on January 26, the United States took no further action against Japan. At this point, both Greene and Price became increasingly frustrated with governmental inaction. Greene vented these frustrations to Eichelberger, upset by the lack of forward planning and inertia in the State Department. A number of possible options were under consideration, but there was no obvious support for any of them. A large part of this dissatisfaction related to the foreign policy message being sent to Japan. Inaction on the part of the United States might encourage further aggression from the Japanese. Price expressed similar irritation with the State Department's "excessive caution."[40]

However, in organizational terms, Greene felt a sense of betrayal: "We adopted our program with the implied blessing of the department, which told us to go out and get popular support. Now that we have a measure of popular support they go back on us." Having built up a clear majority of support for an embargo, ACNPJA supporters were likely to be disappointed by inaction from the government. One implication of that disappointment was a reduction in donations. By February, the ANCPJA had fallen into deficit, and it was by no means certain that incoming funds were sufficient to support an ongoing and open-ended campaign, especially with the nation's eyes on Europe.[41]

Their fears were confirmed when Greene met with Hull on February 6, 1940. Hull made his general sympathy for an embargo clear, but he also made it clear that there would be no movement for an embargo at that time. He did not believe there was sufficient support in Congress; he also feared an aggressive Japanese response and the possibility of war, however remote that seemed. Hull praised the

ACNPJA's efforts, arguing that it had been doing fine work and that it should continue to mobilize and agitate congressional and public opinion. However, this gave little encouragement to Greene. He took "no real satisfaction" from the meeting, as it did little other than reconfirm Hull's support for the committee and agreement with its ultimate objective. The embargo push appeared to have stalled.[42]

Rather than release their frustrations publicly, however, the ACNPJA leaders fell back into line with the administration. Opting to work with rather than break from the administration, they scaled down their expectations to match those of the Department of State. Deciding that any action was better than no action, the committee agreed to back measures short of a full embargo. In particular, it supported calls for restrictions on imports from Japan. Greene reluctantly expressed his revised feelings to Roosevelt, arguing that whatever measure was wisest, "the time has come to do something. Otherwise the Japanese are likely to believe we are afraid of them, and then they may become even bolder, increasing the danger of serious conflict." Roosevelt did not respond, but he clearly did not agree with Greene, sticking for the moment with the line that inaction was the safest course of action. The president did suggest in March that an embargo measure would be passed in the current congressional session, but this reflected his overall sympathies rather than practical realities, and it provided only false hope for the Committee.[43]

In April, it was Price's turn to meet with the secretary of state, and Hull again congratulated the ACNPJA on its "exceedingly valuable" work. Nevertheless, Price could not hide his frustration with the administration's recent lack of action. He outlined in detail the effect of that inaction on China, the encouragement it provided to Japan, and the damage it caused to domestic support. He emphasized pressure from some supporters to stop backing an administration set on a policy of "appeasement" with Japan. Price added that he would prefer to maintain a policy of "constructive support" but that such a policy was increasingly difficult in the face of an intransigent State Department. Hull responded by insisting the country had to move forward step by step. He remained concerned about the possible failure of an embargo bill, especially given the partisan nature of voting in an election year. Price concluded that the State Department was not interested in an embargo law, and that it would become a viable prospect only if the administration could be sure it would be passed without a political storm over "getting the country into war."[44]

After months of excitement about a potential embargo, the sense of disappointment in the winter of 1940 was considerable. For those who retained a focus on the Sino-Japanese War, everything appeared to be conspiring against them. Both Greene and Price increasingly recognized that they were at the mercy of larger forces, both foreign and domestic. The war in Europe dominated the political agenda, overshadowing the war in Asia, lessening the relative importance of an embargo. Domestic political concerns reduced the likelihood of any such embargo. There was a growing sense that further conflict in Europe would make an embargo even less likely. Yet as it turned out, war in Europe would eventually limit American participation in Japanese aggression without the need for embargo legislation.

The failure of the ACNPJA was also a failure of the AUCPE, as the embargo issue was part of its three-point program for the winter. The other immediate part of that program was to support the renewal of the Reciprocal Trade Agreement Act. Here the AUCPE would find success, but without making the same significant contribution to national debate that the NPC had achieved the previous fall. The union's attitude to the trade agreement legislation connected the immediate need for renewal with the AUCPE's long-term peace goals. Yet the long-term, technical nature of the issue meant the union struggled to gain any traction with the public or Congress.[45]

The AUCPE position held that the Reciprocal Trade Agreements Act helped to undercut economic nationalism and "marked one sane effort to keep open that flow of international trade so essential to peace." Not only was economic nationalism a cause of war, but free trade was essential to provide "sound economic foundations upon which to build a new world of law and order." By focusing on the long-term benefits, the AUCPE was true to its goals, but the issue lacked the immediacy of neutrality revision. There was also a lack of urgency, thanks to a sense (picked up by Roger Greene in Washington) that the act would be renewed with relative ease. In the end, the Senate passed it on April 5 by a margin of only five votes; all Republicans and fifteen Democrats voted against it.[46]

Union Now

The AUCPE itself recognized the need for other legislative avenues to pursue. Though it had been very active in the fall, it now lacked a clear sense of momentum. Hugh Moore asked how the union could best express its message of collective security in order to combat "the wave of isolationist pacifism" sweeping the nation. One possible consideration was for it to become a mass membership organization in order to help spread its message and heighten its esteem. In the first instance, the board authorized the creation of a national advisory committee to be composed of individuals and representatives of organizations "covering as wide a geographical area as possible and representing all phases of opinion." But when asked what legislative issues the union could address beyond the trade agreements and the embargo issue, the board was short on inspiration.[47]

The need for inspiration at the AUCPE was in part a result of the limited nature of the phony war. Yet it was intensified by a sense of competition within the broader internationalist movement. This was spurred by the growing popularity of Clarence Streit's Union Now movement. Up to the end of 1939, the drive for a more active foreign policy among organized internationalists had largely stemmed from the overlapping groups of disaffected peace activists that made up the ACNPJA and AUCPE. However, the publication of Streit's popular *Union Now* in 1939 offered an alternative global vision to one based on a Wilsonian international organization.

Streit had been a foreign correspondent for the *New York Times*. Assigned to Geneva in 1929, he saw the failure of the League of Nations up close. Unlike Clark Eichelberger and the LNA, Streit did not see a future for the league or a revised international organization. His plan for federal union, based closely on the United States, differed from that of the discredited league. His plan was for an international federal union of fifteen of the world's "greatest, oldest, most homogeneous and closely linked democracies." Whereas the league was a government of governments, by governments, for governments, the union was to be a government of the people, by the people, for the people. It would have a common citizenship, defense force, customs-free economy, currency, and communications systems. Streit argued that federal union offered a genuine plan for peace that would ensure freedom, democracy, and liberty.[48]

Although Streit was a member of the CSOP, it was clear that his negative view of the League of Nations was likely to bring him into conflict with the AUCPE, and especially its close relative the League of Nations Association. For its part, the AUCPE was concerned by the rise of the Union Now movement, which formally organized in 1939 as the Inter-Democracy Federal Unionists, though it would become Federal Union Inc. in 1940. Eichelberger's attempts to cooperate with Streit in 1939 had failed, and the sense of competition only intensified in the spring of 1940 as the Union Now movement grew while the AUCPE struggled for momentum. In March, Eichelberger found it "very disturbing indeed" that LNA branches were decreasing in number while Union Now branches were expanding.[49]

Eichelberger's biggest concern related to the plan for federal union. While conceding that Streit had made an important contribution to national debate, Eichelberger had a number of criticisms with his plan. First, even if a federation of democracies were created, a universal League of Nations would still be required to deal with universal problems relating to matters that went beyond the union. Second, while he conceded that discussions about some form of union were under way in Europe, they related primarily to economic union rather than ideological union as democracies. Finally, Eichelberger accused Streit of oversimplifying the American historical experience upon which his plan was based.[50]

Streit responded to these concerns by denying that he had any intention of moving away from the ultimate concept of a universal league. Instead, it was a simple case of priorities, and his priority was to start with a union of democratic members and gradually expand from there. As Streit argued, "If the aim is to save what remains of the League, what hope is there of that except through union first of the democracies? You don't need to worry about the League's fate if our union is formed, you do need to if it isn't." The Union Now leader also claimed that he didn't understand exactly what policy Eichelberger was advocating, and that he could not currently support a policy of American entry into the League of Nations.[51]

The other concern of Eichelberger's was organizational and, to an extent, personal. The greatest problem, according to Eichelberger, came from "certain difficulties which Mr. Streit presents in cooperation." It was clear that Eichelberger and Streit did not get on, though this was arguably because the two men were too alike in their single-minded pursuit of a particular international design (less invested in organizational turf wars, William Allen White was notably more open to the Union Now idea than Eichelberger). However, this personality clash was not a problem that was specific to Eichelberger. One Union Now member, William Blake, resigned from the organization in 1940, arguing that Streit wanted "complete control" and accepted support only in a spirit of "blind followership." "It is a bewildering paradox," Blake argued, "that an organization, formed to promote the democratic government of the world along the lines of that great treatise, 'Union Now,' should be run in so totalitarian a fashion."[52]

Nevertheless, Streit's insistence that League of Nations Association supporters abandon their program and support Union Now particularly rankled Eichelberger, especially as he had made some effort to portray the league and union plans as compatible. Streit's insistence on minimizing the League of Nations in order emphasize a federal union was never likely to appeal to a man who had spent the previous decade and a half defending the league. In addition, Eichelberger expressed his frustration that Union Now supporters had, in one case, taken over a branch of the LNA. He suggested that LNA branches cooperate with "the union now people" but maintain their own program. Eichelberger did not wish to be "organization jealous," but he clearly was, urging the branch secretaries to "safeguard the integrity of your organization, its budget and membership."[53]

More than anything, the growing popularity of the Union Now movement threatened the nascent CSOP. The commission had been conceived as a specific project for internationalists to rally around, but it risked being overtaken by the simplicity of the federal union proposal. In early 1940, discouraged by a relatively low public profile and by their unsuccessful efforts to impose an embargo on Japan, the collective-security internationalists needed something to spark their movement back into life. They acknowledged that they needed to be more precise in their proposals, more inspiring in their program, and on the front foot rather than the defensive. Perhaps yet another new organization was required to compete with Union Now, to continue the CSOP on a more permanent basis. A new organization would indeed soon develop, but with a much more urgent short-term focus.[54]

The lessons of the phony war for the internationalists were clear. In terms of public presence and profile, there was a growing need for clear direction and focus that had been missing since the successful conclusion of the neutrality fight. The embargo issue had been eclipsed by war in Europe, Reciprocal Trade Agreements were not an issue of popular concern, and the movement was starting to drift. In the absence of a political fight at home or dramatic events overseas, something new was needed to give real practical momentum to the drive for a more active foreign policy; something that would make a real difference to those fighting against fascist aggressors in both Asia and Europe.

The other key lesson of the phony war was how effective private organizations could be when they were aligned with the administration in power—and how ineffective they could be without administration support, especially if they were working from a policy of what Harry Price called "constructive support." The embargo struggle displayed the limits of organizational effectiveness. Despite popular support for the policy, both domestic political and foreign security reasons left the ACNPJA frustrated and discouraged. The neutrality fight, in contrast, showed what could be done when the interests of the administration and the internationalists aligned. Tragic events in Europe in the spring 1940 saw those interests come together once more, with greater effect than ever.

Chapter 4

Blitzkrieg and the Committee to Defend America by Aiding the Allies

The phony war saw the revision of American neutrality legislation, but that was as far as American opinion was willing to move. The relative lack of military activity in the European theater during the winter of 1939–40 left interested Americans wondering which course the war would take. When movement finally came, it was from Germany, and it was both swift and decisive. In April, Germany invaded both Denmark and Norway. The following month, on May 10, 1940, it invaded the Netherlands, Belgium, Luxembourg, and France. Within six weeks, by the end of June, France had surrendered and the United Kingdom stood alone in western Europe against fascist aggression (which now included Italy, who joined the war in June).

President Roosevelt responded by highlighting the threat posed to the United States, urging the American people to "recast their thinking about national protection." In a message to Congress on May 16, he emphasized the new danger posed by air power, which dramatically reduced the effectiveness of the Atlantic and Pacific Oceans as a defensive safety barrier. In a fireside chat ten days later, he explained the need for building up national defenses, arguing that the nation could no longer close its eyes to the approaching storm. At an address in Charlottesville, Virginia, on June 10, the president referred to the "delusion" that the United States could exist as "a lone island in a world dominated by the philosophy of force."[1]

Yet European events had little impact on public opinion regarding direct American military involvement. In the aftermath of the invasion of Denmark and Norway, only 4 percent of Americans wanted to declare war on Germany.

The number rose after the invasion of France, but only to 7 percent, and even after the fall of France it was only as high as 14 percent. The nation was still strongly against joining the war. Yet the success of the German blitzkrieg threw the tension between the ongoing state of the war and the desired American outcome into ever-sharper relief. Even before the invasion of France, 67 percent of Americans believed that Germany was ahead in the conflict, though only 17 percent believed it would win the war. Given those figures, it was no surprise that a bare majority of 51 percent thought the United States would eventually be drawn into the European war. American involvement was increasingly the most obvious way to ensure a fascist defeat.[2]

However, the strength of non-interventionist opinion ensured that was not an option. As a result, the spring and summer of 1940 saw the debate over American engagement with the war shift from the issue of neutrality to the need to provide aid to those fighting aggression. At Charlottesville, Roosevelt called for Americans to "extend to the opponents of force the material resources of this nation." As early as April, almost two-thirds of Americans polled expressed a preference for the provision of all possible aid to Britain and France except for troops. By the middle of June, 80 percent of those expressing an opinion approved of Roosevelt's decision to sell American military airplanes to Britain and France. It was in the context of this growing national desire to see greater aid to Britain that the Committee to Defend America by Aiding the Allies was born.[3]

The Committee to Defend America by Aiding the Allies

Formed in May 1940, the Committee to Defend America by Aiding the Allies was in some respects a successor to the Non-Partisan Committee for Peace through Revision of the Neutrality Act. Both were chaired by William Allen White (initially at least) and referred to as the White Committee. Both were directed by Clark Eichelberger, who was largely in charge of the day-to-day running of the CDAAA (White had the final say on policy issues, but he rarely disagreed with Eichelberger on other matters). Both enjoyed the administrative support of the League of Nations Association at 8 W. Fortieth Street in New York City. Yet as 1940 progressed, the CDAAA achieved a national prominence that no previous internationalist organization had managed. By the year's end, it was more than a group of internationalist leaders trying to mobilize opinion to influence Congress. It became a well-known national citizens' organization that genuinely represented the American public, with members and local chapters in every state of the union except North Dakota. It was the dominant internationalist organization in 1940 and well into 1941 because, unlike the AUCPE and the CSOP, it focused on an immediate political issue, and, unlike the ACNPJA, it focused on one that had significant popular support.[4]

The CDAAA was inspired in part by the American Union for Concerted Peace Efforts and contained many of the same members. Unlike the NPC, it was not an official creation of the AUCPE. However, the CDAAA quickly rose to such prominence that it eclipsed the AUCPE altogether practically overnight. Immediately after the creation of the CDAAA, the AUCPE agreed to put "all resources of the American Union behind the White Committee." The AUCPE board then did not meet again for more than six months, at which point it reaffirmed its full support for the new organization. After the war, it was acknowledged that following the formation of the CDAAA, the AUCPE "virtually ceased to exist." In effect, it was replaced by the CDAAA regarding immediate concerns and by the CSOP on long-term planning issues.[5]

The CDAAA came together quickly in the spring of 1940, inspired by events in Europe but also by domestic politics and the need to ensure that non-interventionist sentiment did not influence the 1940 election. Searching for organizational momentum in April, the AUCPE proposed a conference similar to the previous year's Conference of One Hundred, with the aim of developing recommendations for both political parties. William Allen White, with whom Eichelberger remained in contact over the winter, was suggested as chairman. An unrelated meeting with the similar aim of keeping isolationism off the Republican platform took place in New York on April 29. Organized by Frederic Coudert, the meeting was attended by Eichelberger and White, James Shotwell, League of Nations Association president Frank Boudreau, and the Carnegie Endowment's Nicholas Murray Butler. In addition to these familiar internationalist names, other significant attendees included Henry Stimson, former director of the Bureau of the Budget Lewis W. Douglas, Republican candidate Wendell Willkie, and J.P. Morgan banker and Roosevelt confidant Thomas W. Lamont. During these conversations, the need for a new "White Committee" came to the fore.[6]

Eichelberger and White were still deliberating when the German advances in May spurred them into action. In the week following May 10, they moved swiftly to create the new committee. In addition to the informal support of earlier conversations, Eichelberger quickly secured the organizational and administrative support of the League of Nations Association. As before, it was recognized that prominent public names added heft and prestige to the organization. After just a week of organizing, telegrams were sent out to significant figures asking them to join the new organization. White argued that the nation must "throw its economic and moral weight on the side of the nations of western Europe, great and small, that are struggling in battle for a civilized way of life; that constitute our first line of defense."[7]

On May 20, a press release announced the creation of the Committee to Defend America by Aiding the Allies. Notable names who had already accepted the invitation to join included Henry Stimson, Frank Knox, New York governor Herbert Lehman, Dartmouth president Ernest M. Hopkins, *The Nation* editor Freda Kirchwey, theologian Reinhold Niebuhr, Bishop Henry Hobson, businessman Will L. Clayton, and playwright Robert E. Sherwood. Hugh Moore was the organization's executive chairman, and Frederick McKee would act as treasurer. The organization contained both Democrats and Republicans who were sympathetic to Roosevelt's foreign policy and the need to aid the Allies in particular. The bipartisan nature of the roster underlined not only the committee's background but its desire to remove the issue of aid from the political agenda in an election year.[8]

Before the CDAAA was announced to the public, Lamont revealed the outline of the new organization in a May 15 telephone conversation with the president. Although Roosevelt had been grateful for the efforts of the NPC, Lamont and White wanted to ensure that their current plans did not clash with any plans or proposals emanating from the White House. Fortunately, the response from the president was positive, confirming that the committee did not run contrary to any government plans. While strictly unnecessary, the decision to run the plan past Roosevelt displayed the policy of "constructive support" that the CDAAA would adopt for its entire existence. Building on the experience of the previous year, and with almost identical views on international affairs, the committee developed an informal but close relationship with the Roosevelt administration. The nature of the relationship was not publicized among the general public, though the nature of White's relationship with the president was known. Nevertheless, the impetus for the CDAAA came from the internationalists, not the U.S. government.[9]

The CDAAA gathered momentum through the end of May and the beginning of June. Initial CDAAA policy emphasized providing as much military aid to Britain (and for those first weeks, France) as possible, but it also urged the American government to speed up war production and preparedness at home. Its calls for aid short of war to help those fighting aggression in Europe gained support as German advances made it clear that aid was urgently required. Yet there was a degree of caution in CDAAA policy. Aid was all that the group initially called for, and the concept of aid "short of war" was vitally important. The committee's name (chosen by White from a list of suggestions written by Eichelberger) was cumbersome, but it deliberately highlighted not only the need for aid but the idea that aid for Britain would remove the need for American military involvement. It also tried—largely without success—to preempt criticisms of warmongering. In addition, White's relative caution and reluctance to move too far ahead of the administration was seen in his refusal to accept Eichelberger's suggestion that the committee call for the repeal of the Neutrality and Johnson Acts.[10]

Despite this caution, the CDAAA firmly arrived in the national conscious-
ness with the publication of a provocative newspaper advertisement on June
10. The full page "Stop Hitler Now" piece, written by Robert Sherwood, urged
the American people to ask their president and congressional representatives for
maximum aid to the Allies. It called for the United States to send planes, guns
and munitions, and food to Europe to avoid the possibility of being left "alone
in a barbaric world." The piece argued that the Nazis would eventually come for
the United States and that "anyone who argues that they will wait is either an
imbecile or a traitor." At a press conference the following day, Roosevelt described
the advertisement as "a great piece of work," giving it a huge publicity boost in
the process. Not everyone agreed. Former *Nation* editor Oswald Garrison Villard
complained to White, arguing that Americans who felt there was no danger from
Hitler were just as loyal as Sherwood. White conceded that that Sherwood phrase
was unfortunate, though he agreed with the rest of the piece. White's unwillingness to move too far ahead of public opinion was revealed, prefiguring later divisions in the organization.[11]

The "Stop Hitler Now" advertisement also brought forward the first conspiratorial claims about the CDAAA. Given the organization's rapid rise and growing
public profile, it quickly faced public criticisms about its motives that the AC-
NPJA had only had to worry about. Democratic West Virginia senator Rush Holt
highlighted that funding for the advertisement came from industrialists, international bankers, international lawyers, and directors of corporations in the United
Kingdom and the British Empire. Such claims were clearly designed to discredit
the committee as a tool of big business in its efforts to drag the United States into
war. In order to counter such criticism, the CDAAA provided the Department of
State with details of those who had contributed financially to the advertisement's
publication and reprinting. This was done to ensure that the "Stop Hitler Now"
piece had been funded by "100% American sources."[12]

However, such accusations of warmongering and profiteering would not go
away entirely. The memory of the Nye Committee was still fresh in the minds
of many Americans, and the CDAAA was seen by some non-interventionists as
a puppet of Wall Street. Their greater concern was with the financial gain that
American bankers and industrialists might achieve in the event of war. Father
Charles Coughlin's *Social Justice* cited the Coudert meeting as evidence that
bankers sought to lead the United States into war, dismissing White as a "sancti-
monious stuffed shirt." Such accusations brought an angry response from Thomas
Lamont. In response to claims that the CDAAA represented a "Morgan party,"
Lamont derided the idea as "tosh," asking incredulously whether the public considered "that my former partners and I are responsible for William Allen White,
or James B. Conant, or Henry Stimson?"[13]

Curiously, non-interventionist concerns largely related to the allegedly perni-cious influence of Wall Street, and there was much less fuss about the suggestion of foreign sources. Unlike the ACNPJA and its anxieties regarding Chinese con-nections, the CDAAA rarely worried about accusations of being a British front, though they did appear on occasion. Of course, it was often accused of being overly pro-British, and there certainly were connections between the CDAAA and Britain. However, whether these connections were overt, such as through the CDAAA's branch in London, or covert, as with links to British intelligence, they did not detract from the fact that the CDAAA was set up by Americans and funded by Americans. For their part, the British recognized that any connections to the British government would undermine the CDAAA's efforts to assist them. As Ambassador Lothian wrote in 1940, "It would be most disastrous to the Wil-liam Allen White Committee were it ever to be established it was communicating and collaborating with any branch of His Majesty's Government." Nevertheless, given the CDAAA's desire to support the British war effort, it would have been more surprising if it had had no connections to Britain at all.[14]

It should be added that the CDAAA was not the only group of Americans who were moved to respond to the crisis in Europe by organizing in May 1940. The American Defenders of Freedom was announced just one day after the CDAAA. Led by Carl Beck of the Chase National Bank in New York, the organization never fully established itself, overshadowed as it was by the CDAAA. Yet despite the conversations that took place between the American Defenders of Freedom and the CDAAA prior to May 20, and despite their agreement on the need to "stimulate preparedness" and "combat isolationist fallacies," it was clear that there were differences in emphasis between the two organizations. The CDAAA em-phasized aiding the Allies: it was the "chief objective" as William Allen White put it, and the idea of defending America was merely a "salesman's talking point" that "shuts up Bert Wheeler." However, the American Defenders of Freedom highlighted the need to defend America, and keeping America out of war was their primary aim. The existence of the American Defenders of Freedom, though short-lived, revealed that the CDAAA members were not the only Americans inspired by events in Europe. It also foreshadowed opposition that would develop later in the year with the aim of defending America first and foremost. In the summer of 1940, though, the CDAAA had the field all to itself.[15]

A Qualitative Approach

Through the summer of 1940 the CDAAA sought to mobilize popular opinion in support of greater aid to the Allies. Like its internationalist predecessors, it sought to do this in two main ways. First, it worked to educate public opinion directly, which would then place pressure on political leaders in Washington. Second, the CDAAA attempted to influence politicians directly through personal connections. In both respects, it was far more successful than its immediate precursors, and as a result it was the most well-known and influential internationalist citizens' group of the era.

With relation to the Roosevelt administration, the CDAAA's connections were stronger than those of its predecessors for two main reasons. First, the personnel involved had greater connections than ever before. Eichelberger was known in the State Department, but his relationship with Roosevelt had been limited prior to 1939. The same could not be said of William Allen White, Thomas Lamont, or Lewis Douglas, all of whom had much closer and more personal relationships with the president, regardless of political allegiances or past differences. Second, as seen in Lamont's contact with Roosevelt, the CDAAA and the White House were pulling in the same direction. The organization had its own aims, but it knew that the best way to pursue those aims was to work with a sympathetic administration. It had been the case with the NPC, and it would be even more pronounced with the CDAAA, which actively sought advice and direction from the White House.

Regarding public opinion, the CDAAA went beyond the NPC and ACNPJA in trying to mobilize the public by actively incorporating them into the committee. The CDAAA rapidly became a mass movement organization with more than three hundred chapters established in every state except North Dakota by the beginning of July. By October 1940 there were seven hundred local chapters; through 1941 there were more than eight hundred. Chapters were also established in the District of Columbia, the Virgin Islands, Canada, and London. Walter Johnson, an early historian of the CDAAA, argued that the group "would have been a paper organization without the local chapters." This underestimates the CDAAA's behind-the-scenes influence on government and overestimates the closeness of the relationship between the national headquarters in New York and the local chapters, but the local chapters certainly helped to give the organization a national profile that the ACNPJA lacked.[16]

While some local chapters appeared as a result of local initiatives, other areas were specifically targeted by the national leadership to develop a sense of scale and full national coverage. Together they gave the impression that the CDAAA had a broad base of public support that stretched from sea to shining sea. However, while the geographic coverage was undeniably broad, it often lacked real depth, especially in the Midwest and Rocky Mountain states. By April 1941, for example, Massachusetts had 137 chapters, New York 53, and California 38. In contrast, Wisconsin had 8 chapters, Missouri only 7, and Idaho just 1. Nevertheless, the committee emphasized its geographic spread to enhance its credibility and to counter criticisms of eastern elitism.[17]

This quantitative expansion in membership and chapter terms helped to establish the CDAAA as a national political force. However, the organization pursued not only numerical strength but also sociological breadth. Its leadership was vulnerable to accusations of being an aging white male, Anglophile, eastern establishment elite that did not fully represent American society. To preempt such criticisms, the CDAAA actively encouraged the creation of national divisions to bolster representation in areas of perceived weakness. It specifically adopted a "qualitative approach . . . to develop support in these 'weak spot' areas in which opposition is most likely to take root." Three sections of society targeted because of divisions within them were young people (and students in particular), women, and labor. By October 1940 there were four national divisions: the youth division, the college division, the women's division, and the labor division.[18]

As those who would have to go overseas to fight, young Americans were perceived to be against any policies that might drag the United States into war. This was especially the case when those policies were promoted by a generation that would be too old to go to Europe and fight. Non-interventionist feelings on campus were particularly strong; the American Student Union, for example, was against any connection with the war. These sentiments created a need for internationalists to develop student opinion behind a more active foreign policy. William Allen White argued for a vigorous approach to America's young as part of an "old fashioned crusade for democracy," highlighting that "Nazis explain Nazism to their youth and we must tell the proper story to our youth."[19]

The fall of 1940 saw the CDAAA develop a college division, which had sixty-eight chapters by June 1941. The most successful of the national divisions, this group created and distributed student-targeted literature, as well as organizing conferences and securing advisers, including journalist Max Lerner and Reinhold Niebuhr. Recognizing that the problem went beyond college campuses, the CDAAA also created a more general national youth division. Compared with the college division, it had limited success in establishing itself beyond New York City, though it was seen as an important area to cultivate support and was flagged as an area to be strengthened.[20]

The national women's division, led by Mrs. Rushmore Patterson, filled another social gap, as internationalist leaders sought to challenge the assumption that women and mothers would take a non-interventionist approach to foreign affairs. To counter well-known pacifist groups such as the Women's International League for Peace and Freedom, the division was created because "women are the home and child builders even more than men, since it is their sons and husbands who will fight if we should go to war, and since if we are faced with peril, it is they who must preserve the home while men are away." It aimed to develop local women's committees throughout the country, and it was hoped that representatives from larger women's organizations such as the League of Women Voters would add weight.[21]

However, the women's division was not a priority for the national leadership. From the outset, while White was happy for Patterson to be part of the CDAAA, he was concerned that a women's group might not adopt the whole program; he was also wary of having the committee "become a museum in which would be stored a lot of relics." Noting the division's focus on "the tea-sipping, cocktail party class" rather than wives and mothers, one observer described the division's efforts as "criminally inadequate." The fact that it was left to organize such trivial activities as the CDAAA poster contest indicates how seriously it was taken and how unimportant it became. Unsurprisingly, it was not as successful as the college division in developing chapters. However, given the number of women working in the regular local chapters, a separate women's division was ultimately redundant.[22]

The national labor division (later known as the trade union division) was created in the knowledge that the memberships of the American Federation of Labor and the Congress of Industrial Organizations were divided in their attitudes toward the war in Europe. However, the national labor division also struggled to spread its activity beyond New York City, despite CDAAA pamphlets highlighting labor's stake in the war and the fact that British trade unions were behind the war effort. Resistance to the committee from labor leaders was in part due to the belief that the CDAAA was a "bankers' committee." However, the division sought to counter that impression as well as more explicitly communist antiwar literature emanating from organizations such as the American Peace Mobilization.[23]

White later admitted that the CDAAA had had limited success with organized labor because it was an overly "middle class" organization that had largely failed to get down to the grass roots. While he admitted that William Green had helped promote internationalist ideas through the American Federation of Labor, Philip Murray had not managed to do the same in the Congress of Industrial Organizations, where former president John L. Lewis's "wig-wagging eyebrows have got most of the proletariat pretty well buffaloed."[24]

The trade union division was the part of the CDAAA with the closest connections to the African American community, a section of society that the CDAAA approached, albeit with caution. Prominent racial divisions remained in the United States, and CDAAA leaders were reluctant to be seen as overly liberal with respect to domestic racial politics or interfering in local politics. However, there was a sense not only that African American representation was important but also that African Americans needed targeting as they were particularly vulnerable to fifth-column activities. There was never any consideration of a separate division: it was unlikely to achieve mass support and could lead to the loss of political support elsewhere. Instead the CDAAA leadership appealed to African American leaders, such as A. Philip Randolph and Ralph Bunche, to join them. Randolph was against the idea of a distinct "colored division," reasoning that there was no need for separate branches.[25]

The CDAAA's caution in this area was best demonstrated by Roger Greene, who suggested African American leaders for the committee but urged that any public announcement of their membership include the announcement of "other leading citizens" (i.e., whites) at the same time. Despite the limited approach to the African American community, the CDAAA still sought their support through pamphlets such as *Colored People Have a Stake in the War*. While the community remained divided, the involvement of some community leaders enabled the CDAAA to show that not all African Americans prioritized domestic concerns.[26]

In addition to these specifically targeted national divisions, the CDAAA took advantage of pockets of professional support to develop five special committees: scientists, historians, physicians, dentists, and an aviation committee. While these may not have been as urgently needed as the college or labor divisions, they added to the broad range of support that the CDAAA could claim within its own ranks. All these special divisions and committees enabled the CDAAA to claim representation from the broadest range of the American public. Overall, the CDAAA took a mixed approach focusing on both quantity and quality: securing maximum membership while also filling in social gaps.[27]

The qualitative approach to expanding the CDAAA's public reach also led to cooperation with targeted organizations that did not normally or specifically deal with foreign policy issues. As with the CDAAA's own national divisions, the sections of society targeted represented "weak spots" in the general profile of American internationalists. In addition to women's groups and labor organizations, highlighted areas included veterans' groups such as the American Legion and religious organizations such as the Church Peace Union, in the knowledge that they were two sectors of society that were deeply divided on the issue of war. These links strengthened the broad image of support provided by the CDAAA's own divisions.[28]

The CDAAA's strategy was again enhanced by the John Price Jones Corporation. The CDAAA had a much closer and longer relationship with the fund-raising and public relations company than did its predecessors. After being employed by the CDAAA in June 1940, the company was retained until August 1941. During that time, it provided detailed advice on fund-raising, publicity, organizational planning, and the committee's strengths and weaknesses through weekly situation reports. The corporation strongly recommended adapting CDAAA strategy to target weak spots and finding existing organizations with similar objectives with whom to cooperate. However, its advice went beyond organizational matters and into the realm of policy and ideas, helping the CDAAA to tailor its message for the American people.[29]

Defining Immediate National Interests

At its heart, from the CDAAA's inception until Pearl Harbor, its message called for greater material and financial aid to the Allies. However, the worldview that underpinned that drive for aid incorporated a broad range of factors. The focus on immediate aid proposals meant that these underlying factors were not always apparent, but they were revealed in CDAAA speeches, literature, and statements. In terms of emphasis, America's national security was clearly the priority. However, it was not the only theme that defined the CDAAA's internationalism. Concerns about the nation's economic future and free trade loomed large, as did political and religious concerns. Given the numerical size and sociological breadth of the CDAAA, there are dangers in generalizing—even among the executive committee members—but there is no doubt that these four freedoms drove the CDAAA's efforts to bring about a more engaged foreign policy.

The issue of America's national security had been raised over the previous two years by the ACNPJA, though it had not been heavily emphasized. However, with the rapid German successes in Europe, an argument that had sounded unconvincing a year earlier now had considerably more weight. In his July 1940 statement on the objectives of the CDAAA, William Allen White argued that Britain was America's first line of defense and that if Britain were not supported, then the United States would be "the subject of an envy that would lead to attack," and "war will come inevitably to the United States." While this line of argument had been raised since September, it had added resonance in the aftermath of the Nazi blitzkrieg, and it paralleled the arguments being made by the Roosevelt administration. Such arguments were repeated again and again over the following eighteen months.[30]

Further CDAAA literature with titles such as *Battle of America* emphasized the direct threat German ambitions posed to the United States and the Western Hemisphere more generally. In explaining exactly *why* Germany would come for the United States, it was argued that Hitler's rule was based on hate and that he must continue to find "new enemies to blame for the hardships *he* inflicts on his people." More specifically, Hitler was quoted as saying that Germany would soon have "storm troopers in America . . . we shall have men degenerate Yankeedom will not be able to challenge." His statement that Germany had no intention of acquiring territorial possession in the Western Hemisphere was contrasted with similar statements he had previously made regarding Austria, Czechoslovakia, Poland, Denmark, Norway, Belgium, and Holland.[31]

Once it was established that Hitler would eventually attack the United States, exactly *how* he would do it was explained. Of crucial importance was the British navy. Without the protection of the British fleet, the United States and its one-ocean navy would be highly vulnerable, and even more so if the British fleet fell into enemy hands. Latin America would then become particularly vulnerable, and internationalists never tired of highlighting the relative proximity of Brazil to Africa, which could be used as a launching point for attacks in the event of a German victory. The fact there were already more than five million people of Italian origin and almost one and a half million of German origin in South America only made the threat more plausible.[32]

It can of course be argued that this threat was exaggerated in order to scare the American public. After all, nothing was more likely to mobilize the public behind the CDAAA than the threat of attack or invasion. While the threat was almost certainly exaggerated, however, it was not deliberately exaggerated, and there is no evidence to suggest that it was done cynically in order to manipulate public opinion. Though it was not clear how long it would take before Germany was ready for an assault on the Western Hemisphere, there was a genuine belief that it was not only possible but highly probable. The suggestion that the CDAAA was engaged in "alarmism" was addressed in the "Stop Hitler Now" advertisement, which admitted there was "no immediate danger" of invasion but that Trojan horses were waiting in both North and South America.[33]

In one respect the rhetoric seemed contradictory. The threat portrayed by the CDAAA was vast and terrifying. In the event of a German victory in Europe, it was argued that the world would be placed on a permanent war footing and that the United States would find itself alone. The need for direct military involvement in South America was described as "virtually certain," and the chance of overall victory was described as limited. The very existence of the United States would be under threat. Yet despite this seemingly inevitable threat, the CDAAA was not asking for a declaration of war. Aid to Britain in both material and economic form was deemed to be sufficient to ensure that a "battle of America" would not take place. While this may have been the most politically viable position, it could be seen as cowardly to let the British fight what appeared to be America's battle.[34]

If there was anywhere that the CDAAA failed to tell the whole truth, it was with regard to the implications of aid provision. Rarely did the group's material admit that one likely outcome of providing aid was that the nation would be drawn into the war sooner rather than later, a possibility that non-interventionists seized upon. The stance that it was "wiser to run even a real risk of war now" than to risk eventual defeat was a largely unspoken one. This again highlighted a flaw in proposing to simultaneously defend America and aid the Allies. In attempting to appeal to all Americans who were sympathetic to the Allies, at risk of war or otherwise, the CDAAA risked spreading itself too thinly. Some would soon come together to emphasize the defense of America, whereas others would assemble believing that mere aid was insufficient.[35]

It is not surprising that the issue of national security dominated the CDAAA's message and underpinned its calls for action. A plausible threat to the nation's security was not easily ignored. Technological advancements of the previous decades had made the world a smaller place, and some Americans no longer felt secure in the Western Hemisphere. However, the fear of a military threat to the security of the United States was just one part of the CDAAA's internationalist worldview. A secondary but significant part of the calls for action related to economic issues, particularly issues of trade and living standards.

The argument that the United States would suffer economically if Britain were defeated was based on the premise that Americans would be "free men in a world of slaves." It was claimed that this would lead to an inevitable fall in the American standard of living, as a free economy could not compete with "military socialism." Germany would dominate global trade with cheap goods produced by state monopolies utilizing cheap slave labor. American goods would be unable to compete internationally, dramatically reducing export trade and leading to unemployment. Access to raw materials in Africa and Asia would be severely reduced, if not eliminated altogether. American gold reserves would be worthless. The threat to the nation's traditional economic system was significant.[36]

Of course, this argument relied heavily on the premise that defeat for Britain also meant defeat for the entire British Empire, but for internationalists committed to reciprocal trade agreements, lower tariffs, and global free trade cooperation, the implications of a British defeat appeared grim for the American economy. Peaceful free trade was needed to help the nation—and indeed the world— out of the lingering depression. Contrary to non-interventionist criticisms of warmongering—and partly to counter such criticisms—the CDAAA argued against an economy based on armament sales, which would represent "a burden of tremendous social as well as economic significance to the American people."[37]

The economic argument emphasized the dramatically different systems of the fascist dictatorships, but it openly highlighted that the United States stood to lose out financially in the event of a British defeat. Even if national security concerns were paramount in 1940, the CDAAA was not afraid to confront this self-interested economic argument directly. Although economic considerations had to be dealt with delicately in the aftermath of the Nye Committee, the CDAAA successfully emphasized the effect such a defeat would have on the American economy and the American people as a whole.

In addition to different economic systems, a more obvious contrast with the fascist dictatorships came with their political systems. William Allen White wrote that the committee had been organized to "uphold democracy" in the face of fascist aggression, but there were fears a German victory threatened democracy within the United States. The shift to a war footing at home would lead to a more controlled wartime society and economy. The ensuing economic and political strain would tear at the nation's social fabric. Fifth-column activities would spread within the United States. Ultimately, the Bill of Rights and Constitution could be threatened. Yet the argument for a political threat to the nation was more vague, less immediate, and generally less convincing than the economic argument.[38]

The overwhelming majority of the CDAAA's work was directed in support of Britain and therefore against Germany in particular. The group saw Nazi Germany as the primary enemy in Europe, the main area of concern. References to Italy and Japan were relatively rare, though Japan was occasionally referred to in the context of Asia. Despite its undemocratic political system, the Soviet Union was barely referred to at all in 1940 as it offered no additional threat to Britain. The CDAAA's primary concern with communism was domestic, as it worked to combat antiwar propaganda from organizations sympathetic to the Soviet Union, which were often strongly anti-imperialist and anti-British.[39]

The greater threat to democracy was of course the threat to Britain itself, which was upheld as a symbol of democratic values. White argued that the British Empire was "the bulwark of democracy," a viewpoint to which most CDAAA supporters subscribed. To critics—especially on the Left—the very nature of the British Empire was undemocratic, but the internationalist viewpoint overlooked Britain's worst imperial excesses. In arguing against focusing solely on the defense of the Western Hemisphere, the CDAAA's Chicago chapter argued that there was "more actual democracy in the British Commonwealth than in Latin America."[40]

The Chicago chapter also made explicit a point that the national committee worked hard to avoid emphasizing: its natural sympathy for Britain. By highlighting that "in race, language and culture we are closer to the British Empire than we are to Latin America," it raised cultural issues that were otherwise actively avoided. The CDAAA made the argument—and genuinely believed—that Britain needed aid for the ultimate defense of the United States. However, there was unquestionably a great deal of sympathy for Britain's plight. This was particularly clear among the leaders, who had direct political, economic, organizational, and business connections to Britain. As with the AUCPE, the CDAAA worldview emphasized a particularly Anglo-American conception of civilization.[41]

A crucial final component of that conception of civilization was religion. Although religion was not as explicit in CDAAA activity as it was in ACNPJA thinking, the fascist threat to freedom of worship was openly acknowledged, and far more than it had been in AUCPE literature. Nazi rhetoric and actions were utilized to show the danger posed to Christian worship. The CDAAA argued that under Nazism any religious activity would be circumscribed and controlled by the state, placing the "Christian church in a straitjacket." Given the number of religious leaders of various denominations in the CDAAA, such appeals had considerable reach and power. And even if domination of the United States was a distant prospect, Nazi successes elsewhere affected those whose faith crossed national boundaries. The group pointed out that the "missionary enterprise in the Near and Far East and in Africa would be terribly handicapped."[42]

While the religious focus was on Christianity, references were occasionally made to the plight of Europe's Jewish citizens, as "the outlook for Jewry will be everywhere desperate." Prominent Jewish leaders were part of the CDAAA, most notably Rabbi Stephen S. Wise of the World Jewish Congress. However, on the whole the CDAAA did not emphasize the appalling treatment of European Jews, at least not in its first year, for fear of mobilizing anti-Semitic sentiment and suggestions that it was in some way a Jewish organization. This concern was reflected in an exchange of letters in June 1940. The Wall Street banker Albert Lord expressed concern to William Allen White that "it was unfortunate to have in as prominent a position as 'director,' a person bearing the name of Eichelberger." Responding on White's behalf, Hugh Moore agreed that "for our purposes it would be fortunate if his name were Moore or Lord, but I do not know how we can correct that." Despite Moore's friendship with Eichelberger and the fact that Eichelberger was in fact Presbyterian, there was a strong desire to avoid any implication that the CDAAA was a Jewish front, regardless of how incorrect such assumptions might have been.[43]

With its concerns for national security, economic well-being, political rights, and religious freedoms, the internationalism of the CDAAA was based on an appeal to immediate national interests. This represented a temporary trade-off for many of the organization's leaders who exchanged long-term concerns about international society for emergency calls for aid to Britain. However, compared with the AUCPE's broader calls for collective security in the previous years, the CDAAA's narrower appeals for immediate aid resonated more effectively with the American people. Despite the previous work of the AUCPE, the ongoing work of the CSOP, and the support of the LNA, there was no discussion of postwar aims or international organizations in 1940. The issue of aid to Britain was controversial enough as it stood. Yet it was this focused approach that enabled the

CDAAA to reach a broader audience and a position of national prominence that its predecessors had failed to achieve.

Moving Forward in Asia and Europe

The rapidly changing nature of the European war and the urgent need for aid to Britain ensured not only that concerns about collective security were downplayed but that the focus was placed overwhelmingly on the threat from Nazi Germany in Europe. Italy was seen merely as a junior partner of Germany, and the Sino-Japanese War was very much in the background. Yet at exactly the same time as the European war expanded, the ACNPJA effectively managed to achieve its long-standing aim of an embargo on war materials to Japan. Ironically, the aim was achieved indirectly as a by-product of the European war, but the effect was much the same. Just as the internationalists of the CDAAA created a mass movement as a result of a narrower focus on immediate national defense, it was national defense that finally secured the long-standing internationalist ambition in Asia.

In response to the rapid success of German aggression in May 1940, Roger Greene wrote to Roosevelt, Hull, and Pittman proposing a general law that "would enable the President to withhold from export any basic war materials and equipment as a means of conserving our national resources." The advantage to such a law was that it would not cause "special offence to any foreign state." For Greene the priority here was Japan, but such legislation could also be used to prohibit the sale of material to Germany and Italy. This shift in argument toward national defense proved effective, and led the United States to pass the National Defense Act, which enabled Roosevelt to prohibit the sale of certain war materials to Japan. Greene and Harry Price were greatly satisfied by the news, informing their members that "our legislative hurdle is passed."[44]

Although they argued that their work was not yet complete, and Japan would continue to purchase materials (especially oil) from the United States, the passage of the National Defense Act effectively brought an end to the ACNPJA. Although the group did not officially fold until February 1941, its work was largely done, and it had been overtaken by events in Europe. Similarly, its narrow focus on stopping the provision of material to aggressors had been overtaken by the need to aid victims of aggression. The question was how to proceed. Greene opted to join the CDAAA, partly as a result of his broader worldview and partly because he believed that a general organization was more effective than a regionally focused one. He quickly became its representative in Washington, and he continued to emphasize the war in Asia and the need to support China. Greene felt that for personality reasons, Price and Eichelberger would not work well together, and Price did not join the CDAAA. Yet both Price and Greene believed that there was space and a need for a broadly conceived organization that could focus on international affairs, and that it was neither the AUCPE nor the Union Now movement. At no point did they consider that there might already be too many similar internationalist organizations.[45]

Despite the implications of the National Defense Act with respect to the war in Asia, the American public's focus remained on Europe in the summer of 1940. In its first two months, the CDAAA tapped into that focus and built popular support for the concept of aid, but despite creating a name for itself in the public sphere, the organization achieved little in the way of concrete aid to the allies. By early July, despite calls for the transfer of Flying Fortresses and torpedo boats to Britain (by now the last Ally standing), only a very limited amount of planes, weaponry, and ammunition had found its way there. The immediate emphasis, understandably, had been on domestic preparedness and developing American armed forces. A more dramatic step forward was needed.[46]

On July 23, in the aftermath of both political party conventions, William Allen White announced the opening of a new phase. With even the Republicans selecting a pro-British candidate in Wendell Willkie, the CDAAA's early concern with ensuring that foreign policy issues were not a crucial part of the 1940 presidential election campaign appeared to have passed. This came just weeks after Republican CDAAA members Henry Stimson and Frank Knox were brought into Roosevelt's cabinet as secretary of war and secretary of the navy, respectively, largely to develop a sense of national political unity on foreign policy matters. The question was how to take advantage of this growing sense of bipartisanship in Washington in order to help Britain, which had just rejected Hitler's cursory offer of a negotiated peace.

White listed four objectives for this new phase of the Committee's work. He urged that the president make ships available to evacuate children from Britain; he called for legislation that would allow the United States to arrange terms of credit to sell agricultural surpluses to Britain; and he urged that the United States prohibit the sale of oil to Spain, much of which was ending up in Germany. However, it was the remaining objective that would have the most dramatic significance for the CDAAA and its efforts to facilitate aid to Britain. White called for the government to allow the sale of "fifty or sixty" overage but recently reconditioned naval destroyers to Britain. Helping the Roosevelt administration find a way to get those ships to Britain provided the focus of the CDAAA's efforts in the late summer of 1940. Much of that effort would be behind the scenes and in conjunction with a new, more interventionist group of Americans, but it would also bring the CDAAA to the attention of Congress and lead to its first serious organized opposition.[47]

Chapter 5

The Destroyer-Bases Agreement and the Century Group

As early as May 15, 1940, just five days after becoming British prime minister, Winston Churchill appealed to Franklin Roosevelt for assistance in the form of naval destroyers. One month later, faced with the imminent fall of France and the loss of the French, Danish, and Norwegian coastlines to Nazi Germany, Churchill asked "as a matter of life or death" for reinforcement on the seas to defend Great Britain, "the only hope of averting the collapse of civilization as we define it." The United States Navy was in the process of reconditioning more than one hundred old destroyers, but there was no guarantee they would be given to Britain. As they were already being reconditioned, the navy clearly felt they were already necessary for the defense of the United States. There was also no guarantee of British survival, especially after the fall of France, which could have seen the destroyers fall under German control. Beyond the military implications, such an un-neutral political step would not come without great debate and controversy. Roosevelt, while sympathetic, was by no means certain that such a move was viable.[1]

Through July and August, the primary task for internationalists was to mobilize public sentiment behind the provision of destroyers to Britain. Regarding public opinion, their role was to make sure that the small majority in support of aid to Britain grew ever larger. In early July, only 53 percent of Americans polled believed the United States should give more aid to Britain. As a result of such fine margins, the summer of 1940 saw a blizzard of promotional material from the CDAAA as it expanded across the country, highlighting the threat posed to America's national interest in all its forms.[2]

Perhaps more significant during the summer of 1940, the internationalists utilized their connections within the Roosevelt administration, working behind the scenes to push for action. In order to help convince the president of the feasibility of action, they exploited the bipartisan nature of the movement to ensure that Wendell Willkie would not make a political issue out of any destroyer transfer or seek to use it against Roosevelt in the run-up to the November election. It was during this period, in the lead-up to what became the destroyer-bases exchange, that the internationalists were most effective in working directly with the administration.

However, despite the rise to prominence of the CDAAA, there was more to the private internationalist movement at this point than one committee. While the CDAAA was the dominant citizens' organization in the eyes of the public, another group of internationalists was meeting privately in New York. The development of the Century Group—or the Miller Group, as it was sometimes known—reflected yet another strand of American internationalism. As before, there was a good deal of overlap between organizations with what William Allen White called "the interlocking directorate of internationalism." Many Century Group members were also in the CDAAA, yet there were no formal connections, largely because there was no formal "Century Group" to join. However, the Century Group was notably more interventionist in its outlook than the CDAAA; whereas the latter organization sought all possible aid to the Allies, the former advocated all-out war, arguing that this was America's war to fight.[3]

With the specific aim of the destroyer-bases exchange to work toward, differences between internationalists were downplayed during the late summer and autumn of 1940. Even as Century Group policy moved well in advance of CDAAA (and indeed Roosevelt administration) policy, their considerable commonalities overshadowed their differences. Their shared aims were emphasized further with the arrival of organized opposition in September, in the form of the non-interventionist America First Committee. Only as the election approached did variations became apparent, and while they were largely differences in tactics in the first instance, differences in attitude toward the war would soon follow.

The Century Group

The beginnings of the movement that led to the Century Group can be found in the work of Francis Pickens Miller. Miller worked for the Council on Foreign Relations, where he was the administrative secretary for the council's War and Peace Studies. He had been asked to join the council as a result of his work with the National Policy Committee, an organization created in 1935 to enhance democratic public engagement with the policymaking process, and a number of National Policy Committee members subsequently played a significant part in both the Century Group and its successor, Fight for Freedom. On June 2, 1940, nine individuals met at Miller's house in advance of a National Policy Committee meeting on the topic "The Implications to the United States of a German Victory." They quickly found that all nine agreed the United States should declare war on Germany immediately.[4]

Having agreed on the need for action in support of the Allies, the group decided to proceed by trying to convince others of that need. It was decided that a public statement was the best way to convince other Americans, so Miller asked his Council on Foreign Relations colleague Whitney Shepardson to produce a draft, which was subsequently entitled "A Summons to Speak Out." The statement, published on June 10 (coincidentally the same day as the "Stop Hitler Now" advertisement), argued that the frontier of America's national interest was now "on the Somme. Therefore, all disposable air, naval, military and material resources of the United States should be made available at once to help maintain our common front." Aid alone was not enough, however. As the United States had already rejected a neutral stance and sided with the Allies, the government should declare "that a state of war exists between this country and Germany." The reasoning given for such action in the brief statement was broad and sweeping: "Nazi Germany is the mortal enemy of our ideals, our institutions and our way of life."[5]

To maximize its effectiveness, the "Summons" was signed by thirty prominent Americans, including retired admiral William H. Standley, bishop of southern Ohio Henry W. Hobson, former *New York World* journalist and playwright John Balderston, and Pulitzer Prize–winning writer Herbert Agar. A total of 127 individuals were invited to sign, but out of the 82 replies that arrived in time, 46 agreed with the desire for aid but not with the proposed declaration of war. Only 6 strongly disagreed with the "Summons." Despite the prominent show of support, the public impact of Shepardson's statement was mixed. This was partly because its release was overshadowed by the Italian attack on France the previous day. However, while the matter of providing aid to the Allies was relatively uncontroversial, calls for a declaration of war were anything but. Subsequent criticisms from the non-interventionist press and individuals were only to be expected, but even some invited signatories who were sympathetic with aiding the Allies saw it as a step too far. Former ACNPJA member Jonathan Daniels publicly spoke out against the "Summons," fearing that "we may embrace fascism at home in the guise of defense against fascism abroad."[6]

A number of prominent CDAAA members also declined the opportunity to sign the statement. Will Clayton was willing to go even further than CDAAA policy but explained that he was unwilling to support a declaration of war on tactical grounds as it went "farther than the American people will follow." William Allen White was less sympathetic, disagreeing with the proposed declaration, which was "about four jumps ahead of my group." Lewis Douglas was more supportive but objected to the organizational overlap with the CDAAA. "Do you think it advisable," he wrote, "to have two organizations directed, in effect, toward the same end?" He conceded that it went "a little bit further" than the CDAAA "and yet its fundamental purpose is identical." Miller responded that those who had signed the "Summons" were sympathetic with the work of the CDAAA and would work to facilitate its efforts. "The signers of the 'Summons to Speak Out' are not a committee and have no intention of organizing a committee."[7]

Yet the statement did spark the creation of a new informal collective, the Century Group. Technically, Miller was correct that the signatories had no intention of forming a committee, as the impetus to build on the declaration came from a man who was disappointed that he had not been invited to sign it in the first place. Henry Van Dusen, a teacher at the Union Theological Seminary and a CDAAA member, enthusiastically contacted Miller, whom he had known for twenty-five years, asking him what the next step was. As he had no idea, Miller suggested they contact the well-connected Lewis Douglas, who could convene a dinner of prominent and politically bipartisan individuals in order to discuss the way forward.[8]

Eleven internationalists attended the dinner at the Columbia Club in New York on July 11, 1940. Miller, Van Dusen, and Douglas were joined by Whitney Shepardson, William Standley, Henry Hobson, Herbert Agar, Will Clayton, Ernest Hopkins, Union Theological Seminary president Henry Sloane Coffin, and publisher Henry Luce. All except Luce would play prominent roles in the organized internationalist movement over the following months, though Luce would contribute in his own way through the publication of his "American Century" article in early 1941. The others held meetings with increasing regularity as 1940 progressed, joined by other like-minded internationalists, including John Balderston, James B. Conant, Robert Sherwood, manufacturer Ward Cheney, and journalists Joseph Alsop and Ulric Bell. They met at the Century Association in New York, which would give the informal collective its informal name.[9]

Those attending on July 11 concluded that "threats to the American way of life and to the interests of the United States in Europe, Latin America and the Far East . . . all stem, in the last analysis, from the power of Nazi Germany." They agreed that the survival of the British Commonwealth was important and that the British fleet was critically important. As a result, the United States needed to act. The suggestion for action did not go as far as the call for a declaration of war issued in the "Summons," but it recommended that the U.S. Navy join in the protection of Britain and its fleet, and that Britain be provided with credit and munitions. The group also proposed that American ships be used to transport food to and evacuate children from Britain. These were measures likely to draw the United States closer to military conflict.[10]

The following day, Miller drafted his conception of the American national interest, and while the draft was not formally used, it revealed a worldview beyond the immediate calls for aid shared by many of his Century Group companions. While conceding that the national interest included "economic, financial, territorial and defense interests," he argued that other, more general interests were involved that related to "faith in the American way of life. In its idealized social version this way of life stems from the Sermon on the Mount and the French Revolution. Even the lowest levels of American society are rarely free from the camaraderie of the egalitarian or the touch of mercy of the humanitarian. In its political and legal version this way of life is deeply rooted in English soil. It includes the representative form of government, the liberties and obligations of the Bill of Rights and a relatively free system of production and trade." Yet again, the internationalist formulation was a mixture of democratic political values, an economic system of free trade, and Christianity.[11]

The distinctly Anglo-American nature of this worldview was reflected in Miller's insistence that "Latin American countries do not practice our way of life. There is no basis—political, cultural, economic, geographic or strategic—for a close alliance between the countries of South America and the United States." By contrast, "the English speaking people, on the other hand, do practice our way of life. . . . The keystone of our foreign policy must be close collaboration with the British Commonwealth of nations." To implement such a foreign policy, Miller called for an offensive strategy from the United States, marked in the first instance by a symbol of an offensive spirit, such as a deal with Britain over "ships and islands."[12]

The Destroyer-Bases Exchange

Over the following two weeks, the nascent Century Group sought to build on its recommendations of July 11, as it began to organize, albeit in a very loose and limited manner. Miller arranged office space for the group in room 2940 at 11 W. Forty-second Street in New York City. A second, larger dinner was held on July 25, at which it was agreed that to ensure America's defense and "reduce the risk of invasion," all possible steps should be taken to prevent German control of the North Atlantic. In particular, given recent British naval losses, it was suggested that the hundred or so recently reconditioned overage destroyers be handed over to Britain immediately. The majority argued that as the action was in America's self-defense, no quid pro quo would be necessary. However, it was also suggested that the destroyers should be offered in exchange for either a guarantee that the ships would be returned to American or Canadian hands in the event of an invasion of Britain or "naval and air concessions in British possessions in the Western hemisphere."[13]

Given existing legal restrictions, a direct transfer of the destroyers to Britain was not possible. The revision of legislation to make it possible was highly unlikely in the face of political opposition, especially given calls for domestic preparedness, and in any event it would take too long. It was decided that the best way to proceed was through executive action by Roosevelt, and given the need for immediate and effective action, the best way to convince the president was to approach him directly. Individuals from the group were designated to visit Roosevelt and convince him of the plan "on the reasonable assumption that Mr. Willkie would go along with him."[14]

Despite the group's priority of direct private representations with Roosevelt, it recognized that a campaign of public education regarding the importance of the British fleet to American interests was also essential. The campaign was to be pursued through all possible channels, including the press, radio, and correspondence with "influential individuals." However, one of the easiest practical steps to accomplish was for the group to cooperate fully with what it called the William Allen White Committee. Miller had already informed White of the group's initial meeting, and while White saw that the Century Group went "a little farther" than the CDAAA, he informed Miller of the CDAAA's priority, announced on July 23, of providing Britain with destroyers.[15]

The relationship between the Century Group and the CDAAA was never closer than during the destroyer-bases exchange in the summer of 1940. The idea provided an immediate focus for action. Whether they supported, like Miller, a declaration of war or, like White, aid short of war, all internationalists were agreed on the need do whatever it took to provide Britain with the destroyers necessary to help it survive. Given their shared aim, it was no surprise that there was soon considerable overlap in personnel between the Century Group and the CDAAA. The Century Group's larger dinner on July 25 included ten CDAAA members, including director Clark Eichelberger. Over the next six weeks, the internationalists combined in every possible way to work toward the survival of Britain.[16]

To acquire an accurate picture of British naval requirements after the July 25 meeting, Miller took the initiative by sending his wife, Helen Hill Miller, with a list of questions for the British ambassador, Lord Lothian. Lothian had known the Millers since their time studying at Oxford, and by sending his wife, Miller put distance between the group and the British government, albeit a very small

amount. The picture painted by Lothian was stark: Britain had lost half of its destroyers available for home defense since 1939, and destroyers and torpedo boats
were the only ones suitable for use in the English Channel against invasion. As a
result, the British asked for forty-eight destroyers, though "if this number could
be augmented to one hundred the chances of successfully repelling an invasion
would be greatly increased."[17]

Convinced of the necessity of some form of destroyer transfer, Herbert Agar,
Ward Cheney, and Clark Eichelberger—members of both the CDAAA and the
Century Group—visited the president at the White House on August 1, 1940.
They informed him of the group's July 25 meeting and the call for immediate
action. Yet while Roosevelt listened, he did not appear particularly enthusiastic,
giving the internationalists a "noncommittal reply." William Allen White wrote
that the president had "lost his cud" since his recent renomination, but Roosevelt
was clearly concerned about the political implications of any such transfer just
three months before the election. The internationalist leaders nevertheless decided to continue to promote the destroyer issue by mobilizing public opinion
behind a transfer, countering the legal arguments against it, and approaching the
Republican presidential candidate, Wendell Willkie. They hoped that together
these actions would be enough to sway the president behind the proposal.[18]

To generate public support, the CDAAA and Century Group arranged radio
broadcasts on Britain's need for destroyers. The first and most prominent was
delivered on August 4, 1940, by General John J. Pershing, commander of the
American Expeditionary Force during World War I. In a speech suggested by
Roosevelt and arranged by Century Group members, the popular and apolitical
Pershing spoke out in support of aid to Britain in a nationwide radio broadcast.
In addition to building up her own forces, he urged, America should "safeguard
her freedom and security by making available to the British or Canadian Government at least fifty of the over-age destroyers which are left from the days of
the World War. . . . They may save us from the danger and hardship of another
war." Pershing's was merely the most prominent of a number of addresses aimed
at convincing the American people of the urgent need for action.[19]

While popular opinion was strongly affected by Pershing's address, elite opinion was significantly affected by a legal opinion suggesting that destroyers could
be transferred to Britain under existing law without further consent from Congress. After meeting with the president, Clark Eichelberger met with Benjamin
Cohen of the Department of the Interior, outlining his earlier conversation and
Roosevelt's reservations. Eichelberger asked Cohen if some kind of authority
could be found to transfer the destroyers. By the following morning, Cohen had
a positive answer, which he soon drafted into a legal opinion. He then conferred
with lawyer and CDAAA member Dean Acheson, who recommended that he

himself and other lawyers not in government redraft the opinion as a letter to the *New York Times.*[20]

It appeared on August 11, 1940, under the heading "No Legal Bar Seen to Transfer of Destroyers," and was signed by Charles C. Burlingham of the New York Bar, former solicitor general Thomas D. Thatcher, former Federal Trade Commission member George Rublee, and Acheson. The lengthy letter dismissed existing legal arguments against a transfer, concluding that "the government should not hesitate to exercise powers under existing law." Four days later, Senator Josh Lee quoted at length from the letter in Congress. For the way the letter opened up the possibility of action without going through Congress, historian Philip Goodhart later described it as "one of the most important letters to the editor ever published."[21]

While the *New York Times* letter represented a collaborative effort between the internationalists and the Roosevelt administration, it was nothing compared with the combined effort used to ensure that Willkie did not speak out against the transfer. Despite the president's noncommittal manner on August 1, it quickly became clear that Roosevelt wanted to facilitate a transfer. However, he wanted to do it on his own terms, having explored all the options, and in a politically secure fashion. In fact, the day after he had met with Agar, Cheney, and Eichelberger, Roosevelt's August 2 cabinet meeting focused on ensuring the sale of fifty or sixty destroyers to Britain. The possibility of an exchange does not appear to have been considered at the meeting, and there was still a strong sense at this point that legislation was required.[22]

As a result, it was agreed at the cabinet meeting that the president would contact William Allen White, who had recently spoken to Willkie on the subject. White was to come to Washington to speak with Roosevelt, Hull, Stimson, and Knox. He was then to get Willkie's approval to speak to and secure support from House Minority Leader Joe Martin and Senate Minority Leader and vice presidential candidate Charles McNary. Later that evening, Roosevelt spoke to White, who claimed that Willkie's attitude was the same as the president's. Roosevelt countered that this was insufficient; "Willkie's attitude was not what counted. . . . Republican policy in Congress was the one essential." All of this highlighted Roosevelt's belief as of August 2 that new legislation was necessary before any transfer, an attitude that did not begin to change until after the *New York Times* letter.[23]

White became the main intermediary between Roosevelt and Willkie, visiting the Republican in Colorado in an attempt to secure his backing. However, despite numerous attempts, White was unsuccessful in his efforts to convince Willkie to publicly support a destroyer sale. Willkie privately supported the action, but he was unwilling to publicly support it without first speaking to congressional leaders. He also preferred to wait until specific legislation was proposed. White subsequently informed the president that he couldn't "guarantee either of you to the other" but "there is not two bits difference between you on the issues pending." Nevertheless, the president could be reasonably certain that Willkie supported the plan in general.[24]

On August 13, the day Roosevelt decided to take executive action to facilitate an exchange, White informed Henry Stimson that he was "confident" Willkie would not say anything in criticism of a destroyer transaction, and that he might even say something in support. When Willkie accepted the Republican nomination on August 17, he did not explicitly refer to the destroyers, though he conceded that the loss of the British fleet would "greatly weaken our defense" and that an Atlantic dominated by Germany would be "a calamity." Yet Roosevelt was already negotiating with the British by that point over the details of an exchange, and he had received the tacit support of McNary without Willkie's assistance.[25]

On September 3, 1940, it was announced that the United States had acquired the right to lease naval and air bases in Newfoundland, Bermuda, the Bahamas, Jamaica, St. Lucia, Trinidad, Antigua, and British Guiana. The first two were gifts from Great Britain, while the other six were in exchange for fifty overage destroyers. Roosevelt was able to justify the exchange on the grounds that it would improve the nation's security "beyond calculation." A State Department official claimed it would "assure this country's safety for a century." As expected, Willkie suggested that the country would support the deal, but he wholeheartedly disagreed with the way it had been done. Some non-interventionist congressmen were even more critical than Willkie; Republican senator Gerald Nye called it a "dictatorial step," while Republican representative Hamilton Fish argued that "it usurps the power of Congress, and violates international laws, the law of the United States and the Constitution. It is virtually an act of war."[26]

Understandably the internationalists were extremely happy with the exchange and the part they played in making it happen. A CDAAA press release commended and congratulated the president. Robert Sherwood summed up the situation best by arguing that the destroyers "will be used for the defense of America just where they will do the most immediate good. The new bases will contribute overwhelmingly to our future security." Frank Kingdon, chairman of the New York chapter, took a more strident tone, claiming the exchange was "a noble and aggressive action." Brooklyn College president Harry Gideonse reflected the CDAAA's bipartisan nature by giving credit to Willkie for the "explicit approval of aid to Britain" he gave in his acceptance address.[27]

For his part, Roosevelt asked press secretary Stephen Early to contact White to "thank him and the organization for all they have done." The subsequent letter to White thanked him and his "very worthy organization" for all their work. The president also told Eichelberger personally that the CDAAA had done a "swell job" and he was deeply grateful for its efforts. There was no doubt that the combined efforts of the CDAAA and the Century Group affected the conduct of the destroyer-bases exchange. By reassuring Roosevelt about Willkie's attitude and by preparing the legal argument to bypass Congress, they worked closely with the Roosevelt administration to ensure that Britain received the naval support it so urgently needed. It represented the closest interaction between the internationalists and the administration during the entire period. Their work to mobilize public opinion was, in this case, secondary.[28]

The Balderston Controversy

Even before the exchange was completed, the CDAAA and Century Group found another way to work together to further the provision of aid to Britain. At a Century Group meeting in mid-August, it was agreed that a news—or propaganda—service was required to provide a newsletter to papers across the country. The purpose of such a newsletter was to clear up factual disputes but, more important, to provide background material for the private use of editors. For example, the urgent British need for destroyers was not fully understood in the United States because the British had publicly downplayed the extent of their losses, but this could be highlighted by the internationalists. Clark Eichelberger attended the meetings where the idea was discussed, and to capitalize on White's name and prominence, it was suggested that the newsletter go out as the "William Allen White News Service."[29]

The service was run by Century Group member John Balderston, former European correspondent of the *New York World*, who came out of retirement to write the newsletter. Beginning on August 22, 1940, the newsletter was provided to fifty newspapers, free of charge. The first came complete with a letter of introduction from White in which he stated that "it is not a propaganda service. Yet it will consist of facts bearing on issues which we are interested in getting before the public and of course will bear on the causes we are trying to further." During the destroyer-bases debate, the newsletter revealed the extent of British naval losses and background to the slow progress of negotiations. For a brief period, it appeared to offer an effective and influential tool for reaching the press.[30]

In the immediate aftermath of the destroyer-bases exchange however, Balderston issued a statement that went too far for White's liking. Arguing that fifty destroyers were not enough to save Britain, Balderston urged the supply of further material in seven essential areas in order of priority and need: twenty torpedo boats, flying boats, Flying Fortress bombers, tanks, airfields for training British pilots, 250,000 Enfield rifles, and the new American Norden bomb sight. While

Balderston conceded American military authorities would argue that these items were necessary to defend the United States, he countered that failure to provide them would lead to the fall of Britain. It was therefore necessary to bring public opinion to bear on the issue to ensure new executive or legislative action that overruled the military authorities.[31]

Upon reading the release, White said it was "superb" but asked that it be held until the following morning, when he would be in Washington to discuss it. Balderston went ahead and released it on September 4. The following day, White contacted the *New York Herald Tribune* to repudiate the newsletter. He claimed that neither he nor the CDAAA was in favor of sending war material to Britain that was deemed necessary for national defense. He also admitted the list was a little drastic in the aftermath of the destroyer exchange, clarifying that Balderston's list was purely a list of British needs and that it did not represent a new CDAAA program.[32]

The spat was a relatively minor one, and it did the CDAAA little immediate harm. Balderston continued in his role until he moved to Hollywood the following month. Yet it revealed the tensions within the internationalist movement that had been hiding under the surface since May and that would only become more prominent from this point onward. The relatively small and closed leadership groups of the ACNPJA and the AUCPE meant that those in charge of the organizations controlled their direction. However, as the CDAAA grew in numbers, and as it grew closer to the Century Group, it became harder and harder for White to keep control of the organization's message. Without an obvious and immediate policy to work toward—such as the destroyer exchange—disagreements over direction were more likely to occur.

Balderston later admitted that he "tried to maneuver White into a more advanced position than he then wished to take." Yet he was not alone in thinking White had been too cautious in this instance. While there were some in the CDAAA who felt that Balderston was a loose cannon likely to do the committee more harm than good, others highlighted the valuable nature of his service, thanks to his writing ability and his connections. Clark Eichelberger, usually in tune with White's thinking, disagreed with him in this instance, believing that Balderston was indeed useful. Balderston himself admitted that those in high places were talking openly to him "as I never found them before."[33]

The nature of Balderston's connections led to a second spell of controversy at the end of September. This time, it was a far more public and external storm that saw the background to the CDAAA and Century Group revealed to the public, leading to the most open criticism of the movement's connections to Britain. The disclosures came in a *St. Louis Post-Dispatch* article by Charles Ross on September 22. Ross had written the piece with cooperation from members of both groups, who believed that a full objective history of the movement would preempt more sensationalist exposés from non-interventionist critics. There was always an element of risk. While the CDAAA was nationally well known, the Century Group was not, and it relied far more on behind-the-scenes connections. Will Clayton had previously argued that once the existence of the Century Group was known, "their influence from that time forward will be practically nil."[34]

The Ross article was an extremely full account of internationalist activity since May 1940. While there was very little the internationalists could disagree with— Miller thought Ross did "a superb job"—there was rather too much information, which paved the way for opposition attacks. Describing the movement as a "propaganda engine" in the headline did not help. The story provided an account of the recent internal disagreement between Balderston and White and repeated Balderston's wire service call to sway American military opinion. It also highlighted that Balderston was in touch with the British embassy, claiming that it was "no secret and has no special significance." Non-interventionist critics begged to differ, and the Century Group—and Balderston in particular—was soon under attack in Congress.[35]

The day after publication, the article was inserted into the appendix of the *Congressional Record* by Senator Bennett Champ Clark of Missouri, who raised the issue in the Senate again on September 26. Describing the article as "a remarkable piece of reporting," Clark, along with other non-interventionist senators including Gerald Nye, Rush Holt, and Burton Wheeler, proceeded to criticize the internationalists and their "interlocking system of propaganda." In the midst of a lengthy critique of the organized movement as a whole, Senator Holt highlighted Balderston's role, stating that he "is not interested in preserving America but is directly under the British Ministry of Information." Holt went on to emphasize Balderston's 1940 *Who's Who* entry, which listed his London address ahead of his Beverly Hills home.[36]

Balderston responded angrily in October with a privately distributed twenty-three-page memorandum entitled "The William Allen White Committee News Service and a Little 'Smear Campaign' in the Senate." He described Holt's accusation that he was a foreign agent as "a deliberate lie," though one made under the cloak of senatorial immunity so that Balderston had no legal opportunity to sue. Not only was he not paid by Britain, but he was not even paid by the CDAAA, as all of his work for the news service came out of his own pocket except for wire toll charges. His *Who's Who* entry included his former London address for work reasons. Yet his main resentment was a result of Holt's comment that he had been overseas working for a propaganda agency during World War I; what Holt deliberately omitted was that the agency was the United States government's Committee on Public Information. Balderston described the attacks as "copperhead" smears, and although he subsequently stepped back from the movement, the non-interventionist opposition continued with much greater strength and numbers, and not just from opponents in Congress.[37]

The America First Committee

On September 4, 1940, the day after the announcement of the destroyer bases exchange, the America First Committee was formed. Up to this point, despite the strength of non-interventionist feeling in the United States, the CDAAA had had no real adversary. No equivalent citizens' group had been created specifically to mobilize public opinion *for* a greater emphasis on American national defense and *against* the idea of greater aid to Britain. Such a group arrived with the creation of the America First Committee, and the public debate expanded dramatically. The debate grew in intensity, peaking early in 1941 with the Lend-Lease debate and continuing until the attack on Pearl Harbor.

The origins of the America First Committee can be found in May and June 1940 as German successes focused American attention on events in western Europe. However, unlike those internationalists who were sparked to call for greater assistance to Britain or a declaration of war, Yale student R. Douglas Stuart sought a way to ensure that the United States stayed out of the European conflict. In June 1940, he led a group arguing for greater concentration on hemispheric defense and noninvolvement in European affairs. As the summer progressed, Stuart contacted General Robert E. Wood, chairman of Sears Roebuck and Co., about developing a non-interventionist organization, and a list of prominent names to serve as a national committee was established through July and August.[38]

The first public statement of America First outlined its principles. It argued that no foreign power or group of powers could successfully attack a prepared America. Therefore, it argued for the building of an impregnable defense for the United States while also claiming that the provision of aid short of war to others not only weakened national defense but risked dragging the country into war. More broadly, it argued that staying out of the European war was the only way to preserve American democracy. The committee aimed to provide sane leadership, avoiding hysteria, and to unite all Americans who shared such views, with the exception of "Nazists [*sic*], Fascists, Communists, or members of other groups that place the interest of any other nation above those of own country." Most important, it aimed to direct non-interventionist opinion at both the president and Congress, in much the same way as the organized internationalists did.[39]

The acting chairman of the America First Committee was General Wood, and Stuart was its national director, but the committee lacked a chairman with the national prominence and bipartisan appeal of William Allen White. It relied far more than the CDAAA on politicians for publicity, regularly utilizing congressional figures such as Clark, Nye, Holt, and Wheeler. Its most prominent member was Colonel Charles Lindbergh, whose personal history and fame made him the most popular member of the America First Committee. However, Lindbergh initially declined the offer of becoming chairman, not formally joining the national committee until April 1941. Nevertheless, America First quickly grew in popularity, developing chapters across the country, with particular strength in the Midwest and Chicago.[40]

On September 5, America First was launched to national attention with a radio address by General Hugh Johnson, who highlighted the limited nature of American military preparedness and the need to focus on defending America first. On October 3, the committee placed advertisements in the national press, again arguing for the need to stop aid to Britain and giving the new organization greater publicity. The advertisements sparked an internal CDAAA memorandum analyzing the America First position. The response politely conceded that the members of America First "are no fifth columnists" and "are known for their honesty and patriotism." That said, it was argued that America First was ignoring one crucial fact: that it would take time—"years not months"—to build an impregnable defense. According to the CDAAA's analysis, the only way to ensure time to build up American defenses was for Britain and its fleet to hold out for as long as possible.[41]

The CDAAA then offered responses to the key principles of America First that were firmly in line with earlier CDAAA pronouncements. It stated that the United States could not be made impregnable independent of Canada, Mexico, and South America, and even then, America's newly drafted army (created by the Selective Training and Service Act of September 1940) would not be trained until 1942, and a two-ocean navy would not be complete until 1945 at the earliest. It argued that a group of powers could in fact attack the United States, especially if the combined strength of Germany, Japan, and Italy were supported by the manpower of Europe, Asia, and Africa, even if the United States were fully prepared. As a result, it made sense to provide aid to Britain to buy time for greater preparedness activity. The only alternative was to "trust in appeasement." Regarding the suggestion that American democracy was threatened, the CDAAA argued that the best chance of ensuring democracy was to make certain that the war remained in Europe.[42]

This first reference to America First was surprisingly civilized given the heated rhetoric that followed. The non-interventionist comments of military generals Wood and Johnson were countered with remarks by General Pershing, Admiral Standley, and former army chief of staff General Douglas MacArthur, but they acknowledged that Wood and Johnson had "served this country well." Yet while arguments were often made with evidence and reason, the conversation between the internationalists and non-interventionists rapidly deteriorated. By the end of the year, the America First Committee was accusing the CDAAA of warmonger- ing; the internationalist response was increasingly to emphasize the less salubrious elements within the America First orbit, particularly with suggestions of Nazi sympathies.[43]

One clear effect of the developing debate was to solidify the lines between non-interventionists and internationalists. Earlier in the year, the lines were not so clearly drawn. Some CDAAA members—most notably its chairman, William Allen White—genuinely believed that keeping Britain safe was the best way to ensure the United States remained out of war. Yet in the final months of 1940, as the debate over American foreign policy developed without a particular legisla- tive focus, the long-term implications of CDAAA policy came under question. Was the accusation of "warmonger" a fair one? Was the CDAAA willing to sup- port Britain at risk of war? In the end, such questions led to divisions within the internationalist movement itself.

Awakening the American People

Just days after the conclusion of the destroyer-bases exchange, the Battle of Brit- ain entered its most destructive stage, as German bombers attacked British cities with unprecedented ferocity. As the CDAAA and Century Group looked to the future, the exchange was already seen as merely a first step. For the CDAAA, the issue was how to ensure more aid for Britain. Looking to the government for direction, Eichelberger visited briefly with Roosevelt, who emphasized the Brit- ish need for torpedo boats, and William Allen White contacted Henry Stimson to ask what more the CDAAA could do to help the government help Britain. As a result of these exchanges, the CDAAA built on its earlier plans, with White informing members days later of the need to supply Britain with "twenty-five flying fortresses and as many planes as possible, and twenty mosquito boats." The Flying Fortresses and mosquito/torpedo boats matched Balderston's earlier list of British needs. More broadly, White urged his members to use all their remaining energy to support the government in "sending every bit of material that can be spared to help Britain resist invasion from air and sea." The message remained much the same over the following three months.[44]

In early October, Thomas Lamont contacted White reiterating the need for all possible aid to Britain, while adding suggestions for further consideration. First, Lamont suggested the CDAAA push for repeal or further amendment of the Neutrality Act to enable American ships to carry goods to Britain. Second, regarding Britain's increasingly low dollar reserves, Lamont proposed that the United States finance the British war effort: "The coffers of the Government of the United States should be opened, and loans, without stint, made to England by the Government itself." Lamont admitted both suggestions were "premature," and neither suggestion made it into a confidential CDAAA update a week later that focused on Flying Fortresses and Flying Boats. This reflected reluctance on the CDAAA's part to advance too far ahead of public opinion. Yet it is likely that Lamont's message came from the administration, as it made almost identical suggestions to the Century Group that same week.[45]

The situation for the Century Group was somewhat different from that of the CDAAA. As it had been established just prior to the destroyer exchange, there was brief consideration of whether the group had any reason to continue. There was never really any doubt that it would continue, however; the real questions were what form the group would take and how it would proceed. At a September 5 meeting it was decided that two committees would review what the group could contribute to the present crisis. The first, chaired by Allen Dulles, examined the coordination of productive effort in the Anglo-American community; the second, chaired by Herbert Agar, looked at how best to awaken the American people.[46]

A week later, it became clear that awakening the American people was to be the group's main task moving ahead. Agar's subcommittee argued that the job ahead was to show the public "the meaning of the revolution that is sweeping the world." The group needed to continue because the CDAAA was insufficiently advanced and "too big and slow" for the job of mobilizing the people. The group was also necessary in order to create public demand for action, which was just what the government wanted. The idea of a more formal public organization was rejected at this point, and it was hoped that ultimately a more substantial organization such as the CDAAA would take over the group's work. Yet for now it was clear not only that the efforts of room 2940 needed to continue in order to apply pressure "effectively for specific and easily defined ends" but that an expanded role was necessary for the group.[47]

On one hand, the Century Group continued—like the CDAAA—to stay in close contact with the Roosevelt administration. With Francis Miller taking a step back to focus on Council on Foreign Relations activity in October, the group's office was increasingly led by Ulric Bell, who was just as keen to stay in close contact with the government. In early October, a conversation with Cordell Hull's assistant, Cecil Gray, revealed the Department of State's preferred priorities for the group, which almost matched those given to William Allen White by Thomas Lamont. These included staying in touch with the British purchasing mission to see what was needed and in what quantities, looking at further revision or repeal of the Neutrality Act, and carrying forward the general education of the public (especially with regard to the possibility of Britain's running out of dollars). All of these were prominent on the group's agenda over the following months.[48]

However, regarding the general education of the public, the group aimed to influence the public far more broadly than before, with a qualitative approach similar to that of the CDAAA. Specific sections of society were targeted in order to break down non-interventionist sentiment. In particular, the initial focus was placed on the Catholic Church—"the steadiest and strongest force for appeasement in the country"—and women's groups. Herbert Agar's brother William led the effort to sway Catholic opinion, while Katherine Gauss Jackson, daughter of Dean Christian Gauss of Princeton, was to work within women's organizations. Organized labor and colleges were also to be targeted as bastions of non-interventionism. Magazine writer Helen Everitt was enlisted to utilize the press to help spread the group's broader message: halting the "slow unconscious murder of America," in Agar's vivid phrase.[49]

The focus of both organizations remained firmly on events in Europe, even after September 27, when Japan, Germany, and Italy signed the Tripartite Pact, agreeing to cooperate with each other in the establishment of a new world order. The Century Group in particular kept its focus tightly on aiding Great Britain. After discussions with the State Department in early October, the CDAAA announced an unchanged policy in the face of the new Axis alliance. Although the alliance was deemed to have united two wars into one, the key policy remained the "survival of Great Britain. If Britain wins the Pacific area can be taken care of. If Britain loses the aggressors will be victorious all over the world." China was an ally to be aided but very much a secondary one, to be given all possible financial and material assistance "without lessening the tempo of our aid to Britain." While Roger Greene was relieved that the CDAAA called for a complete embargo on war materials—such as oil—to Japan, his hopes that the CDAAA would take over the work of the now-dormant ACNPJA were largely disappointed.[50]

One European issue that greatly concerned both the CDAAA and the Century Group in the autumn of 1940 was former president Herbert Hoover's plan to send food to the starving civilian populations of Europe. Having spent months trying to ensure maximum aid to Britain, they now found themselves fighting against the idea of aid to those in occupied Europe. Despite a natural sympathy for those suffering under fascist rule, internationalist sentiment was best expressed by William Allen White, who argued that the American people must be aware that their "humanitarian instincts can be used as a front for appeasement propaganda." Most believed the food would be appropriated by the Nazis; all recognized that it would undermine the British blockade. Hoover's comparison to 1914, when he oversaw food relief in Belgium, was dismissed as flawed given German dominance of the continent. The religious leaders of the Century Group—Hobson, Van Dusen, and Coffin—were particularly active in countering religious calls for humanitarian aid, organizing statements signed by prominent individuals. Much to their satisfaction, Hoover's plan was not adopted by the government.[51]

Nonpartisan Challenges and the Election of 1940

In the absence of any specific new plans for aid, the internationalists spent much of the autumn on the defensive, countering anything that might undermine the British war effort, whether it was a specific proposal such as Hoover's or noninterventionist sentiment in general. Yet a further key focus of attention was November's presidential election. The selection of Wendell Willkie as the Republican contender ensured that both candidates were internationalists. However, neither candidate wanted to be portrayed as a warmonger, so there was little progress in terms of new plans for aid in September and October. In fact, in a desperate late attempt to catch Roosevelt in the polls, Willkie actually criticized the president's foreign policy as one that would send American boys to fight in Europe. Roosevelt famously responded in Boston on October 30: "Your boys are not going to be sent into any foreign wars."[52]

White outlined the CDAAA position at the beginning of September, though it was a more ambiguous statement than might have been expected. He confirmed that the committee's position was strictly nonpartisan, though he added rather unnecessarily that the CDAAA supported the president's foreign policy, not because he was a Democrat, but because he was president and commander in chief and because "his foreign policy is one that we can enthusiastically support." More generally, the national committee was split fairly evenly, and on a personal level among the leaders, White publicly supported Willkie, whereas Eichelberger supported Roosevelt. The fact that the CDAAA was accused by each side of favoring the other suggests that on the whole it got the balance right. However, given the lack of consensus, it was hardly surprising that problems arose at the local level, most notably in New York City.[53]

Despite White's attempts to keep the CDAAA nonpartisan, and despite the committee's official policy of noninterference in elections, members of the New York chapter actively sought to defeat New York Republican representative Hamilton Fish. Fish was a staunch non-interventionist in line to become chairman of the Foreign Affairs Committee if the Republicans gained control of the House. Building on existing CDAAA activity, the New York chapter organized to defeat Fish. Led by Newark University president Frank Kingdon and journalist Herbert Bayard Swope, the chapter recognized that while presidential candidate Willkie was an internationalist, many congressional Republicans were anything but, and that if the CDAAA existed to aid Britain, one way to ensure such aid was to defeat congressmen who opposed it.[54]

The Non-Partisan Committee to Defeat Hamilton Fish was created in late October, but despite the attempt to distance itself from the CDAAA, the connections and overlapping memberships came back to trouble the committee and White in particular. White resented the partisan nature of Kingdon's group and the fact it had singled out Fish among the many non-interventionist Republicans. White personally contacted Fish explaining that any use of the CDAAA name against him was unauthorized. Days later, Fish released the letter from White, which also stated, "I hope as Republicans we are united in our support of the Republican ticket from top to bottom in every district and state." The letter made it look as if White was in fact partisan and that his attempts to quell the New York chapter were for the benefit of the Republicans. In fact, White had simply failed in his efforts to separate his personal views from that of the committee he chaired.[55]

White had to make amends for his statement. He quickly if reluctantly released a telegram stating that "our committee is non-partisan. As such we wish to see the Republicans and Democrats elected who support a program of aid to Great Britain." The statement appeared to give individual chapters a free hand, and the whole incident revealed the challenges in remaining nonpartisan. White subsequently wrote that the activities of the New York chapter were one of the "chief headaches" of his job. He suggested that these might be the result of the "New York complex," which made the chapter think it had rights and privileges above those of other chapters.[56]

More broadly, White was struggling, and the internationalist movement was leaving him behind. It was obvious by this point that in terms of both general strategy and specific tactics, White was not at the forefront of his own committee. In addition to being more restrained in his broader suggestions for aiding Britain, White was less forceful in devising and supporting tactics to speed that aid along. He struggled to reconcile his desire to stay out of war with his desire to aid Britain, his support for Roosevelt's foreign policy with his history as a Republican, and his CDAAA leadership with his personal views. Focused on the larger issue of aid to Britain, White lost touch with the domestic political implications of his committee's position.

While his position appeared shaky, White still believed that the work of the CDAAA was not yet done. Even before the election result was in, a drafted appeal letter from the "rooster on the cowcatcher" argued that there could be no rest for the committee "so long as the gangrene of totalitarianism continues to threaten the lives of free men and free institutions." Preparation began for a postelection drive regardless of the result, one based upon revision of the Neutrality Act, co-ordination of American and British defenses, and the adoption of the status of nonbelligerency. Yet on the eve of the election, White rejected a call from Eichelberger to condemn suggestions—such as those by Willkie—that if Roosevelt were reelected he would take the United States into war. In fact, White stepped back from the CDAAA in the last two weeks of the election campaign to focus on local politics in Kansas.[57]

The situation regarding the election in the Century Group was much clearer. To begin with, while a small majority of Century club members were Democrats, a larger majority preferred Roosevelt's foreign policy. In addition, while they had been disappointed with Roosevelt's campaign addresses emphasizing his dislike of war, they were even more dissatisfied with Willkie's criticisms of Roosevelt. Willkie's politically expedient flirtations with non-interventionism may have made for a closer presidential race, but they lost him internationalist support. Looking back, it is clear that both candidates were erring on the side of political caution but that the winner would have greater room to maneuver after the election. After Roosevelt's reelection on November 5, the issue was which direction the president would take.[58]

From the summer of 1940, the combined internationalist force of the CDAAA and the Century Group had brought considerable success. The CDAAA had a growing public profile, and both organizations had influence behind the scenes. This was seen most clearly in the case of the destroyer-bases exchange. That strength was increasingly necessary as organized non-interventionist opposition had developed in the shape of the America First Committee. However, with Roosevelt still in the White House, there was hope for greater aid to Britain and a more active foreign policy moving into 1941.

Yet in addition to the successes there were clearly differences growing within the internationalist movement. The Balderston controversy and the more belligerent style of the CDAAA's New York chapter revealed tactical differences within the CDAAA, making it more difficult for the leadership—especially White—to control the organizational message. The Century Group, of course, was even more forceful. Much of the difference came down to a disagreement over what role such groups and committees should play in society and how closely they should be linked to the government. For now, the internationalists were still largely working with the administration, sticking closely to its policies rather than pushing out in advance. The months after the destroyer exchange showed how the movement was least unified when there was no clear direction to follow. It soon had a new policy to support, but not before divisions had taken their toll on the CDAAA chairman.

Chapter 6

Maximum Aid and the Battle for Lend-Lease

In the aftermath of Franklin Roosevelt's reelection, many internationalists expected a more active foreign policy in the form of greater aid to Britain. With an unprecedented third term in office ahead, it was hoped that the president's caution on the campaign trail would be rejected in favor of an initiative to deliver more boats and planes to an increasingly beleaguered Britain. However, there was no immediate initiative to support. Given the strength of non-interventionist sentiment, Roosevelt was reluctant to confront the two legislative barriers to further aid: the Johnson Act barring loans to nations in default on their debts and the Neutrality Act, which required nations to pay cash for munitions purchased from the United States.[1]

In the six weeks during which Roosevelt deliberated on how to proceed, the organized internationalist movement began to drift. With no clear direction from the White House, different voices and opinions came to the fore that both reflected and exacerbated existing divisions. In an attempt to forge ahead, the CDAAA released a new policy statement at the end of November. Yet confusion over the implications of the statement, combined with greater pressure from belligerent members of the Century Group and personal attacks from the CDAAA's New York chapter, ultimately led to William Allen White's resignation as chairman in the first week of 1941.

Yet despite the very public downfall of the internationalist figurehead, the months following his resignation saw the CDAAA achieve its greatest public profile in the debate over Lend-Lease. While the beginning of 1941 saw 88 percent of Americans preferring to stay out of the war rather than join it, 60 percent felt it was more important to help Britain at the risk of war than to stay out completely. That help was provided through the Lend-Lease bill, foreshadowed by Roosevelt in late December and introduced to Congress on January 10, 1941. The bill was passed on March 11 but not before a heated public debate that saw the bill's supporters and opponents most visibly represented by the CDAAA and the America First Committee. While much of the effort in support of the destroyer-bases exchange had been undertaken privately, the Lend-Lease debate saw the CDAAA maximize its ability to bring public pressure to bear upon Congress.[2]

The debate saw the internationalist movement mobilize a significant network of internationalists to counter non-interventionist resistance to the bill. The support of women, students, and religious leaders was emphasized to counter the argument that those segments of society were firmly against the bill. More generally, the CDAAA worked through published material, speeches, and radio addresses and organized rallies to promote the bill in the face of suggestions that Lend-Lease would draw the United States much closer to conflict. With the bill's successful passage in March securing an unlimited amount of aid for Britain, the CDAAA had arguably fulfilled its raison d'être.

The Need for Direction

After Roosevelt's victory, internationalists sought to move beyond the partisan feuds of the election and unite the nation behind a more active foreign policy. A drive for national unity was created, with internationalist leaders such as William Allen White calling for bipartisan support for aid to the Allies, a policy that had been broadly promoted by both candidates. White also wrote to the president hoping that the CDAAA "may still be of service" to him in the coming years, despite White's personal campaign support for Willkie. Harry Price was even more forthright, urging that more "vigorous measures" be taken to increase aid to both Britain and China, but despite the continued efforts of both Price and Roger Greene to link the Asian and European conflicts, the national focus remained firmly on Europe. The main question was how best to secure greater aid to a British government that was fast running out of dollars.[3]

The CDAAA was still by far the most prominent internationalist organization after the election, but as the months prior to election had shown, differences were growing within the movement. These differences, and the challenges facing the CDAAA more generally, were revealed in a private John Price Jones Corporation assessment of the committee's own strengths and weaknesses. On the positive side, it was acknowledged that the CDAAA was the leading organization supporting aid to those fighting fascist aggression; indeed, it was the only national organization with a network of local committees mobilizing support for a more active foreign policy. That established position brought with it a certain amount of prestige and, on a more practical level, volunteer personnel and financial support. The committee was also seen to benefit from the nationwide respect for William Allen White and from the "crusading" leadership of Clark Eichelberger.[4]

However, the number of perceived weaknesses was troubling. Regarding its central message, the fact that both presidential candidates were in support of maximum aid to Britain suggested that the CDAAA now lacked a clear "fighting objective." Where it was once out ahead of general public opinion, the events of the previous six months had overtaken the committee and seen it fall behind. In fact, the "short of war" angle, so important at the committee's beginning, was now seen as a liability that was increasingly difficult to define. The most logical course was the one most likely to ensure the nation's "ultimate national safety," though it was impossible to tell whether that course could be pursued without recourse to war. The CDAAA was also seen to be lacking in organizational terms. The committee lacked an obvious successor to take over the leadership if White could no longer continue. It also relied far too heavily on White for its public statements, unlike the Century Group, which was more successful in mobilizing lists of significant names behind causes. More broadly, it lacked both a clear plan of action and the type of cohesive "brain trust" group to develop a future program.[5]

Subsequent months proved that all these perceived weaknesses were very real, and there would be only a limited amount of success in overcoming them. The exact meaning of "short of war" was already contested by non-interventionists, who felt any further support for Britain was likely to lead to war, and by the small but growing number of belligerent interventionists who felt that nothing less than war was now required. Unfortunately, the problems with the central message and the implications of further aid led to even greater problems on the organizational side, revealing just how dominant White had become as the public face of the CDAAA. While it was understandable that the CDAAA would seek to capitalize on White's prestige and renown, relying so heavily on one individual was always a risk, especially given the number of other prominent members.

Ironically enough, there was a larger brain trust at work in the offices of 8 W. Fortieth Street in New York, but true to the CDAAA's deeper roots in the League of Nations Association, its members were focused on the less immediate but equally complicated issue of the future peace. Recognizing that the preparations for peace could not be ignored—despite the fact the United States was not yet at war—the Commission to Study the Organization of Peace issued its preliminary report in November. In a relatively brief and general statement, the CSOP advocated a world federation "stronger and more adjustable than the League of 1919." League of Nations Association president Frank Boudreau saw the work of the CDAAA, CSOP, and LNA as deeply intertwined, and he urged LNA branches to continue to give their full support to urgent ongoing work of the CDAAA.[6]

For its part, the CDAAA recognized the need for direction and attempted to provide it with an official statement of policy on November 26. It argued that appeasement was not an option as the world "cannot live four-fifths slave and one-fifth free," and that the only chance of avoiding war was to give "all material assistance to Great Britain and her allies immediately." In dramatic language, it was claimed that "the fate of human freedom, freedom of thought, of religion, of individual initiative, is dependent upon victory of Britain and her allies." If Britain fell, war would come to America. Instead, it was time for democracies to reaffirm their faith in "a world of peace based upon justice and the security of nations."[7]

In addition to its previous calls for Flying Fortresses and torpedo boats, the committee argued for three further steps. First, it urged a vast increase in arms production, to be done under a state of national emergency if necessary. The second and most controversial point argued that the sea route between Britain and the United States was a lifeline for Britain. As a result, "under no circumstances must this line be cut and the United States must be prepared to maintain it." Exactly how it was to be maintained was not made clear. Third, Congress was urged to catch up with the national mood in providing greater aid to Britain through revision of the nation's "international policy." This proposal clearly referred to the existing Neutrality Act, which William Allen White knew Roosevelt was reluctant to try and revise for fear of a non-interventionist backlash.[8]

A second part of the statement acknowledged the global nature of the conflict in the aftermath of the Tripartite Pact by recommending a firm foreign policy in the Pacific. Roger Greene had recently become associate director of the CDAAA, and he would have been encouraged by the new emphasis on the Pacific, including the call for the United States to introduce embargoes on all war materials to Japan. However, this emphasis was primarily a result of the implications of Japanese expansion for Britain. All possible material and financial aid for China was promoted, as long as it was done "without lessening our aid to Britain." In addition, Britain and the United States were specifically encouraged to open their Pacific naval bases to each other's fleets. More generally, the statement encouraged the two nations to establish a naval understanding in order to "permit the two fleets to be placed in the most advantageous position to protect the Atlantic for the democracies and to stop the spread of war in the Pacific."[9]

Less than two weeks later, national headquarters felt it necessary to issue a memorandum to local chapters clarifying two points from the official policy statement. The first related to the naval lifeline across the Atlantic and how it was to be maintained. The response provided little in the way of clarity, claiming that "how far such action should go cannot be decided now," though the possibility of providing Britain with more destroyers was explicitly mentioned. The second point related to the concept of a naval understanding between Britain and the United States, and the clarification again clarified little. Greater naval cooperation between the two nations was urged, but "how far such an understanding should go is a question that only the Government can decide."[10]

Both "clarifications" suggested the CDAAA was unwilling to admit the possibility that the active foreign policy it promoted might be more likely, not less, to lead the United States into war. The memorandum specifically argued that naval cooperation in the Pacific would make it more likely that the United States could avoid war as it made further Japanese expansion less likely, though non-interventionists believed the opposite was true. The more obvious unwillingness to engage directly with the likely course of action in the Atlantic in the event of a British collapse indicated that some committee members saw war as the probable outcome. In either case, there was ambiguity over the short-of-war concept and confusion over the likely implications of new CDAAA policy.[11]

Internationalist Divisions

The person most concerned about that ambiguity and the general direction of the CDAAA was William Allen White. White was particularly concerned with the committee's proposal to revise the Neutrality Act. Not only had Roosevelt personally informed him that he was opposed to revision or repeal of the act, but that same message was now coming from the State Department with added detail. After consultations with the department's Herbert Feis at the beginning of December, the CDAAA's Livingston Hartley informed White of the administration's intention to put the question of aid to Britain directly to Congress, rather than attempting to revise either the Neutrality or the Johnson Act. As a result, Hartley suggested that any CDAAA campaign should "steer around entirely any question of revision." This was White's position, which increasingly put him at odds with the rest of his committee.[12]

Despite his own concerns about the CDAAA's direction, White stumbled into controversy of his own making at the end of November. In a speech to the National Association of Accredited Publicity Directors, White spoke about the CDAAA's role as "organizers of the great majority of public opinion" in securing the destroyer exchange. However, an editorial in the *New York Times* chose to highlight White's comment that the committee's objectives had been approved in advance by the U.S. Army and Navy, suggesting that the government was attempting to influence opinion through the CDAAA. In addition, it picked up on White's comment that "the really smart trick we pulled was that after Lindbergh made his speech we put his mother-in-law [Mrs. Dwight W. Morrow] on the air—and was that a face card? It was!" The editorial suggested that the reference to smart tricks exaggerated the CDAAA's role in the destroyer-bases transaction and "may needlessly arouse suspicions and injure the future usefulness of his committee."[13]

White responded with a public letter to the *Times* objecting to the editorial's failure to understand that he was not boasting about playing a trick on the American people but rather that he had taken a trick, a different figure of speech underlined by the "face card" reference. He again used the opportunity to claim that the CDAAA had done nothing more than crystallize existing public opinion. *Times* editor Arthur Hays Sulzberger justified his decision to run the editorial by asserting his belief that White had misspoken. As the *Times* was sympathetic to the British cause, it was "anxious to protect the thing in which both you and we were interested." In the eyes of the *Times*, White was damaging the credibility of the CDAAA.[14]

Yet Sulzberger's concern was not just with the CDAAA but with the internationalist movement more broadly. He confessed that the *Times* had been "very much disturbed by the emanations from 'Room 2940'"—the Century Group. He recognized that while White was not part of the group, given the overlapping memberships of the two organizations, it contained many of his associates. During this period, the Century Group focused on fighting Hoover's food plan and on urging Roosevelt to remove Joseph Kennedy from his position as ambassador to Britain on account of his pro-appeasement stance. The group's overtly pro-British positions on all issues, not simply the question of further aid, left it open to criticism.[15]

There was a certain irony in Sulzberger's view of White and the Century Group working together, for although White had recently attended his first Century Group meeting, he had been deeply concerned by what he observed. Both White and Eichelberger attended a small Century Group dinner on November 20, which focused on the need for an open demand on Roosevelt to repudiate Joseph Kennedy and the Hoover food plan. Ulric Bell's minutes of the meeting record White agreeing that the CDAAA should adopt a more militant stance on the food question. Yet White's subsequent comments reveal that the generally militant stance of those at the meeting made him profoundly uncomfortable.[16]

Two weeks later, White informed Eichelberger that the Century Group had him "worried all the time." Despite the overlapping memberships of the two organizations, White wanted to separate the two completely, adding "the further we get away from that crowd the happier I will be." He described the difference as largely one of approach, with White admitting his strategy was to stay "fairly abreast" of public sentiment without getting too far ahead of it. But White was even more critical in speaking to Thomas Lamont, expressing his annoyance with the group and his concern that its members were "radical" and "far in advance of us." Highlighting Herbert Agar, Ulric Bell, and Herbert Bayard Swope as the leaders, he expressed his frustration at the "multiplicity of statements" and the need to take a radical position on every possible minor issue. He was also increasingly concerned that the energetic Eichelberger was being swayed by the activity of the Century Group, which was "likely to get us [the CDAAA] into trouble." He asked Lamont to pass his concern on to other less belligerent CDAAA figures such as Lewis Douglas, Frederic Coudert, and Frank L. Polk, whose influence he hoped would keep the organization on the right track.[17]

Staying on track was proving increasingly difficult given the uncertainty over what the right track actually was. In addition to the differences between the CDAAA and the more belligerent Century Group, there were differences within the CDAAA as well. Not only was there ambiguity regarding the implications of the organization's recent policy statement, but there was disagreement between the CDAAA executive committee and the New York chapter, which was led by the Century Group's Swope and Frank Kingdon. Swope was particularly defensive about the extent of the chapter's achievements, though White saw many of them as unnecessary projects that detracted from the main issue of aid to Britain.[18]

The divisions within the movement worked on a number of levels. In some cases they were based on simple personality clashes, but the main disputes came down to questions of organizational focus and strategy. For White and many other CDAAA members, especially more conservative ones, the focus was getting aid to Britain; every other issue was a distant second. For others, especially those in the CDAAA's New York chapter and the Century Group, but also including Eichelberger, issues such as Hoover's food plan and Joseph Kennedy were all part of the same larger picture of keeping Britain alive. Getting the internationalist leaders to agree on the desired end was not a problem; the exact means for achieving that end were open for surprisingly heated debate.

Also under debate was the best way to mobilize the public. White always claimed that he was simply crystallizing existing opinion, though the CDAAA clearly existed to mobilize new opinion. However, it was also clear that White was reluctant to move too far ahead of public opinion. In contrast, many internationalists believed the best way to develop public opinion was to get ahead and lead it. This internal debate was complicated by a desire to please the Roosevelt administration. Most private internationalists, working from a position of constructive support for the president, were willing to restrain their views at times if they thought it was what the White House would prefer. Yet as private organizations they could also advocate advanced policy positions that were politically problematic for the administration to promote.

To complicate matters, supporters of both approaches believed they were doing what the president wanted. Many took the line followed by actor and prominent CDAAA member Douglas Fairbanks Jr., who believed the job of the internationalists was to get out ahead of Roosevelt and build up support for greater aid to Britain. Fairbanks recalled Roosevelt's urging the internationalists to "build up huge public support for a particular bill or law, and that will 'push' the leader. . . . Now go out and get the public to push me!" White, on the other hand, relying on his personal conversations with Roosevelt, believed that restraint was the best way to proceed. Yet a display of restraint that made him lose touch with the committee he supposedly led brought his resignation.[19]

The Resignation of William Allen White

The timing could not have been more unfortunate. Just as divisions within the internationalist movement were coming to the fore, a policy they had been working toward started to take shape. At a December 17 press conference, Roosevelt raised the idea of aid to Britain for the first time since the election. Hinting at Britain's financial difficulties, he expressed his desire to "get rid of the silly, foolish old dollar sign" and in so doing set in motion the Lend-Lease bill. The president famously explained his idea with the analogy of lending a garden hose to a neighbor whose house is on fire. The urgency of the situation means no money changes hands. Instead, when the neighbor has extinguished the fire, he returns the hose; if it is damaged, he will replace it. The simple illustration hid the complex debates within the administration over the previous six weeks on how best to proceed and carefully sidestepped the Neutrality and Johnson Acts. It was immediately lauded by an internationalist movement waiting for a policy to support. White sent a telegram to Roosevelt the following day in support of the plan, adding "our committee wants to help."[20]

However, any momentum the CDAAA might have taken from the announcement was lost when White was outwitted in an exchange with Roy Howard of the non-interventionist Scripps-Howard newspaper chain. Upon hearing that Howard was going to attack the CDAAA as a group of warmongers, White wrote to Howard, claiming "the only reason in God's world I am in this organization is to keep this country out of war." He added that the CDAAA was not in favor of repealing either the Neutrality Act or the Johnson Act and declared, "If I was making a motto for the Committee to Defend America by Aiding the Allies it would be 'The Yanks Are Not Coming.'" White agreed that with a few minor revisions the letter could be published, and it appeared in Scripps-Howard papers on December 23.[21]

White's comments triggered significant responses from all sides of the debate. Unfortunately for White, non-interventionist leaders eagerly stepped forward to praise his views. Both Charles Lindbergh and Robert E. Wood highlighted how White's statement offered a basis for national unity. Wood welcomed White's remarks on behalf of the America First Committee, as he was "in essential agreement with our position." Lindbergh took the opportunity to try to force a split in the internationalists, noting that White's comments confirmed that the CDAAA as a whole did not agree with the interventionist views of some of its members. By emphasizing the need to avoid war over the need to provide aid at the risk of war, White's remarks certainly moved him closer to the non-interventionist end of the political spectrum.[22]

Needless to say, this did not go down well with his fellow CDAAA members. Many of the ordinary rank and file were just as disappointed with White as were the more interventionist members of the New York chapter. Telegrams came in from across the country from members who felt that White had shifted too far across to a stance of appeasement. Unsurprisingly, though, the CDAAA executive committee—and not just the interventionists—was extremely disappointed at how White had allowed himself to be tricked into such a position. While he was almost certainly trying to send a message to the more belligerent wing of his organization, he had clearly gone too far. His support for the Neutrality and Johnson Acts placed him at odds with the CDAAA's November 26 statement. Also, his comment that "the Yanks are not coming" suggested they were not coming under any foreseeable circumstances, a point that did not reflect White's own views about the possibility of war in the future but was by no means clear in his comments. Swope quickly informed Roosevelt that White had fallen into a deliberate trap, but he claimed that a statement would be issued to save the organization from what he described as a "threatened and serious split."[23]

However, the statement never came. The executive committee made numerous attempts to convince White of the need to repudiate his statement and respond to Wood and Lindbergh. CDAAA treasurer Frederick McKee actually flew to Emporia on Christmas Day, but White refused to issue a further statement. Subsequent telegrams from Eichelberger, Swope, Lewis Douglas, and Frank Boudreau convinced White to produce a response, but his draft was not deemed to be clear enough, and he was asked not to release it. On December 28, he informed Lewis Douglas that his resignation seemed inevitable in order to save the CDAAA from embarrassment and harm.[24]

Further embarrassment came the following day, however, with the publication of a highly critical letter to White from New York mayor Fiorello LaGuardia. In a reference to the French collaborator, LaGuardia described White as "doing a typical Laval." He suggested that the CDAAA should divide into two groups: White could lead a "Committee to Defend America by Aiding the Allies with Words," while the rest could form a "Committee to Defend America by Aiding the Allies with Deeds." Written on December 26, the extremely personal attack appeared in the press on December 29. To add insult to injury, it was publicly supported by Swope the following day. This was no great surprise, as Swope and Kingdon had already issued a strong statement on behalf of the New York chapter in support of maximum aid, though it did not refer to White by name. Eichelberger attempted to minimize the damage, rushing out a statement denying a rift and claiming that the organization was united behind a program of "all possible aid to Great Britain and her allies." Behind the scenes, however, it was now clear that the damage was irreparable and that too many key figures felt White had to go—including White himself.[25]

The division came at the worst possible time for the internationalists, as they sought to prepare the ground for Roosevelt's latest statement on aid. In the knowledge that the president's forthcoming fireside chat to the nation was to address the subject, Roosevelt was informed on Christmas Eve of a forthcoming telegram, organized by James Conant and Lewis Douglas, which was to be signed by more than 170 citizens urging maximum aid to Britain. The purpose of the letter was to prepare the way for Roosevelt's leadership. In addition to supporting the president's nascent Lend-Lease idea, the Conant-Douglas round-robin asked for clarification on "the nature of the conflict which threatens to wipe out the sort of Christian civilization in which men may be free from the restraints of intolerance, from the fear of injustice and from the menace of arbitrary power." The CDAAA formally endorsed the letter on December 28. Tellingly, given his comments to Roy Howard, White was not initially asked to sign the letter. When he learned of its existence, however, he added his name to the list.[26]

Roosevelt thanked Douglas and Conant for the letter before delivering his December 29 fireside chat on national security, in which he took a position almost identical to that of the CDAAA. After stating that it was his job to keep the country out of war, he claimed that "never before since Jamestown and Plymouth Rock has our American civilization been in such danger as now." In the aftermath of the Tripartite Pact, the Axis powers had proclaimed there could be no peace between Axis powers and the rest of the world, and while the United States was safe for now, it would be living "at the point of a gun" if Britain fell. To keep Britain alive, Roosevelt called for greater levels of material aid from the United States. Arguing that "there can be no appeasement with ruthlessness" he called for the United States to become "the arsenal of democracy."[27]

Unsurprisingly, the CDAAA's public reaction was one of strong support, endorsing "every word" of the president's address. At the same time, in a not-for-publication letter to chapter representatives, Clark Eichelberger emphasized the need to work with the administration: "This is the President's program. This is our program. It is our task to mobilize public opinion in support of the President's program." With reference to the ongoing controversy over White, Eichelberger underlined (literally) that there had been no weakening of the CDAAA's program. In fact, White himself also expressed his support for Roosevelt. Prior to the speech, he informed Roosevelt that the country was with him; after the speech he pledged the CDAAA's full support for the president's "magnificent call." Roosevelt responded personally with thanks, urging White to keep up the good work.[28]

Of course, White was unable carry to on as chairman of the CDAAA, and he resigned on January 2, 1941. He did not withdraw fully, remaining as honorary chairman until a new chairman was announced and as a member of the executive committee. But it was clear that his time as the figurehead for the internationalist movement had passed. Describing the CDAAA as an "adventure in democracy," he urged that the organization continue under the leadership of a younger man who did not have the responsibility of running a Kansas newspaper. Hugh Moore accepted his resignation on behalf of the executive committee with the greatest reluctance, praising White's leadership in the cause of aiding Britain. Privately, Thomas Lamont informed White that he deplored his resignation, though he understood it in light of the actions of Swope and the New York chapter. He also passed on the president's "indignant" response to LaGuardia's comments.[29]

Lamont was the CDAAA member most responsible for keeping the Roosevelt administration in the loop regarding White's resignation. He had already asked Cordell Hull to intervene on White's behalf, and the day after White's resignation he asked Roosevelt if he would meet with Clark Eichelberger to pass on advice and counsel from time to time. Lamont also warned Roosevelt that the New York members failed to understand the need to replace White with another significant figure from the Midwest. On January 11 White personally expressed his regret that he would no longer be able to help the president. Roosevelt responded that he was disturbed at the loss of White's leadership of "this very great movement for saving America by helping to save our type of civilization and government." He also added that his resignation was unfortunate because White's name had become "so clearly fixed in the minds of all the local organizations."[30]

There is a certain paradox to White's leadership of the CDAAA. On the one hand, it cannot be denied that he was the official leader of the organization. He was its chairman, primary spokesman, and figurehead. The organization would continue to be referred to as the William Allen White Committee by some commentators through 1941. This deep connection had reached a point where any personal statement released by White was seen as a statement of the CDAAA. Yet at the same time, White did not truly represent the group. He was more than a "stuffed shirt," but Eichelberger ran the office, and as 1940 progressed White became more and more removed from the executive committee, both temperamentally and tactically. Even his geographical distinctiveness—one of his key advantages at the outset—became a drawback as White increasingly saw himself as a more cautious midwesterner at odds with the Atlantic coast.

The timing of White's resignation meant its significance for the movement was not as dramatic as it might have been. Fortunately the imminent Lend-Lease bill provided a much-needed focus of attention for all those in support of a more active foreign policy. What White's resignation did was to emphasize the divisions within the movement, especially between those who genuinely believed war could be avoided with further aid and those who believed war was a likely result of such aid. It also highlighted the strength within the movement of those who felt it was necessary to move ahead of the Roosevelt administration in order to mobilize public opinion. White held firm until the end that the CDAAA should not get ahead of the president, but he was clearly now in the minority. The main question for the future would be how far ahead of the president to go, but for now the focus was on regrouping in support of Lend-Lease.

Regrouping for Lend-Lease

On January 6, 1941, in his annual message to Congress, Roosevelt reiterated his call for the United States to be an arsenal for those fighting aggression. He clarified that such aid would be a type of loan, to be repaid not in money but in similar materials after the cessation of hostilities. In so doing, he sought to create a world founded on four freedoms: freedom of speech and religion and freedom from want and fear. Those closely paralleled the political, religious, economic, and national security principles upon which the private organizations' conception of internationalism was based. Four days later, the Lend-Lease bill to provide such aid was introduced to Congress as S. 75 and the patriotically numbered H.R. 1776. Given the need to mobilize all possible support for the bill, the CDAAA moved quickly to replace White and get the organization back on track.[31]

The debate over reorganization and replacement had begun even before White's formal resignation. One immediate outcome (previously hinted at by the John Price Jones Corporation) was the decision to share the leadership responsibility so that it did not lie solely on the shoulders of one individual. It was decided that the CDAAA executive committee would be enlarged to make it more representative, and that the advisory policy committee would meet more frequently than before (at least once a month) and that it would function as a national policy board. This would lift some of the burden from White's replacement to make it less of a one-man organization.[32]

The obvious choice to succeed White was Wendell Willkie. As a prominent internationalist Republican from the Midwest, Willkie would have provided a like-for-like replacement. Unfortunately for the CDAAA, he was not interested in the position, and few obvious alternatives remained. The eventual choice was lawyer Ernest W. Gibson from Vermont, who had briefly served as senator for his home state in 1940 when he filled the vacancy caused by the death of his father. While in Washington, Gibson had notably given an impassioned debut speech in support of the selective service bill. Prior to 1940 he had served for seven years as secretary of the Vermont State Senate. Gibson was an internationalist Republican, but he lacked the national standing and reputation of White or Willkie. Nor was he from the Midwest. The White House was informed of and approved the decision, though Lamont went back to Roosevelt asking for better suggestions, ideally including a liberal-minded midwestern Catholic. Lamont damned Gibson with faint praise as "all right enough" but dismissed him as "not known west of the Alleghenies."[33]

Lewis Douglas was quickly chosen as chairman of the new national board to provide an additional position of support for the new chairman. Douglas had been a key part of the CDAAA from the beginning, from the destroyer exchange through the recent round-robin letter. Like many internationalists, he believed that international peace required an open economic world and free markets. For Douglas, the nationalism of the Great War and subsequent decades was responsible for the current global crisis—including that of the United States. He also shared the religious view of many of his CDAAA colleagues, seeing Christian civilization underpinning a stable and prosperous world order.[34]

The Writers' Anti-War Bureau weekly *Uncensored* offered a scathing summary of the changes. The non-interventionist journal dismissed Gibson as a "political nonentity," arguing that in reality Douglas would be the new leader of the organization. The promotion of Douglas was seen to represent a victory for the interventionists in the "ex-White Committee," and it was noted that White's statement endorsing the new arrangements failed to mention Douglas at all. It also described the succession of Gibson and Douglas as a defeat for the CDAAA's liberal wing (represented by the New York chapter). However, this analysis failed to take into account the overlap between the New York liberals and the Republican interventionists within the organization, not to mention the consensus within the CDAAA to have Republican leadership for the sake of bipartisanship.[35]

Yet while Gibson and Douglas were the new public faces of the CDAAA, executive director Clark Eichelberger remained as the organizational driving force, supported by Hugh Moore as chairman of the executive committee, Frederick McKee as treasurer, and Roger Greene as associate director. Despite his earlier cautious comments on Eichelberger's excessive enthusiasm, White had been particularly generous about Eichelberger upon standing down, commending him to the new chairman. Describing him as "indefatigable" with boundless energy, "honest as daylight" and "loyal to the core," White claimed that "a son could not have been more helpful and kind." Although he had been content to sit back and allow White to take the limelight in 1940, Eichelberger's public prominence grew considerably through 1941.[36]

Gibson gave his first address as chairman on January 18, in which he reiterated the national security, political, economic, and religious arguments that drove the CDAAA forward. Stating that the sole purpose of the committee was to defend America, Gibson again said that the only way to stay out of war was to provide material aid to Britain and her allies. Responding to those who saw the committee as warmongers, he argued that CDAAA policy was "the only policy that has a chance of keeping this country at peace," as the United States would be next. Highlighting German influence in Brazil, Argentina, and Chile, the new chairman made it clear that the Western Hemisphere was part of Hitler's plan for global domination.[37]

In addition, Gibson argued that totalitarian domination of the rest of the world had both political and economic implications. He disagreed with those who felt the country could exist as a free democracy with the rest of the world in chains. He also countered those who felt the United States would be able to compete in a world of slave labor: "The standard of living of everyone in this country would be lowered to the starvation point." Borrowing from Lincoln, he claimed the world could not exist half slave and half free. Yet he also highlighted the "spiritual side" to the conflict beyond American self-interest that could not be ignored. Invoking Cain and Abel in one of a number of biblical references, he argued that "man was not so created that he might gaze unmoved upon his brother's pain." Moving back to American interests, Gibson emphasized the Nazi threat to religion in the United States, with God as "the center and soul of our world whom the Nazis would destroy." In sum, the immediate message was clear: the way to ensure the defense of the United States was to pass the Lend-Lease bill as quickly as possible.[38]

The Lend-Lease Debate

From January 10 until the passage of the Lend-Lease bill on March 11, a heated debate about the implications of Lend-Lease raged across the nation. Yet although the two-month debate was impassioned, there was a sense from the very beginning that the bill would pass. The CDAAA fought to ensure not only that it passed but that it did so as quickly as possible without reservations. The organization's position was clear from the outset: standing "squarely back of the

President's plan for aid to Britain and to the other nations now fighting against aggression." Responding to criticisms that the bill would give the executive an unprecedented amount of power, the statement from Gibson and Douglas countered that "only large powers will serve to meet the growing threat to our safety." The following day, however, Gibson openly conceded that Lend-Lease might not be enough: "If our aid to the Allies isn't sufficient we certainly are going to get into the war."[39]

Indeed, the primary reservation of the non-interventionist movement was not the concept of aiding Britain or victims of aggression but the vast amount of power being handed over to Roosevelt. The non-interventionist *Chicago Tribune* referred to Lend-Lease as the "war dictatorship bill" for the duration of the debate. The bitter tone of the debate was set on January 12 when Senator Burton K. Wheeler, an America First Committee member, infamously described Lend-Lease as "the New Deal's Triple-A foreign policy—it will plough under every fourth American boy." Roosevelt responded by dismissing the statement "as the most untruthful, as the most dastardly, unpatriotic thing that has ever been said. Quote me on that. That really is the rottenest thing that has been said in public life in my generation."[40]

Present at the debate where Wheeler made his remark was the Century Group's Herbert Agar, who responded to Wheeler's suggestion that Lend-Lease would bring war by arguing that the nation was already at war. Agar, like all Century Group members, fought to ensure the bill's swift passage. Based on information from his Washington connections, Ulric Bell reported that Roosevelt wanted external support on the Lend-Lease debate because party lines would be formed against the bill, which would lead to delay or worse. The Century Group members worked hard behind the scenes to mobilize opinion behind the bill, but they left the CDAAA to lead the drive for public support. The group spent much of the debate assessing the new CDAAA leadership and considering how to proceed once the bill had passed. In particular, its members were looking to create a new organization building on the previous year's "Summons to Speak Out" and on Agar's assertion that the nation was already at war.[41]

In the meantime, the CDAAA accepted Roosevelt's call for external support with enthusiasm. The support was not entirely external, as the organization remained in contact with the administration throughout the debate. Not only was there a meeting between Roosevelt and Eichelberger, but the CDAAA California vice chairman, Douglas Fairbanks Jr., utilized his fame as an actor to meet with both the president and Cordell Hull to discuss CDAAA activity. With the bill already under consideration, there was little of substance to discuss. The CDAAA knew that its task was to mobilize support to ensure the bill passed through Congress as quickly as possible.[42]

Most of the organization's effort was focused on directing public support for the bill to Congress. Ernest Gibson was able to give the CDAAA's position directly to Congress in a statement of support presented before the House Committee on Foreign Affairs. More generally, the organization utilized press releases, radio addresses, and public events to express its message of support for Lend-Lease and to counter the bill's opponents. Eichelberger used a radio debate against 1936 Republican presidential nominee Alf Landon to appeal for bipartisan support for the bill. "The people want quick, practical action," Eichelberger argued. "They will have little patience with the politicians who do not like the lend-lease bill because President Roosevelt is for it. Wendell Willkie looms as a greater Republican today than the members of his party who oppose the bill on party lines." Having failed to secure Willkie as chairman, the organization tried unsuccessfully to get him to speak under CDAAA auspices during the debate but was still pleased by Willkie's full support for the bill.[43]

The CDAAA also provided legal support to the Lend-Lease bill, much as it had during the destroyer-bases exchange. The group released a statement by George Rublee, one of the signatories of the *New York Times* letter of the previous August, specifically refuting charges made in the minority report of the House Foreign Affairs Committee. Rublee refuted the charge of dictatorship leveled at the bill, adding that "the Bill of Rights will still operate. This measure does not add to the powers the President already has as Commander in Chief of the Nation's armed forces, and under which powers he could get us into war today, if he wanted to."[44]

Gibson reiterated the CDAAA's support for the bill at the beginning of February, claiming there were two reasons why it should pass: because the German minister of propaganda, Joseph Goebbels, had broadcast a message against it and because the *Chicago Tribune* was against it. It was not the first time Gibson had connected non-interventionism with Nazi leaders, having previously noted that "our committee is thoroughly disliked by Hitler and Dr. Goebbels and that the America First Committee has the blessing of these two." The references reflected both the heated nature of the Lend-Lease debate and Gibson's belligerent leadership. When asked if convoys might be necessary for material to reach Britain, Gibson again replied yes, if it was necessary, but not at the present time. Such questions could wait, but the immediate focus was passing Lend-Lease.[45]

While the CDAAA focused squarely on the Lend-Lease bill, the Century Group was reasonably confident of its passage and already looking ahead to the future. Its immediate focus was on a counterproposal to Hoover's food plan. Under the plan to provide food relief to beleaguered democracies, the United States would become not only the arsenal but the larder of democracy. In the meantime, the Century Group's influence on the Lend-Lease debate was largely through three affiliated organizations created in December and January that sought to represent traditionally non-interventionist segments of society: women, students, and religious groups.[46]

The Women's Committee for Action operated on an informal basis alongside the Century Group and organized a letter-writing campaign in support of the bill. Working in conjunction with the Women's Committee for Action in order to represent America's youth was the Student Defenders of Democracy. The organization was based at 8 W. Fortieth Street in New York alongside the CDAAA, and it quickly adopted a position of support for Lend-Lease. Finally, religious groups came together in the Inter-faith Committee for Aid to the Democracies, led by the Century Group's Henry Sloane Coffin. Consisting of 143 leading Protestant, Catholic, and Jewish clergymen, the Inter-faith Committee made its position clear in a letter to Senator Walter F. George, chairman of the Senate Foreign Relations Committee, in which it urged "speedy and unanimous passage and enactment of the Lend-Lease bill." All three organizations had the appearance of independence but were in fact closely connected to existing internationalist organizations.[47]

The proliferation of citizens' organizations stepping forward to promote Lend-Lease nearly continued in February with the announcement of United Americans. Proposed by Orville McPherson, editor of the *Kansas City Journal,* the new body aimed to support Roosevelt's policies and complement the CDAAA by filling the gap left by William Allen White's more cautious leadership. McPherson claimed the CDAAA was hampered in the Midwest by a sense that it was a pro-British organization. Using the CDAAA's name as an illustration, United Americans supported aid to the Allies but claimed to put the emphasis "where it perhaps more properly belongs—on the defense of America." Ernest Gibson supported the new group, though Eichelberger admitted off the record that its program was identical to the CDAAA's. Many Century Group members were asked to join, and there was concern about the growing number of groups and the duplication of effort (though this was in part because of the embryonic plans for the Fight for Freedom committee). However, despite plans for a national premiere, including a radio address by the president, United Americans never fully materialized.[48]

Two other existing citizens' organizations with a focus on the threat to American democracy also contributed to the Lend-Lease debate. Friends of Democracy, established in 1937 by the Reverend L. M. Birkhead, promoted a movement to protect democracy from threats on both the political Left and Right. Its rhetoric was particularly aggressive. A notable brochure in March described the America First Committee as a "Nazi Transmission Belt," emphasizing that the Nazis endorsed America First policies and suggesting that the group's supporters were often members of pro-Nazi organizations. The Council for Democracy took a slightly broader approach, focusing on the promotion of democracy as an idea.

Created in October 1940 with C. D. Jackson of *Time/Life* as president and radio commentator Raymond Gram Swing as chairman, it adopted what the historian Mark Chadwin described as a "lofty moral" tone. It lacked a grassroots organization and rarely discussed specific foreign policy issues. But the council frequently worked with the CDAAA and the Century Group, and it counted William Allen White, Lewis Douglas, Herbert Agar, Frank Kingdon, and Henry Van Dusen among its members.[49]

By mid-February, the successful outcome of the Lend-Lease debate was not in doubt, but the network of citizens' organizations promoting the bill effectively countered non-interventionist public sentiment and appeared to be ensuring the bill's swiftest possible passage through Congress. Even the CDAAA was looking beyond the debate to its next steps. Gibson and Eichelberger wrote to Roosevelt proposing that he give another stirring public address explaining how the nation should function "industrially and morally as a nation at war." For once, the CDAAA was moving too far ahead of Roosevelt in claiming that the American people were waiting to hear how the economy was to be mobilized for war. Roosevelt was not ready to ask the American people to make sacrifices and abandon business as usual. The president did, however, acknowledge that a public address of some kind would be useful. A similar letter to Secretary of the Treasury Henry Morgenthau proposing an educational campaign on sacrifices and agitation for the freezing of all foreign assets was met with a similarly noncommittal response.[50]

The CDAAA's focus was firmly back on Lend-Lease by the end of February, as the Senate debate dragged on and concern grew about the threat of a filibuster. Noting delays in the Senate, Clark Eichelberger argued that the date for a vote should be set and the threat of endless debate stopped. He demanded that debates begin earlier and end later, that senators stick to the minimum amount of time available to speak, and that unnecessary amendments be avoided so that the bill could pass speedily. He added that through their repeated references to the likelihood of war, "the handful of isolationists who are trying to obstruct the passage of this bill are the real war-mongers."[51]

Eichelberger was merely the first internationalist to speak out as the organization mobilized its forces against congressional delay. The New York chapter urged Vice President Henry Wallace and New York senators Robert F. Wagner and James M. Mead to call for an immediate vote on the bill. It sent the same request by telegram to Senate majority leader Alben W. Barkley. Signed by twelve prominent citizens, including former presidential candidates James M. Cox and John W. Davis, the telegram declared that every further delay "will be paid for by the blood of those who are fighting to stop Hitler beyond the Atlantic." Ernest Gibson insisted the country needed to get on a wartime basis immediately because Germany could take Brazil "by telephone" if Britain fell.[52]

The filibuster never materialized, and the Senate passed the Lend-Lease bill on March 8 by a vote of 60 to 31. The House of Representatives approved the revised Senate version on March 11 by a vote of 317 to 71, and Roosevelt signed it into law that afternoon. The act authorized the president "to sell, transfer title to, exchange, lease, lend, or otherwise dispose of . . . any defense article" to "any country whose defense the President deems vital to the defense of the United States." In a subsequent address, Roosevelt announced that "we have just now engaged in a great debate. It was not limited to the halls of Congress. It was argued in every newspaper, on every wave length, over every cracker barrel in all the land; and it was finally settled and decided by the American people themselves." The CDAAA had been at the very heart of that debate.[53]

As the passage of the Lend-Lease bill ensured maximum aid to the Allies, the CDAAA had arguably fulfilled its purpose. Some, including those in the Chicago chapter, considered the possibility of winding down and closing up. However, it was clear that for the majority of CDAAA members—and for the overwhelming majority of the leadership—this was not a viable option. A telegram from William Allen White was released to local chapters, expressing his hope that the committee would maintain its identity and continue to act as a vehicle "giving hundreds of thousands of American citizens the opportunity to make their private sentiments public opinion in matters related to the new position of the United States in world affairs." Eichelberger congratulated the membership on its efforts, acknowledging that while passage of the bill had been almost certain from the outset, the work countering delaying tactics in the Senate had been particularly effective.[54]

Eichelberger added that the policy board was meeting that week and that there was much for the CDAAA to do—"probably even more in the future than in the past." Yet even before the bill was passed, Gibson had written to the CDAAA membership to comment on the organization's future. He highlighted the need to put the country on a wartime basis to maximize the production of material aid and the need for "proper amounts" of that material to reach Britain. While its leaders were vague on detail, it was clear that the CDAAA planned to continue in a way that would consider both the domestic implications of war production and the question of convoying material across the Atlantic. It was simply a matter of waiting for the right time politically.[55]

Not only was the CDAAA convinced of the continued need to assist Britain, but the group was clearly still needed domestically to fight the forces of non-interventionism. The America First Committee had grown in popularity and influence during the Lend-Lease debate, and the antagonism between the two organizations had only increased in January and February. The conflict took on a new intensity at the beginning of March when Senator Burton Wheeler accused the CDAAA of being a tool of international bankers and an instrument of British war propaganda. Gibson publicly responded that the America First Committee and groups like it were "a strange conglomeration of business appeasers, Bundists, Communists, Fascists and some sincere but misguided Americans." On March 10, the CDAAA released a full list of all contributors who had given over one hundred dollars, challenging the America First Committee to release details of their financial supporters. The CDAAA list did reveal contributions from bankers such as J. P. Morgan, but it also revealed a diverse array of individuals from industry, labor, publishing, stage and screen, and former government positions. In doing so it helped the CDAAA's image as an organization that reflected many walks of American life.[56]

The beginning of March saw the CDAAA at its organizational zenith. It had survived the loss of its leading figurehead and achieved its primary goal, and it was now more prominent than ever. Yet while the CDAAA felt the Lend-Lease debate had been a success, the Century Group looked at the CDAAA with a growing sense of frustration. It members had been waiting to see how the organization would act after White's departure, but despite Lend-Lease success, they were still not satisfied with the CDAAA's cautious overall message. By the time the debate was over, the Century Group had decided a new organization was necessary.[57]

The idea had been floating around since the previous autumn, but the division within the CDAAA over White's resignation sparked the group into serious discussion. Despite the assurance of Lewis Douglas at a January group meeting that the CDAAA was united behind whatever was needed to defeat the Axis, Francis Miller was not satisfied. He requested a new manifesto along the lines of the "Summons to Speak Out." Believing that the war was America's war and that the nation's role in it needed to be made explicit to the American people, Miller asked for a statement based on the slogan "fight for freedom."[58]

Chapter 7

Deliver the Goods and Fight for Freedom

The passage of the Lend-Lease Act in March 1941 confirmed that the United States was willing to provide all possible material aid to Britain and any other allies fighting against the fascist aggression of Germany, Italy, and Japan. However, it did not mean the end of debate over the nature of America's relationship to the war. Instead, it merely changed the issues being considered. Rather than whether or not the United States should aid Britain, the main issue in the spring of 1941 was about how that aid should reach Britain. Once it had agreed to act as the arsenal of democracy, was it up to the United States to ensure that aid crossed the Atlantic? For most American internationalists, the answer was clearly yes. Lend-Lease alone was insufficient. From their perspective, what was the point in lending and leasing armaments to Britain if they ended up at the bottom of the Atlantic?

This represented yet another public opinion battle for the internationalists to fight. While there had been consensus on Lend-Lease, the country was still deeply divided over the broader issue of the war. In the week Lend-Lease was passed, a Gallup poll revealed that 83 percent of Americans would vote to stay out of a war against Germany and Italy. A month later in April, a similar poll revealed that 81 percent would vote to stay out, despite the fact that a question asked in the same poll revealed that 82 percent believed the United States would ultimately end up in the war. Although they could see war looming inexorably, the vast majority of Americans were in no hurry for it to arrive.[1]

On the issue of using the U.S. Navy to guard ships transporting war material across the Atlantic to Britain, the opinion divide was much closer. In the middle of April, 50 percent of Americans said that the navy should not be used for convoying whereas 41 percent thought it should. However, if it appeared that a British defeat would be inevitable without American naval protection, the number in support rose to 71 percent. A month later the numbers had almost reversed, with 52 percent for convoying and 41 percent against, but it was hardly a conclusive majority. The implications of convoying were also unclear. When asked how they would respond if U.S. ships were sunk in the act of convoying, 50 percent of those polled claimed they would still not be in favor of war, with just 40 percent in favor. The message from the American public as a whole remained clear: they wanted to help Britain as much as possible while at the same time staying out of the growing global conflict.[2]

Much of the popular debate in March and April of 1941 focused on the issue of convoying. For one group of internationalists, however, there was little point in arguing over convoying as it missed the bigger picture: the United States was already effectively at war. With this view in mind, the Fight for Freedom committee was announced in April as an out-and-out interventionist organization. Evolving from the Century Group into a formal national organization, it took the argument for a more active foreign policy to the extreme. The new committee argued that in acting as the arsenal of democracy the United States was already at war, that it was cowardly to suggest otherwise, and that further action was required immediately to keep Britain alive.

With the creation of yet another organization seeking to mobilize public opinion, the debate moved closer and closer to conflict. Fight for Freedom saw itself as the ultimate opponent of the non-interventionist movement and the America First Committee. It also saw itself as the new standard bearer for supporters of Britain and a more active American foreign policy, as the CDAAA appeared to have achieved its stated goal of maximum aid to the Allies. However, the CDAAA continued to operate, following a more moderate path close to that of the Roosevelt administration, whereas FFF forged strongly ahead of public opinion. Yet while there were numerous tactical, bureaucratic, and personal differences between the two organizations that severely limited their cooperation, they also had a great deal in common when it came to the factors supporting their different approaches to internationalism.

Delivering the Goods

With Lend-Lease passed, the CDAAA immediately sought to find a clear new message. Despite a sense of relaxation over the bill's passage, Chairman Ernest Gibson argued that the job was "very far from done." Just days after Congress passed the Lend-Lease bill, the CDAAA released a new policy statement outlining five aims to make the new legislation as effective as possible. It asked for revision of legislation to allow Americans to serve in the armed forces of America's allies, freezing of all foreign assets in the United States (with particular reference to the Axis powers), a firm policy in the Pacific against Japan, and greater efforts to combat totalitarian propaganda in the Americas. Most important, the CDAAA argued for full economic mobilization in support of production of war materials for Britain, including the convoying of Allied ships with American naval vessels if necessary. The organization's new slogan was "deliver the goods to Britain now."[3]

In taking this position, it argued that if Britain fell, "the survival of our world is at stake." The United States would be barred from "the external world," lacking access to all essential resources, and would thus be left under the threat of invasion. The organization acknowledged that its policy carried the risk of war but argued that it offered a lesser danger of war and a greater chance of peace than failure to act. To force home the threat to the United States, the group quoted Hitler's words from the previous December: "Two worlds are in conflict, two philosophies of life. . . . One of these two worlds must break asunder."[4]

A subsequent letter to members from Gibson on March 28 emphasized a three-point program: speeding production, delivery of war materials, and the study of the organization of peace. In urging heightened production rates, the CDAAA demanded that the nation abandon "business as usual." Instead, industry needed to put itself at the disposal of government production agencies, and labor needed to make war material production its chief concern. Strikes were to cease immediately, and Americans were to accept higher tax burdens. The CDAAA tried to do its part by bringing labor and business together locally, and on a national scale it was proud to highlight that CDAAA policy board member Frank Graham had been appointed to Roosevelt's Labor Mediation Board for the settlement of strikes.[5]

Given the CDAAA's origins and its relationship to the League of Nations Association and the Commission to Study the Organization of Peace, the third element of Gibson's program was no great surprise. It highlighted the long-term collective security worldview of the CDAAA that had been somewhat hidden during the immediate fight for Lend-Lease. In early April, Clark Eichelberger wrote to Roosevelt urging him to begin preparing plans for the postwar peace table in order to create "a New Deal for the world." Roosevelt replied by encouraging Eichelberger to place any suggestions before Cordell Hull (who actually drafted the letter), but what Eichelberger did not know was that at exactly the same time, the Department of State's research staff was just beginning—albeit in an embryonic way—to consider postwar issues.[6]

Just over two months later, Eichelberger's CSOP issued its own postwar statement of aims entitled "A Statement of American Proposals for a New World

Order." The commission drew upon the four freedoms, urging the preservation of freedoms of speech, assembly, and religion, as well as freedoms from want and the threat of war. Reasoning that "permanent peace rests upon social justice," the CSOP called for a substitute for war in settling disputes, freer commercial interchange and more equitable labor and living standards, an international Bill of Rights to uphold democracy, guarantees for minorities, free interchange of ideas, and a commitment from the United States to utilize its resources to drive postwar reconstruction. While the statement made no reference to a world organization, it did state that as "part of the world community," the United States could no longer ignore its global duties or responsibilities.[7]

A further long-standing issue commanding the attention of the CDAAA in March and April was Herbert Hoover's suggestion of providing food to occupied Europe. Gibson wrote to both the president and the secretary of state to express the committee's disapproval of suggested plans to provide food for unoccupied Vichy France. (Consistent with its position of the previous autumn, the Century Group's Ulric Bell also expressed his dissatisfaction to Hull.) The CDAAA argued that the United States must not feed the Axis war machine, but the Roosevelt administration was in fact willing to allow some food and medical supplies into Vichy France. In this instance the British vetoed all proposals, though some material was allowed through later in June.[8]

The number of different issues emphasized by the CDAAA in March and April revealed a lack of immediate focus and direction, but it was the issue of convoying material across the Atlantic that was most prominent in both CDAAA literature and public discourse. In many ways it was the obvious issue in the aftermath of Lend-Lease, and there appeared to be no time to lose. After the German invasion of Greece and Yugoslavia on April 6, Eichelberger pleaded with CDAAA members to do everything possible to spread the "desperate facts" about the shipping situation and the need for the United States to ensure delivery of war material to all the Allies. Convinced that the American public was ready to support convoying to ensure delivery, he urged chapters to inform the president of this support.[9]

Unfortunately, not only was the American public deeply divided on the issue of convoys, but Roosevelt also had reservations. Those were in turn based on his perceptions about the nature of public opinion. Believing that the public had united behind Lend-Lease on the basis that it would keep the nation out of war, the president feared the idea of convoying would shatter the fragile popular consensus. Instead of moving ahead with the new idea of convoying, Roosevelt simply expanded the existing area of Atlantic patrols to twenty-five degrees west, including the Azores and the Greenland.[10]

Roosevelt's view was expressed to the CDAAA by Thomas Lamont, who advised against "waving too much the provocative slogan of immediate 'convoys.'"

Noting that neither Roosevelt nor Hull had actually used the word "convoys," Lamont suggested waiting for the president before pressing ahead in support of them, as he knew best whether the country was ready. To emphasize the point, and despite his professed support for the CDAAA's work to date, Lamont argued that it was "not for us private individuals" to decide on issues such as convoying and that the Committee should wait until Roosevelt's forthcoming meeting with Ernest Gibson for counsel. For his part, Lamont believed that it was too soon to expect support from the country west of the Alleghenies.[11]

Lamont's view was supported by William Allen White, who thought the committee's policy statement in support of convoying was a mistake. White shared Lamont's view that it was of no value to the administration for the CDAAA to move ahead of its policies, arguing that he would support convoys only when the president did. The response of both Lamont and White highlighted yet again their positions on the more conservative end of the CDAAA spectrum, but it also emphasized their belief that the CDAAA worked best when it worked hand in hand with the administration to support specific aims. More general efforts to change the national mood were to be encouraged unless—as in this case—they went counter to thinking in the White House. The disagreement over convoying (along with his wife's illness) led to White's final quiet resignation as honorary chairman in April, severing his ties with the CDAAA that had been nearly synonymous with his name.[12]

Despite the views of Lamont and White, the CDAAA continued its calls for convoying, albeit with a certain amount of restraint that suggested the White House view was not completely ignored. Even with that restraint, the leadership sensed a change in the relationship between the CDAAA and the administration. Partly because there was no specific policy to support and partly as a result of the disagreement over convoying, there was a sense within the CDAAA that despite its previous effectiveness, it was no longer of use to the president. In April, Mrs. J. Borden Harriman, the former minister to Norway and newly appointed CDAAA vice chairman, openly appealed to the White House to throw its weight behind the CDAAA. She argued that supporters of the president's policies were overconfident in the aftermath of Lend-Lease, which had led to a reduction in financial contributions. She specifically requested that the administration spread the word to those who had not donated to the committee that it was important and worthy of support. Suggested names for the administration to approach included the financiers Clarence Dillon and Bernard Baruch; Myron Taylor, industrialist and current envoy to Pope Pius XII; philanthropist Vincent Astor; and the Rockefellers.[13]

The CDAAA's finances were certainly in dire need of a boost. Despite their having raised $343,244.16 since May 17, 1940, the available balance as of April

14, 1941, was $561.86. An estimated $150,000 was required for the next six months of operations, but weekly expenses were considerably higher than weekly income, and drastic reductions in staffing were considered. Internal situation reports suggested the general public was inclined to feel that the CDAAA was no longer needed and therefore did not require further funding. Donations rose at the end of April, but by June the committee's financial situation was again in a state of crisis, and would remain so until December 1941.[14]

The CDAAA attempted to take the initiative itself with yet another new statement of policy in May, calling for a full state of national emergency, use of American naval and air forces to secure the lifeline to Britain (by convoying if necessary), military cooperation with the Allies, aid to China, freezing of Axis assets, and a declaration of intent from the United States to take full responsibility in organizing a peace based on political, social, and economic justice. The statement added little to the one issued less than two months previously, but it was given added publicity by being released on the same day as the CDAAA's Freedom Rally at Madison Square Garden in New York. The rally, featuring speeches from Wendell Willkie and Fiorello LaGuardia, was attended by a capacity audience of twenty-two thousand, with almost as many listening through loudspeakers outside.[15]

The CDAAA also attempted to revitalize itself with a change of name. Recognizing that "aid to the Allies" was national policy and therefore somewhat passé, the executive committee agreed in May to shorten the organization's name to the Committee to Defend America. A number of subheadings would follow under this main title to make the name reflect the organization's aims more comprehensively. The change had the odd effect of simultaneously simplifying and complicating the name—shortening it yet expanding an already cumbersome name still further. Despite some dissent, the majority of chapters were in favor, and the change went ahead at the beginning of July. The organization's new full name was the Committee to Defend America: by Aiding the Allies, Defeating the Axis Powers, and Developing Means for Permanent Peace.[16]

While the CDAAA continued its support of convoying and made headlines and radio addresses on its own, it still sought administration approval, with little success. The president was quietly informed of the committee's feeling that he no longer cared about their cooperation. Eichelberger told Secretary of the Interior Harold Ickes of his failed appeals to the White House and his frustration with a general unwillingness of anyone in the administration to speak out without Roosevelt's prior approval. Ernest Gibson asked Roosevelt's assistant William Hassett to tell the president the CDAAA was a "better organization than he realizes." The CDAAA still openly supported Roosevelt's May 27 fireside chat in which he proclaimed an unlimited national emergency, but it felt unappreciated despite a response from Stephen Early. In June, Eichelberger wrote directly to the president, openly conceding that the CDAAA needed guidance and direction: "How can we most effectively support the policy upon which you have decided and which the country supports overwhelming [*sic*]?" He admitted that the very future of the CDAAA was at stake.[17]

The CDAAA was struggling for a number of reasons. It appeared to have achieved its main goal and needed more than a cosmetic name change. It suffered from a lack of both financial support from the public and moral support from the administration, whose post–Lend-Lease caution was not helping. In May it also suffered yet another change in leadership. After just four months in office, national chairman Ernest Gibson was called up for active service in the army. Clark Eichelberger took over as acting chairman, and in June it was agreed that Wendell Willkie should again be approached to take the position on a permanent basis. Once again Willkie declined the post, claiming he could be of greater service without holding a formal position. The organization continued without a figurehead until Eichelberger was formally announced as national chairman in October 1941. Though he was well known in certain influential circles, he lacked the national standing of Gibson, let alone of William Allen White. The CDAAA's inability to replace White with a figure of similar renown undoubtedly had an effect on the organization's relative decline in prominence after Lend-Lease. Yet perhaps the biggest reason for the CDAAA's dip in fortune was the arrival of a new internationalist organization in the form of Fight for Freedom.[18]

Fight for Freedom

Created in April 1941, Fight for Freedom represented a natural outgrowth and expansion of the more informal Century Group that had existed since the previous July. Frustrated by the relative caution of the CDAAA, the Century Group supported a more muscular internationalism and had been considering the issue of a bold new manifesto from the beginning of the 1941. By the end of January, it had produced a draft promoting a national policy of defeating Hitler. With more aggressive and provocative language than that of the CDAAA, the draft claimed that "there is no peace. There is only revolution—flaming, world-wide revolution—aimed at the moral basis of our life. We must resist it with everything we own. . . . We must use our full strength to beat the Axis." While the draft conceded that it was not known where and when that strength would be applied, it endorsed the use of such strength as soon as possible. Though it was never publicly issued as a statement, over the next two months the draft became the basis of the new and more interventionist organization.[19]

Francis Miller had called for the new manifesto in January, but although he took on the title of FFF vice chairman, other commitments meant his role was limited. Instead, it was Ulric Bell who was the individual responsible for driving the new organization through 1941. Bell had been Washington correspondent for the *Louisville Courier-Journal*, the newspaper he had worked for since 1910. He had a connection to the Roosevelt administration, having accompanied Cordell Hull to the Montevideo Conference in 1933, and he remained in touch with the secretary of state through 1941. Though Bell naturally preferred to remain off stage and off the record, Miller suggested he take on a bigger and more formal role. As chairman of the executive committee, Bell was primarily interested in organizational practicalities and getting things done, leaving the big ideas to others. He was ably supported in the Rockefeller Center office by former advertising executive F. H. Peter Cusick as executive secretary and Wayne Johnson (formerly of the Inland Revenue Service) as treasurer. In many respects, Bell was to FFF what Eichelberger was to the CDAAA: the man in charge of daily organizational operations and the power behind the throne, though unlike Eichelberger, he remained in the background throughout.[20]

It was clear to the FFF organizers that they would need a nationally well-known chairman. In fact, they chose two. As honorary chairman, they secured respected Virginia senator Carter Glass. A southern conservative Democrat, Glass supported an active internationalist foreign policy. Despite the fact that he had never previously allowed his name to be used by a citizens' organization, he made an exception after an approach from fellow Virginian Francis Miller. Glass provided a name of national standing, but he provided little else, insisting that organizational demands on his time be kept to a minimum. Needing a more active chairman to act as the public face of FFF, the organizers chose Henry W. Hobson, the bishop of southern Ohio. Like Glass, Hobson was a Democrat, but unlike Glass he was willing to speak out regularly against dictatorship overseas and what he saw as isolationism and appeasement at home. He had played a key role in the development of religious opinion as a member of the Century Group, and despite being based at home in Cincinnati, Hobson took on a significant burden as the FFF's main spokesman.[21]

The choice of Glass and Hobson as figureheads revealed that FFF did not fully share the CDAAA's concern with the need for bipartisanship or Republican leadership. Indeed, the FFF leadership was on the whole more liberal than that of the CDAAA. FFF also differed from the CDAAA in the geographical origins of its leadership. Rather than representing the northeast, the core of FFF leadership was from the south in the cases of Miller and Glass, and west of the Alleghenies in the cases of Hobson, Bell, and Bell's former *Louisville Courier-Journal* colleague

Herbert Agar. Of course, despite their geographic origins, almost all the FFF leaders had a college education, many of them at elite institutions (Bell, without a degree, was a rare exception).[22]

Fight for Freedom went public with a radio address from Hobson on April 19, 1941, the anniversary of the Battle of Lexington. Making a clear historical analogy with the Revolutionary War, he argued that as in 1775, the moment had come in which Americans must "fight for our freedom or lose it." Just as then, he claimed, the right of Americans to be free to speak, write, listen, worship, and govern themselves was under threat. He went on to state that FFF believed in four things. First, that freedom itself was worth fighting for. Second, that believing Hitler's defeat was essential was an immoral position unless Americans were willing to "face the dangers and sacrifices which others are suffering in this struggle for freedom." Third, that providing material aid to Hitler's enemies was dishonest "without facing and admitting the fact that we are in this war." Finally, unless the United States acted immediately to do whatever was necessary to ensure Hitler's defeat, the war would be lost.[23]

Having experienced war in 1918, Hobson claimed that no one hated it more than he did. He therefore took offense at the characterization of FFF as "warmongers" seeking to betray the country by leading it to war. Instead he countered that "following the isolationist way we would be left alone to face the final onrush of aggression from all sides in total war. . . . For this way leads not only to the greater loss of life, but to the destruction of courage, faith, the spirit of sacrifice, heroism and loyalty." As a bishop, he also confronted criticism of his actions from a religious perspective. "I have taken my stand," he argued, "because I believe that Hitler, and the forces he has marshaled in his violent aggression against all mankind, have chosen that state of blasphemy against the Spirit of God which makes any appeal to them on a Spiritual basis ineffective. I therefore favor the use of force, as the only weapon available, to bring about their defeat."[24]

Newspaper reports the following day listed a number of prominent individuals who had already agreed to join FFF, many of whom had been Century Group members or had connections to the Roosevelt administration, including Herbert Agar, Allen Dulles, John Balderston, Colonel William J. Donovan, and banker James Warburg. Notable by their absence were any of the CDAAA leaders. Despite invitations to join, almost all declined. While agreeing with much of FFF's argument, Hugh Moore could not bring himself to join an organization favoring war. Neither could Herbert Bayard Swope, one of the more aggressive members of the CDAAA, who claimed that the statement was "bad and unnecessary," and represented an attempt to be "consistent with personal rather than national policy." Despite having attended Century Group meetings, Lewis Douglas and

Clark Eichelberger also chose not to join, focusing on the ongoing efforts of the CDAAA.[25]

Just three days later, a Century Group dinner meeting acted as an informal first meeting of the new organization. The decisions made at the dinner reflected how poorly developed the organization's plans were at that stage. Given the support for Hobson's speech, the group chose an executive committee, agreed to the need for a finance committee, and recognized the need to develop a policy. Despite calls to support specific policies such as convoying, Wayne Johnson argued that FFF shouldn't be a convoy committee as it was "the war committee." Calls for a declaration of war were rejected, however. Robert Allen argued it was too soon, and that they must first "set the stage." Despite all the rhetorical references to the immediate need to fight, it was in fact October 1941 before FFF formally called for a declaration of war. Given the group's name and its rhetoric, however, most observers assumed this had been FFF policy from the outset.[26]

Within days, the new organization was again in the headlines. Just two days before the unveiling of FFF, Charles Lindbergh gave his first speech as a member of the America First Committee. Acquiring the famous aviator was a significant propaganda coup for the non-interventionist organization, and when Lindbergh made a further speech in New York on April 23, FFF felt it necessary to reply. In a radio address, banker James Warburg vehemently countered Lindbergh's suggestion that Britain was losing the war and that the United States was invulnerable to attack. Reiterating the new organization's cause, he claimed the war was not a foreign war. It was in fact "our fight—for us to win or for us to lose."[27]

Like the CDAAA, FFF was frequently attacked with exaggerated suggestions that it was a front for the financial interests of Wall Street. Confronting such criticisms directly, Warburg began his address that night by noting that a number of people had contacted him urging him not to speak because he was Jewish. Since he had been invited by Hobson, he told listeners that he had asked the bishop "to consider the anti-Semitic party line against Jews and bankers," a line Hobson dismissed as irrelevant. "Jew or Gentile," Warburg argued, "an American can say only this to Charles Lindbergh: your second non-stop flight has taken you to a strange destination." Throughout 1941 FFF's opponents continued to make war-profiteering arguments that were occasionally marked by anti-Semitism.[28]

FFF was also frequently accused of being pro-British, which of course it was, and for which it made no apology. The organization had extremely close connections to the British government, most notably through the British Press Service, which had been set up in 1940 as a propaganda bureau to build relations with the American press and public. It was located just twenty-two floors above FFF in the same Rockefeller Center building, which facilitated regular contact by telephone and in person. This enabled Bell and Cusick to find out the latest news from London, which they could then utilize in FFF material and speeches.[29]

The President's Advance Guard

Of course, it was with the American government that FFF was particularly interested in cultivating close relations. In this respect it followed a path similar to the CDAAA's, working to influence the Roosevelt administration both through personal connections and through the broader education of public opinion. The biggest divergence from the CDAAA was of course the decision to move much further ahead of the administration's policies in order to force the government—and the rest of the public—to catch up. While FFF saw itself as working from a position of constructive support, its leaders had a different understanding of the concept from the old CDAAA method; William Allen White's strategy of waiting for the president to act did not apply. Instead, FFF believed the best way to support Roosevelt was to act as an advance guard. There were drawbacks to this approach, most notably that it left them wide open to accusations of warmongering. However, it was clear that the administration was sympathetic and that many within it found FFF a useful ally—including the president.

While Roosevelt had almost no direct connections to FFF, there were numerous connections between the organization's leaders and members of his administration. Secretary of the Interior Harold Ickes went as far as attending an informal dinner on April 30, subsequently stating that had he not been a member of the government, he would have joined the organization. Some individuals directly connected to the administration did join FFF, including James B. Conant, Admiral William H. Standley, and (briefly) William J. Donovan. Ulric Bell and Francis Miller were both invited to informal conversations organized by Vice President Henry Wallace on American war aims. As historian Mark Chadwin has noted, a number of men around Roosevelt viewed FFF as "an unofficial propaganda instrument for the administration." This was a role that FFF was happy to play and one that kept the group in close daily telephone contact with the White House. The organization also used more conventional tactics, including regular telegrams and letters to the president and secretaries of state, navy, and war. In a telegram following Roosevelt's May 27 fireside chat, Bell pledged the organization's "loyal and wholehearted support. We endorse in advance whatever actions you may take toward finishing the job in hand."[30]

Despite the belligerent stance of FFF, it was willing to listen to the Roosevelt administration and temper its stance when appropriate. Much like the CDAAA, FFF did not make a particular issue out of convoying in April and May. Despite

asking the nation to acknowledge a state of war, it chose not to make loud demands for convoying at the White House's request. Both organizations limited
their calls for convoying and regarding war in the Atlantic more generally until
the unprovoked sinking of an American ship, the *Robin Moor,* by a German sub-
marine in June. At that point, Stephen Early removed his request for the organizations to withhold judgment, and both were subsequently more aggressive. More
generally, though, Roosevelt was happy for FFF to take a more aggressive line
and get out in front of public opinion to move it forward. James Warburg later
recalled writing a promotional advertisement for FFF that was deemed by others
to be particularly strong in its language. When Ulric Bell showed the draft to the
president, he replied, "If you're going to give me hell, why not use some really
strong language?" before adding that "pusillanimous isn't such a bad word!"[31]

Roosevelt's personal appreciation of FFF and the role it could play is indicated in a presidential memorandum from May 1941. That month, Roosevelt
established the Office of Civilian Defense. Led by Fiorello LaGuardia, the office
had a broad mandate that included bolstering national morale. At that time, a
memorandum from Roosevelt urged Lowell Mellett, director of the Office of
Government Reports, to meet with LaGuardia, Secretary of the Interior Harold
Ickes, and Ulric Bell regarding "the whole subject of effective publicity to offset the propaganda of the Wheelers, Nyes, Lindburghs [*sic*], etc." The idea was
quickly rejected by Ickes, though this was due to his concerns about LaGuardia's
ability to lead public morale and the fact that Mellett was "abysmally ignorant on
the subject matter" rather than any reservations about FFF and Bell.[32]

Along similar lines later in August, former CDAAA member Adlai Stevenson
(now assistant to Secretary of the Navy Frank Knox) contacted Bell regarding a
proposed joint government-public organization to foster national unity and support for the administration, while countering the non-interventionist rhetoric
of the America First Committee. The projected organization was to consist of
two parts. The first part was a government liaison committee, including Stevenson, Assistant Secretary of War John J. McCloy, William Elliot from the Office of Production Management, Coordinator of Information William Donovan,
and a representative from the Office of Civilian Defense. The other half was
a public liaison committee, which was to include Bell (representing FFF) and
Clark Eichelberger (on behalf of the CDAAA). Nothing came of the proposal,
which effectively called for a domestic propaganda branch, but it reflected the
administration's belief in the worth of such organizations when mobilizing public
opinion.[33]

When it came to mobilizing popular opinion, FFF again adopted an approach
similar to the one used by the CDAAA. Bell argued that his organization was
necessary as the government was not equipped to mobilize public opinion, and

he openly admitted that FFF was a propaganda organization selling truth to the American people. That message then needed to be passed on to Congress, with FFF persuading "our great representative body to be representative" by telling them what the grass roots were saying. To prove FFF truly represented the real grass roots of the American people, it was vital to show quantitative strength through the support of as many local chapters as possible, and there were 372 by the time of the Pearl Harbor attack.[34]

The quality and diverse nature of that support were crucial. In his address announcing the creation of FFF, Henry Hobson claimed those who joined represented "every phase of American life." A memorandum outlining FFF's history proudly listed the number of different sectors of society involved, including actors, architects, artists, military and government officials, authors and dramatists, businessmen, bankers, clergy, directors, educators, journalists, labor officials, lawyers, musicians, publishers, scientists, and women. Although both the CDAAA and FFF sought both the broadest and deepest public support, FFF tried to take a different line. FFF officials argued that their approach was targeted at the common man, or a broader perception of the mass public "via Main Street." This was contrasted with what they saw as a more top-down approach from the CDAAA, who "gather in the bigwigs, and then try to work down," leading to a "society complexion" that FFF claimed to avoid. However, while this criticism may have been valid in larger cities with greater degrees of social stratification, it was less effective in smaller communities, and FFF continued to emphasize connections to prominent members of society.[35]

FFF also created special divisions to focus on the same type of "weak spot" areas targeted by the CDAAA in what Chadwin described as "a carefully cultivated attempt by a determined minority to give the impression of size and spontaneity." In fact, it focused on the same groups: labor, women, and youth, but with an additional focus on African Americans. The most successful appeal was to labor, in part as a result of FFF's open support for collective bargaining but also because labor was more firmly behind the internationalist cause. Targeted FFF advertisements emphasized Nazi criticism of free trade unions in order to attract support from organized labor. The group was inadvertently assisted in appealing to workers by the America First Committee's regular criticism of the Roosevelt administration, which of course had vast labor support. Thanks in part to the assistance of Harold Ickes, FFF also secured the support of Daniel J. Tobin, who as president of the International Teamsters Union was seen as the most important labor leader to bring on board.[36]

There was one brief incident in which FFF's support for domestic issues in the form of collective bargaining nearly backfired. When Rear Admiral Emory S. Land suggested using troops to open strikebound San Francisco shipyards in

May, Bell replied on behalf of FFF with a strident telegram claiming Land did not speak for the administration. This led to a complaint to the honorary chairman, which caused Carter Glass to engage in a rare piece of FFF correspondence. Glass believed the organization should "keep its hands out of capital-labor disputes and all matters extraneous to the one big job." However, the regular FFF leadership clearly disagreed, and it benefited from greater labor support as a result.[37]

Aside from the labor division, FFF's efforts to reach "weak spot" areas lacked the organization and coordinated effort put in by the CDAAA. FFF did not create a women's division until November 1941, and it barely had time to organize before the United States was at war. However, prior to that it had worked informally with the Women's Committee for Action, which saw itself as opposition to "the influence of the women lobbyists for peace who are giving Congress very effectively the idea that all women are against war and help to Britain if it involves any danger to ourselves." It was, however, a far less public operation than the CDAAA's women's division, with no drive for mass membership. Instead, it worked largely behind the scenes, as it did during the Lend-Lease debate to create the youth organization Student Defenders of Democracy.[38]

The Student Defenders of Democracy was just one of a number of efforts made to appeal to American youth to counter the idea that those of fighting age were against the war. However, as with its efforts to appeal to women, FFF was slow to organize and initially relied on these more informal adjunct organizations. When it did create its own "First-to-Fight" youth division, it was not particularly successful. The division eventually came together with other youth-focused organizations to create American Youth for Freedom. This umbrella organization of twelve national youth groups had little time to achieve anything before Pearl Harbor beyond sponsoring a rally at the Waldorf-Astoria Hotel in New York on Armistice Day, which included as speakers Herbert Agar, Clarence Streit, and columnist Dorothy Thompson.[39]

When it came to the African American community, FFF's intentions were more laudable than its efforts. As with the CDAAA, FFF's approach was to directly contact prominent community leaders such as A. Philip Randolph and Adam Clayton Powell. FFF even went a step further in creating a Harlem division, though financial pressures limited its effectiveness and eventually forced the branch to move to midtown. Despite the extra effort (and the generally more liberal outlook of FFF policy compared with the CDAAA's), the internationalist movement was largely unable to convince the wider African American community that issues abroad were more pressing than those at home.[40]

Overall, FFF had an uneven record in mobilizing opinion during its eight-month existence. On the one hand it created a national profile and began embedding itself in American society. By adopting a mass membership approach and focusing on Europe at a time of heightened tension, it had a far higher national profile than the ACNPJA had ever held. However, it failed to establish itself to the same extent as the CDAAA, for a number of reasons. These included a relative lack of time and internal bureaucratic disorder, which made it harder to establish an organizational infrastructure; the fact that the CDAAA remained in existence and that there was considerable overlap in support between the two; and its inherently more belligerent outlook on world affairs, which ensured that it remained a minority cause. Its significance as an organization is primarily due to its inside connections to the Roosevelt administration, connections that had existed and arguably functioned just as effectively in its previous incarnation as the Century Group.

Confronting a "World Revolution"

The immediate internationalist aim of FFF was explicitly stated in its title: the need to fight for freedom. The freedom in question was broadly defined, but its nature was revealed in the organization's literature and statements throughout 1941. Without referencing Roosevelt's speech directly, it was clear that the group's conception of freedom corresponded closely to the four freedoms outlined by both the president and the broader internationalist movement. In addition to the national security concerns that represented freedom from fear, economic and political considerations were prominent. However, beyond national security concerns, the most significant element of FFF's conception of internationalism was religion. This was not only in the sense of freedom of worship but also in the broader sense of concern for the future of Western or Anglo-American Christian civilization. FFF argued that modern civilization had developed in a particular historical fashion, one located specifically in the American experience, and that the war was part of a global revolution against that very civilization.

This broad freedom-based conception of internationalism can be traced back to the Century Group in 1940, via Francis Miller's call for a statement based on the slogan "fight for freedom" that came just days after Roosevelt's "four freedoms" State of the Union address, through Henry Hobson's opening address in April 1941 and beyond. Hobson, of course, introduced the organization by speaking broadly about the concept of freedom, arguing that the freedom for Americans to speak, write, listen, worship, govern themselves, and determine their own destinies was under threat. Appealing to the memory of the War of Independence, Hobson claimed that fighting for freedom in 1941 was firmly in the tradition of those who had fought 166 years earlier. Now the fight was against "a dictatorship which threatens our country, as it threatens the world, because it denies the right of man to live as a free child of God."[41]

That broad threat to American security was at the emotional heart of immediate appeals for war (or maximum support to Britain in all possible forms). The possibility of a direct threat to American life and territory was still the most effective argument for war, and with the United States taking an increasingly un-neutral stance, the likelihood of being drawn into war grew as 1941 progressed. Just as Ernest Gibson had, Hobson used Hitler's provocative statement about two worlds in conflict to convince Americans they were next on Germany's list. In his speech responding to Charles Lindbergh, James Warburg dismissed those who claimed that Hitler had no designs on the Western Hemisphere and that the United States was safe behind two oceans. Warburg argued that the myth of invulnerability had been exposed by America's military leaders, and he cited Russian-American aviator Alexander de Seversky as a well-known expert to counter Lindbergh's famous status.[42]

Rex Stout, the author and regular FFF speaker, was even more belligerent in his denunciation of Lindbergh, taking the two-worlds thesis to its logical conclusion. He argued that Americans had little choice in the face of fascist aggression but to control or be controlled, to give orders or take orders. For Stout, there was no need to be apologetic for using phrases such as "domination" or "world mastery." Appealing yet again to the past, he argued that any American who claimed "we are not imperialist" and that all the United States wanted was to dominate the continental United States "does indeed need a dose of history, beginning with the words of Washington, Franklin, Jefferson and Lincoln." While Stout hoped the time would come when a viable world police force existed, for now the oceans were going to be controlled by a great power, and that power controlled the world. If you were convinced by the logic of the two-worlds argument, it was clearly better to have the United States controlling the world than Germany.[43]

The national security argument used by FFF was similar to that used by the CDAAA, but the claim that the United States was already at war made the FFF argument much simpler. The United States was under imminent threat of attack and already effectively at war—therefore, it should go to war and fight. The FFF argument was far less concerned with details about *how* any attack would actually occur against the United States. The CDAAA detailed how war might come to the United States through Latin America, but accepting a belligerent position from the outset made such details redundant. Of course, it also made the argument less convincing at a time when most Americans—despite their sympathy for Britain—did not want direct involvement in the growing global conflict. The majority of Americans simply did not agree with the concept that the United States was already at war.

Of course, concern for national security was just one line of argument proposed by FFF. Concerns about other key American freedoms underpinned the group's belligerent internationalism. As with both the ACNPJA and the CDAAA, economic considerations were an important part of the FFF worldview. Once again, the core argument was that the American way of business—capitalism—was under threat and that the nation's high standard of living was therefore at risk. In May, William J. Donovan claimed that German domination of Europe would leave the United States in a dangerous economic position. A German empire had the potential to dominate Europe, Africa, and Asia and would have no obligation to trade with the United States. Its exports, produced by low-paid conscript labor, would undercut American production and affect living standards. Even in 1941, as the United States slowly recovered from the Great Depression, Donovan argued that "the very height of our standards makes us vulnerable."[44]

A similar argument was promoted in a 1941 book written by Douglas Miller entitled *You Can't Do Business with Hitler*. As commercial attaché at the American embassy in Berlin from 1925 to 1939, Miller had a close view of Nazi Germany and used his book to warn Americans about the New Order in Europe and Nazi plans for world domination. Miller argued that in the event of a German victory, America's foreign trade would "come almost to a standstill" and the United States would have to revise its economy accordingly. FFF produced a condensed version of the book in pamphlet form for widespread distribution and enlisted Wendell Willkie to write to fifteen thousand American businessmen urging them to read the book. Willkie argued that a negotiated peace with Germany would destroy America's economic system. Herbert Agar also claimed that a deal with Nazism would "condemn the American economic system and the American business system to death."[45]

To further promote the idea that it would be impossible to do business with Hitler, FFF produced a one-page newspaper advertisement with the views of twelve national businessmen, including FFF's own Ward Cheney and George Watts Hill, and also the CDAAA's Lewis W. Douglas. Douglas was particularly forceful in arguing that Hitler needed to be beaten, contending that American business was based on trust and promises, whereas the Nazi system was based on lies and force. He also highlighted that "business, as run by totalitarian governments, *doesn't have to make a profit*." Harold Connett, chairman of the Tanners' Council of America, emphasized that it was "essential to the economic existence of this country that we be permitted to trade freely in world markets" and that such trade would not be possible in an Axis-dominated world.[46]

Once again, the economic argument was engaged openly by internationalists who recognized the potential threat posed to the American way of life. For those struggling to secure their freedom from want after more than a decade of economic depression, the argument was effective. The economic argument was less emotional than national security concerns, but it was more convincing as a German invasion of the United States was not required in order to affect American living standards. The economic argument highlighted the threat to the United States that would come with a simple negotiated peace. The aim was to persuade American businessmen who believed that war was not good for business that the long-term implications of a strategy of appeasement were even worse.

The economic argument relied partly upon the belief that a defeat for Britain meant a defeat for its empire, but much like the national security argument, it divided the globe into two worlds that were inherently in conflict. This division gave the internationalist argument a simplicity that made it more threatening and arguably more persuasive. If the public was convinced by the FFF's portrayal of the world as one of "them and us," then the logical conclusion was to support whatever measures were necessary to ensure a victory for "us." This approach also added a further level of moral clarity to the argument. Of course, the non-interventionist position held that the two worlds need not necessarily be in conflict, but that position became more and more difficult to hold as the United States provided more and more support to Britain and its allies.

Britain was regularly highlighted by FFF as one of the remaining democracies fighting for freedom against Germany, and the political distinction between democracies and totalitarian fascist regimes was another way in which the two worlds were differentiated. FFF stated that if Americans did not want their democratic form of government enough to fight for it, then they would lose it. The group argued that if Germany defeated Britain, the United States would inevitably end up with a military dictatorship of its own in the face of a hostile world. If Germany ultimately defeated the United States, it would impose a dictatorship as in France. "The only way to save our democracy is to see that Hitler does not win, isolationists, pacifists and fifth columnists notwithstanding."[47]

The non-interventionist counterargument was that the onset of war would inevitably see an end to democratic government. In response, FFF used historical examples to show that this was not the case. It maintained that the Revolutionary War had won the nation its freedom and seen the development of its democratic form of government. Subsequent involvement in World War I had not led to the loss of a democratic way of life (though wartime restrictions such as limits on civil liberties were left unmentioned). Britain and its dominions also emerged in 1918 with democratic governments intact, so a loss of democracy in wartime was not certain if Americans were "worthy sons of worthy fathers."[48]

While the hope of a more democratic world was a key part of the FFF message, the more progressive elements of the organization's leadership hoped not just for greater democracy overseas but for a strengthening of democracy at home. This represented the personal views of leaders like Herbert Agar and Ulric Bell rather than the general membership. But Bell's crusading spirit had already been seen in his support for organized labor, and it was reflected in his claim that democracy could not be fulfilled until all Americans rid themselves of "the touch of fascist many of us have." Examples of those doing their bit for fascism at home included the American "who runs a sweatshop, who wants the little fellow to pay all the taxes, who tries to bilk the government into making him a millionaire through defense contracts, who mistreats his neighbor because he belongs to another race or creed." Rex Stout agreed that in this sense it was a "two front battle."[49]

Of course, such ideas were hardly a central part of the group's message. As Chairman Carter Glass had already indicated, domestic affairs only complicated matters and distracted from "the one big job." Bell's interest in labor freedoms were countered by those who supported the freedom to work and create jobs. In addition, Glass—like many members—would certainly not have supported any efforts to discuss civil rights issues under the FFF banner. So while Herbert Agar used one speech to openly discuss the failure of Americans to support civil rights after World War I, most considerations of democracy were made in contrast to the lack of democratic freedom in Germany.[50]

The biggest drawback to promoting the conflict as a war for democracy was the undemocratic nature of the British Empire. An issue often criticized by non-interventionists who argued the war was between rival imperialisms, it was a point the internationalists confronted directly, if not wholly effectively. FFF chose to emphasize the empire's "independent democracies" of Canada, Australia, New Zealand, and South Africa, though it also maintained that there was no chance of Indian independence with a German victory. The rest of Britain's empire was ignored. However, Britain was still very much part of America's world of freedom. Unlike the CDAAA, FFF openly admitted its sympathy for Britain. While acknowledging Britain's shortcomings, the FFF described it as the "mother of our ideas of freedom and justice; of the 'founding fathers' of the Republic; of our language and culture."[51]

That shared Anglo-American conception of Christian civilization made up a significant part of the FFF message. Perhaps the most important part of the shared culture was religion. Such ideas had been promoted from the earliest days of the Century Group, particularly with Francis Miller's ideas about the relationship between the United States and Europe and the shared civilization of Britain and the United States. Two of the founders of the group, Miller and Henry Van Dusen, promoted an activist view of Christianity informed by the Social Gospel movement, and that was visible in the actions of both the Century Group and FFF, where the torch was carried by Henry Hobson.

The religious arguments of FFF were drawn out more explicitly when considering the specific threat to Christianity in the United States. FFF claimed that Hitler sought to "destroy Christianity," and as a bishop, Hobson bore most of the responsibility for defending the organization's position. He often repeated the stand he had made in his opening address, stating his belief that there were times when physical force was necessary to fight evil; in fact he saw it as his Christian duty. Of course, part of the reason for the strongly religious argument was the need to counter the traditional peace argument of the church. Religious groups were still at the heart of the peace movement, and it was clear that one way to reach them was through church members like Hobson. Another was to take samples of religious views in Europe. Herbert Agar spoke of the fear of Catholic bishops in Germany for the future not only of the church in Germany but of the church itself. For him, the idea that the traditionally conservative Catholic Church was so concerned proved that the very existence of Christianity was stake.[52]

FFF produced a variety of material to highlight the Nazi threat to religious freedom. One particularly scaremongering FFF newspaper advertisement included a picture of two small frightened children praying to a bust of Hitler under the heading "Repeat after me Yank: Adolf Hitler, hallowed be thy name." Another FFF pamphlet focused specifically on religion was reprinted with the suggestion that it might contain material of interest to ministers and form the basis of sermons. It claimed that "freedom's eldest and most cherished child is religion" but that religion was one of the "fruits of civilization that the Nazi war machine would devour." The presence of ministers, priests, and rabbis in German concentration camps was seen as evidence that the true design of the Nazis was "the extermination of religion." Acknowledging that the church was committed to peace, FFF conceded that there might be an obligation to fight for peace if necessary.[53]

The reference to rabbis was one of a few references to the treatment of Jews in Germany and occupied Europe, but there were very few references to the plight of European Jews before the autumn of 1941. Given the comments of James Warburg in April, this was due in large part to domestic concerns regarding an anti-Semitic backlash from the America First Committee and the non-interventionist movement more broadly. Suggestions that international—Jewish—bankers were attempting to draw the United States into war continued through 1941, and internationalists sought to avoid controversy over the issue (a notable exception was the response to Charles Lindbergh's comments about American Jews in September 1941).[54]

Overall, the FFF rhetoric suggested a near-apocalyptic vision of the future. Portrayed in more emotional and impassioned language than previous arguments from the CDAAA, the alternative to fighting for freedom was seen as devastation. Despite focusing narrowly on the threat from Germany—with minimal consideration given to Italy and Japan—FFF combined the threat to American democracy, living standards, and religion into what Herbert Agar described as a "world revolution." Agar's philosophical argument was that this counterrevolution against human history would lead to the destruction of civilization itself. Those who supported the "new order" failed to recognize that it was not possible to build a new order on the destruction of the old. If Americans were not willing to defend their civilization, man would revert to the primitive. There is little doubt that men like Agar genuinely believed their own rhetoric, but there is also no question that their language was chosen deliberately to sway Americans by appealing to both their ideals and their fears.[55]

Yet FFF's conception of internationalism was rarely presented in such abstract and philosophical terms. Whenever possible, the economic, political, and religious freedoms promoted by FFF were presented in real terms through a short-term focus on the immediate threat of German aggression. There were few considerations of the long-term future. Agar acknowledged that the United States had something to contribute of "genuine importance to world history," but he focused on the more immediate fact that it would not be in a position to contribute to the postwar world unless it contributed to the war itself. However, there was agreement that the United States needed to support its words with deeds. Building on the lessons of the previous war, Agar noted that America needed to live up to the promises it had made. Similarly, at a meeting with Henry Wallace attended by Francis Miller and numerous other FFF members, it was agreed that that Roosevelt's four freedoms would have little impact unless the United States became "not only the arsenal but the champion of an expanding area in which those freedoms operate."[56]

What was not clear was exactly how those freedoms were to be championed. While it was obvious to internationalists of all types that "isolationism" was to be rejected and the United States needed to fulfill its global responsibilities, the exact nature of the future peace was still open to question. The immediate national security concerns of the United States were understandably top priority, but ensuring America's freedom from fear in the long term was barely an issue. With its rhetorical two-worlds approach, FFF offered a case for American leadership in the face of an unacceptable alternative, but little more. Just days before the Pearl Harbor attack, Roger Greene suggested to Ulric Bell that FFF develop a statement on how the postwar order might be organized and maintained. By contrast, the CDAAA, which spent much of its first year ignoring abstract questions of peace, began to return to those questions in the spring of 1941. This move reflected the origins of the CDAAA leadership and could be seen in the organization's expanded name (Developing Means for Permanent Peace). It also marked an attempt to differentiate the two internationalist organizations.[57]

Tensions of Internationalism

The CDAAA and FFF shared a great deal. Their conceptions of internationalism were very similar. They had overlapping memberships. They had a common organizational foe in the America First Committee. Yet despite all this, relations between the two were fraught. While the difference between the CDAAA and the more belligerent Century Group had been acknowledged in 1940, it had caused no significant problems as long as the Century Group remained behind the scenes. William Allen White and Clark Eichelberger even attended group meetings. Once FFF became a formal organization in April 1941, however, the relationship became considerably cooler. Their disputes were based upon different public attitudes toward the war (and how far to push ahead of the Roosevelt administration), as well as more private bureaucratic and personal disagreements.

The CDAAA considered its relationship with FFF in the week immediately following its formation, when the executive committee authorized Clark Eichelberger to discuss the possibility of cooperation between the two organizations. A meeting was held between the groups in which it was agreed that the two organizations shared a common aim in the defeat of Hitler. They therefore needed to avoid any sense of competition at the national or local levels. Though competition was largely kept behind the scenes, it nevertheless existed and grew as 1941 progressed.[58]

Initially, the CDAAA leadership was not overly concerned about FFF. Conceding that the position of both organizations was "about the same" on immediate issues such as convoying, Eichelberger believed that FFF would really appeal only to the minority of Americans who supported an immediate declaration of war. However, many CDAAA members supported a more aggressive stance, and a number of chapters threw their support behind FFF. This in turn led to bureaucratic problems. FFF represented a new and dynamic organization that threatened the more established and (politically and strategically) conservative CDAAA. The CDAAA's Irwin Jaffe argued that the CDAAA had outlived its usefulness and should merge with FFF as soon as possible before the internationalist movement split into two factions. FFF also had concerns about the overlap between the two groups. Despite an initial belief in the need for both organizations, Henry Hobson quickly found that many supporters disagreed, especially after the CDAAA's May policy statement.[59]

Attempts to come to a satisfactory agreement were unsuccessful. The CDAAA did not want FFF to steal CDAAA chapters and members, urging it to stick to "virgin territory." Nor did it want to alarm its more cautious members by pushing for war, feeling a merger would alienate more members than it might recruit. Its executive committee was almost entirely against the idea of a merger, instead proposing close functional cooperation. Frederick McKee argued that the arrival of FFF had the advantage of presenting the CDAAA as the great "middle of the road" organization in popular debate, with FFF and the America First Committee on the extremes. He was also concerned that FFF might not regard "the organization of the machinery of peace" as an essential part of future work.[60]

For its part, FFF had no desire to limit its organizational efforts purely to avoid offending the CDAAA. Bell and Agar argued that they should be free to win over anyone convinced by their argument, whether he or she was a CDAAA member or not. Nor did FFF want to water down its forthright message for the sake of a merger. Its leaders were largely supportive of a merger but only if it was on their terms. The FFF leadership increasingly saw the CDAAA as an organization that followed opinion but never took the lead in developing or creating opinion. As a result, it had become a hindrance that was "almost as great a handicap as the America First Committee." The comparisons with America First showed just how much both organizations had lost sight of the bigger picture on domestic opinion at the expense of bureaucratic differences.[61]

There were exceptions to the disagreement, most notably in New York City, where the CDAAA's New York chapter and FFF agreed to unite in June to issue a joint statement in support of Roosevelt's unlimited national emergency fireside chat. Later in August, those same two parties merged into the comprehensively titled New York Fight for Freedom Committee to Defend America. Yet even this merger between FFF and the CDAAA's most belligerent chapter (which was in large part responsible for William Allen White's resignation) did not come easily, as earlier efforts in July to bring about a merger had been unsuccessful.[62]

July saw the most concerted efforts to arrange cooperation on a national scale. A tentative agreement was reached that ensured each organization would maintain its own identity, but a coordination committee was to be created to arrange for fund-raising and speakers and to issue joint statements whenever possible. Local organization was still an area of significant disagreement, as FFF felt that cooperating with existing CDAAA chapters gave the established organization an advantage, while CDAAA chapters asked to cede operations to FFF felt insufficiently recognized for their year of effort. Nevertheless, the CDAAA hoped its chapters would cooperate with FFF groups and FFF would in turn avoid creating duplicate offices where the CDAAA already existed. The two organizations could then divide up remaining communities. It was also suggested that the two organizations would issue a joint statement saying they shared the same objective: the defeat of Hitler.[63]

Unfortunately, the FFF leadership was no more interested in compromising on organizational matters than it was on the question of war. It saw no advantage to a full merger, nor did it see any advantage in a halfhearted "merger that isn't a merger." Many FFF members failed to understand the CDAAA's need to continue, with Herbert Agar suggesting that the CDAAA still believed there was a way to defeat Germany without the need for war. Efforts to issue a joint statement continued without success until Pearl Harbor, even though both groups recognized that bureaucratic issues were taking up valuable time that could have been spent on larger objectives.[64]

The ongoing failure to reach an agreement led to personal bitterness between Eichelberger and Bell. The two men were temperamentally opposed; Eichelberger was bureaucratic, while Bell was more practical. Bell became increasingly annoyed with Eichelberger's rigid territorial stance toward the CDAAA and inability to see the bigger picture. When Eichelberger accused him in November of turning FFF into a political machine to support a third party for Wendell Willkie, Bell declared it was "war" from that point onward. For his part, Eichelberger became increasingly frustrated with FFF's efforts to take over CDAAA chapters, and he condemned the "intolerable tactics and disrespect of their field men." By early December, as Eichelberger was drafting yet another proposed joint statement, Bell was arguing that a merger was desirable but "impracticable" with the CDAAA's existing policy. On the eve of Pearl Harbor, Bell believed that FFF was recognized as the largest opposition to the America First Committee, but much of his time in the previous eight months had been spent competing with the CDAAA.[65]

Although the two organizations failed to come together with a joint message in 1941, they did both work through the summer and fall of 1941 to promote an even more active foreign policy. In doing so, they highlighted key foreign policy issues to the American people and provided informal support for the Roosevelt administration. In addition to promoting the fight for freedoms overseas, they fought the forces of non-interventionism at home, both in Congress and in the America First Committee. However, they struggled to make serious inroads into the majority of American opinion that still wanted a British victory without the cost of American involvement.

Chapter 8

The Battle of the Atlantic from Barbarossa to Pearl Harbor

In the summer of 1941, the United States slowly moved closer to war in the Atlantic. For many internationalists, the progress was too slow. Having expanded the area of Atlantic patrols in April, President Roosevelt reiterated the need to reduce attacks on shipping in his May 27 fireside chat. However, with the notable exception of the arrival of U.S. marines in Iceland, there was little concrete action. Even the sinking of the *Robin Moor* had failed to spark a sense of public outrage, and Roosevelt was reluctant to force such an incident into a pretext for more aggressive measures. He still believed the nation was divided on the issue of war.

Opinion polls largely supported the president's assessment. By the beginning of July, 79 percent of Americans believed the country should not enter the war, though 56 percent now thought the U.S. Navy should be used to convoy material across the Atlantic. The numbers did not change dramatically before the Pearl Harbor attack. In mid-November, 63 percent of Americans opposed the idea of a congressional declaration of war against Germany, with just 26 percent in support. The situation was more complicated when Americans were asked whether it was more important to keep out of war or to ensure that Germany was defeated. In September, 70 percent argued it was more important to see Germany beaten, though by the middle of November the number had in fact shrunk slightly to 68 percent. Americans still wanted to see Germany defeated but ideally without having to go to war.[1]

The focus of American debate throughout 1941 remained primarily on the battle of the Atlantic and the threat from Germany. However, the potential threat from Japan was increasingly recognized through the latter half of the year. In

October, 64 percent of Americans thought the United States should take steps to prevent Japan from becoming more powerful, even at the risk of war. By the beginning of December, 52 percent believed the country would go to war against Japan in the near future. Yet the focus of the public, and the internationalist movement in particular, was very much on Europe with events in Asia a distant second.[2]

However, with a cautious Roosevelt administration, the internationalists had few major initiatives to promote. The previous year showed how effective the movement could be when it worked alongside the government in support of a particular policy. Close connections remained with the administration, but with few remaining policy shifts short of war, there was little of substance to get behind. This left both the CDAAA and FFF to find issues where they could in order to continue the slow shift of public opinion. Regarding the war, they fixed their attention primarily on the battle of the Atlantic and any measures that supported the delivery of aid to Europe.

Domestically, the internationalist organizations focused on fighting the forces of non-interventionism, both within Congress and in the wider public as represented by the America First Committee. Here, in the absence of legislation to debate, the arguments became particularly heated. The rhetoric of FFF in particular became more and more emotional as it presented almost all matters as a battle of two worlds, good and evil. However, the view of the war as good versus evil and as a war for freedoms of speech and religion was seriously complicated in June by the German invasion of the Soviet Union.

The War for Democracy and Operation Barbarossa

All three major internationalist organizations portrayed the war—whether in Europe or Asia—as one of totalitarianism against democracy and political freedom. The ACNPJA argued that China was a fledgling democratic state, and both the CDAAA and FFF downplayed the undemocratic nature of the British Empire. Despite their imperfections, both China and Britain were closer to the American ideal than the totalitarian alternative. The two-worlds argument made this divide between the free world and the fascist totalitarian alternative particularly clear. FFF even made the case that the war was to improve democratic freedoms at home. The conflict was sold as one for the freedoms of speech, expression, and religion.

None of the organizations dwelled on the issue of communism. While minority elements of the ACNPJA were sympathetic, the vast majority of the organized internationalist movement was against the idea of communism just as much as fascism. For the most conservative leaders of the CDAAA as well as the more progressive members of FFF, communism represented just another type of totalitarianism. In one of few earlier references to the Soviet Union, William Allen White equated Soviet tyranny with that of Nazi Germany following war with Finland. It was no surprise, then, that the internationalists were unsure of exactly how to act when Germany initiated Operation Barbarossa and attacked the Soviet Union on June 22, 1941.

One issue they were certain about was that they did not wish to be tainted by communism themselves. Many communist sympathizers within the United States had spent the previous two years arguing against intervention in a war that was portrayed as one of competing imperialisms. With the Soviet Union under attack, however, many immediately changed sides and argued for American aid for the communist nation. However, the internationalists had no desire to welcome communists into their organizations. They had used the existence of communists within the America First Committee as a way to discredit its actions and quickly realized that communist support could now be used to discredit their organizations too.

For once, FFF did not want to expand its support base. A statement from F. H. Peter Cusick on June 23 made the organization's position clear: "We repudiate here and now any support which comes from members of the Communist party or their sympathizers. We are fighting for freedom. In such a struggle, those who advocate totalitarian doctrines for this country can, of necessity, have no part in our movement." Confirming the organization's wish to see Roosevelt's four freedoms realized throughout the United States and throughout the world, the statement concluded that "this is a war to extend democracy, not limit it." Tellingly, the statement focused on domestic communist sympathizers; it made no suggestion as to what American policy should be toward the Soviet Union, as the FFF leadership waited to hear how Washington responded.[3]

The organization soon received queries as to whether its repudiation of communist support meant that it repudiated Soviet support of the anti-Nazi cause. With Roosevelt's announcement of support for the Soviet Union on June 24, the answer became clearer. In a letter to the *New York Times*, Robert Spivack of the FFF press bureau clarified that the organization welcomed any nation willing to take up arms against the Nazi regime. It was not an ideal position, but the enemy of America's enemy had become its friend. In a rather limited defense, Spivack highlighted that "neither Greece nor Poland came up to our standards of democracy, but in the common cause we are all united."[4]

The CDAAA's initial statement focused on the implications of the German attack on the Soviet Union. It emphasized Hitler's desire for world domination and his willingness to break any agreement to achieve it, the increased threat to Britain if Germany were successful in securing Soviet oil supplies, and the "increasingly grave" threat to the United States. As with the FFF statement, no reference was made to official American policy toward the Soviet Union, though a subsequent letter from Clark Eichelberger suggested America's attitude "should be one of realism." The "unexpected assistance" of a fighting response from the Soviet Union would distract Germany from the Atlantic and allow more material to reach Britain. The attack therefore represented an opportunity for the United States to help defeat Germany.[5]

The CDAAA soon adopted a line similar to FFF's regarding collaboration with American communist sympathizers. Eichelberger warned his chapters that communist-leaning groups such as the American Peace Mobilization were now looking for cooperation with the CDAAA. Yet despite acknowledging the assistance of the Soviets in winning the fight against Germany, the CDAAA was not willing to cooperate with groups who "put Russia ahead of the United States and who were opposed to American preparation and aid to Britain when Russia was playing with the Axis and have now changed their line simply because Russia has changed its line."[6]

Both internationalist groups remained wary of communist support, even if some branches might have been infiltrated by communist sympathizers. FFF was particularly vigilant against such intrusion, recognizing that communist support would "furnish to the enemies of an allied victory in this country the necessary red paint with which to splash the allied cause as a communist one." FFF later argued that it was not interested in working with individuals or operations whose opinions were "signed and sealed in the Kremlin." In its simplest form, FFF was "not for Stalin, we are against Hitler."[7]

This view—and the general ambivalence of internationalist support for the Soviet Union—was reflected in the fact that neither organization made a significant promotional push for aid to the Soviets. To offer support to the Soviet Union went against the ideals of most internationalists, leaving them feeling awkward and uncomfortable. Despite the vast push for aid to Britain over the previous year, there was no similar effort for the Soviets in late 1941. Instead, both organizations emphasized the importance of the Atlantic and the need to ensure the successful delivery of aid to Britain. For many internationalists, the eastern front of the European war was first and foremost an opportunity to secure Britain's survival and defeat Germany.

Battle of the Atlantic

In July, the CDAAA focused its efforts on a new campaign to win the battle of the Atlantic. In particular, the organization supported the use of the U.S. Navy to "clear the Atlantic" and keep the lifeline to Britain open. The group seized upon the recent remarks of Secretary of the Navy Frank Knox, who argued that "the time to use our navy to clear the Atlantic of the German menace is at hand," noting the Germany attack on the Soviet Union provided a window of opportunity for effective action. The message was passed on to the CDAAA's 866 chapters to mobilize public sentiment and pass that sentiment on to Washington. The campaign was spread through all media, including a notable full-page newspaper advertisement proclaiming "Okay, Mr. President, Go Ahead 'Clear the Atlantic.'"[8]

Despite the forceful message of the new campaign, the CDAAA was specific in rejecting calls for a declaration of war. Instead, the campaign worked on the basis that the United States was already in a state of undeclared war with Germany, claiming that "most Americans realize that we have, to all practical purposes, been in the war for some time." The newspaper advertisement explicitly stated that the American people "know the difference between an undeclared war and a declared war." This new logic enabled the CDAAA to continue to move in line with the majority of American opinion that supported convoying but not a declaration. When it came to a decision on war, the committee would wait for leadership from the White House. The stance also maintained a small degree of distance between the CDAAA and FFF.[9]

Of course, while FFF's name suggested it supported of a declaration of war, it had yet to officially come out and call for one. As a result, its policy in July was much the same as that of the CDAAA. It came out in strong support of the arrival of American troops in Iceland, claiming that this showed how democracy moved faster and more effectively "than the crafty Nazi fuehrer." FFF also publicized Secretary Knox's recent quote to help legitimize the group's position. As an additional aside to justify the action, it explicitly highlighted Iceland as the first democracy in the Western world.[10]

An executive committee meeting underlined that FFF's "major job" was to "clear the Atlantic." Minor issues included the desire to sever relations with Vichy France and the growing threat from Japan, but these were deemed secondary. A prominent FFF newspaper advertisement urged immediate action in the Atlantic while Germany was concentrating on the east: "Don't wait for the whites of their eyes!" Promoting the organization's program in broad terms, the advertisement called for the Atlantic to be cleared, the severing of diplomatic relations with the Axis powers, occupation of all Atlantic islands, and repeal of the Neutrality Act under the provocative subheading of "Shoot first! Shoot now!"[11]

It was clear that FFF felt official policy was moving far too slowly by this point, and the executive committee even began to draw up a statement attacking the "appeasement clique" of the State Department. Herbert Agar suggested it was impossible to find a rationale for the department's lethargy as it acted "like a neurotic man trying to get a divorce. There always seemed to be some new obstacle that bothered him." Particular criticism was directed at Secretary of State Hull—"old squirrel hunter himself"—who was deemed too slow and obstinate. Robert Allen claimed the department never functioned better than it did when Hull was out sick. Allen Dulles countered that there was little point in criticizing Hull as he was little more than a "messenger boy" for the president, who was really in charge of foreign policy. Dulles was largely correct about the workings of the administration, and the next major policy initiative came from the president himself.[12]

While both organizations grew frustrated with the lack of military action in the Atlantic, both were largely satisfied with the results of the Atlantic Conference between Roosevelt and Churchill in August. The two leaders met for the first time to discuss a joint declaration of war aims despite the fact that the United States was not yet at war. The official statement of the conference, known as the Atlantic Charter, stated eight principles shared by the United Kingdom and the United States "on which they base their hopes for a better future for the world." These included calls for avoidance of any territorial aggrandizement, no undemocratic or enforced territorial changes, the right of all peoples to choose the government under which they live, equal access to trade and raw materials (with "due respect for . . . existing obligations"), international economic collaboration for improved economic advancement and social security, a peace promising freedom from fear and want, freedom of the seas, and an abandonment of the use of force.[13]

The CDAAA in particular was happy to see the democracies go on the "moral offensive" in outlining an ideological justification for the war. In Eichelberger's words, Roosevelt and Churchill had "raised the curtain of the future and have given the world the general principles of the world order which a democratic victory will make possible." The Atlantic Charter also justified the CDAAA's stance of promoting the need to win the peace as well as the war. The war aims suggested they were two sides of the same problem and that the best way to build morale and support for action was to "give the peoples of the world a picture of what they are fighting for."[14]

The CDAAA was not entirely satisfied, however, as the conference had not done enough to reveal how the war was to be won. Eichelberger urged chapters that "our participation in the conflict should be speeded up." The reason for such urgency was the fact that only American involvement in the war could justify American involvement in the subsequent peace. Unless the United States joined the war, it would have no right to a say in the building of the postwar world. The Atlantic Charter saw the CDAAA take the offensive, and in arguing that "the time has come for the American people to throw their full weight into this conflict," its position was now almost identical to that of FFF.[15]

It was not surprising that the response of FFF to the Atlantic Charter was almost identical. Henry Hobson proclaimed that the joint declaration represented "our victory code," though he did not emphasize the future peace to the same extent as Eichelberger. Instead he emphasized the more urgent need for action, as the code could be implemented only "after we start shooting at the enemy of all mankind." Unlike non-interventionist critics, both organizations chose not to dwell on the shortcomings of the charter, such as the deference to the British Empire over "existing obligations" or to the Soviet Union regarding the lack of any reference to freedom of religion. However, the issue of the charter had no significant impact on public opinion, failing to move the debate forward one way or the other.[16]

The most likely event to significantly affect policy or public opinion was a direct attack on an American ship. One came on September 4 when the American destroyer *Greer* was attacked in the North Atlantic. After being informed of the location of a German U-boat by the British, the *Greer* tracked the German vessel for a number of hours. The U-boat fired torpedoes at the *Greer*, which responded with depth charges. Neither craft was hit, let alone sunk, but Roosevelt gave a strong response a week after the attack in the form of a fireside chat. In it, the president omitted to mention the *Greer*'s tracking of the U-boat and instead described the German submarines as "rattlesnakes of the Atlantic." As a result of the attack, he instigated a new shoot-on-sight policy to protect American ships and the freedom of the seas. The president may have been sympathetic to the internationalist argument through the summer, but he was unwilling to take dramatic action in the Atlantic without the provocative incident provided by the *Greer*.[17]

In taking such action, Roosevelt of course had the full support of both the CDAAA and FFF, who had called for such a policy for months. Describing the attack as "startling," the CDAAA used the *Greer* incident to reenergize support behind the battle of the Atlantic campaign and stress the need for immediate action. On behalf of FFF, Francis Miller dramatically proclaimed, "This is *der Tag* in the eyes of the power drunk gangsters who have struck their opening blow at the Western Hemisphere." Frank Kingdon, chairman of New York's Fight for Freedom Committee to Defend America, urged the public to pledge its full support to Roosevelt.[18]

The CDAAA's new September policy statement explained its position in depth. With more forceful language than ever before, it showed how far the organization's position had advanced in the nine months since William Allen White's departure. Supporting Roosevelt's new shoot-on-sight policy in waters necessary for American defense, it noted with approval that the area of those waters was not limited and encouraged full collaboration with the British navy. It argued that since the "fascist powers have made war on us," the only hope left was "a courageous course of positive action. . . . Our nation must recognize that economically, industrially, financially and in the use of our diplomatic and naval power we are already in the war. We are now pledged as a nation to victory and the destruction of Hitlerism."[19]

The recommended course of positive action was a comprehensive ten-point policy. Two related to fascist governments in Europe: sever diplomatic relations with Germany and recognize the Free French government in areas under its control. Three related to the battle of the Atlantic: deliver the goods across to Britain, prevent Axis control of Atlantic or African bases, and use American garrisons on outlying bases. Two points related to Asia: reject any agreement with Japan that would sacrifice open-door principles in China or America's existing position in the Pacific, and promise to limit Japanese expansion in Singapore, the Dutch East Indies, Thailand, and Siberia. One policy was domestic, supporting one-man control of defense production. The final two looked to the postwar future: study the conditions of peace based on the Atlantic Charter and ensure American cooperation in the international world after victory.[20]

Despite the comprehensive nature of the new policy, two notable issues were missing. First, the CDAAA did not ask for a declaration of war. On this issue it stuck to its policy of support for undeclared war, waiting for presidential leadership on anything more formal. Eichelberger's view was that despite the need to get into the shooting war as soon as possible, a declaration of war might take time and bring with it "very considerable and bitter debate." Despite the CDAAA's role in that debate, Eichelberger preferred to sidestep it if possible asking, "Is a declaration of war the most modern devise [sic] to use to participate in the shooting and is it necessary, even though highly desirable at the present time?" While this stance could appear undemocratic, Eichelberger argued the president had public support. As for suggestions it was unconstitutional, he referred to the president's policies as an "Atlantic Doctrine"—a companion to the Monroe Doctrine, forbidding aggression on the ocean.[21]

The second missing issue was an explicit reference to neutrality revision. Once again, on this issue the CDAAA was waiting for movement from the White House. It did not have to wait much longer, as after the sinking of the American-owned *Pink Star*, Roosevelt informed a September 23 press conference that he was looking to amend the Neutrality Act. Three days later, the CDAAA launched its campaign for outright repeal in order to "recapture the freedom of the seas." Using language similar to that in the policy statement, the organization reiterated that the United States was not neutral and was dedicated to destroying Hitlerism; it was therefore time to repeal "the miscalled Neutrality Act."[22]

On October 9, Roosevelt asked Congress to repeal part of the Neutrality Act and authorize the arming of merchant ships. Further revisions were added in the

Senate, but there was to be no full repeal. This frustrated internationalists, who wanted the symbolic victory of full repeal, but the administration did not want to antagonize non-interventionist forces in Congress any more than necessary. In the end, the internationalists fell behind the administration's efforts to remove "all of its restrictive provisions." The repeal effort was undoubtedly assisted by the loss of 11 Americans in the attack on the destroyer *Kearny* on October 16 and the loss of 115 American sailors in the sinking of the *Reuben James* on October 31. The final vote was closer than expected, however. In mid-November, neutrality revision passed the Senate by 50 to 37 and in the House by just 212 votes to 194.[23]

Ulric Bell described revision as "the beginning of the end for Hitler," suggesting that "this will mean war and a declaration of war will and should follow." Yet despite the successful outcome, the close nature of the vote on partial neutrality revision suggested that both Roosevelt and Eichelberger were right to assume there would be no declaration of war from Congress in the immediate future, and any attempt to secure one would bring with it prolonged and bitter debate. Neither the president nor the CDAAA leadership wanted to take a divided nation to war, but it would clearly take a more significant and dramatic provocative incident from overseas to unite the country behind a declaration. Domestic appeals alone were not enough.[24]

That was not a view shared by FFF. Having worked since April to set the stage for a declaration of war without formally calling for one, the FFF leadership began its final push for a declaration in August. It had avoided calling for a declaration for many of the same reasons that the CDAAA had, including a belief that it would lead to prolonged national debate. Yet in mid-August, a letter from Henry Hobson, Ulric Bell, and Francis Miller canvassed opinion for a declaration, arguing it would make the organization's position clear-cut and distinguish it from "avowedly short of war groups"—a reference to the CDAAA, whose policy was increasingly similar to that of FFF. More controversially, the letter argued that the move would unite the country.[25]

One theme emphasized in the letter was how FFF had "worked through the executive branch of the Government because they could get things done." Given its connections to the administration, it was no great surprise when FFF delayed its final push by a month once it was informed that Roosevelt was moving on neutrality revision. After waiting through September to avoid embarrassing the president, the group finally announced its new policy in early October. At its two-day Continental Congress for Freedom in Washington, it finally passed a resolution calling for a declaration of war against Germany.[26]

This remained the primary policy distinction between the CDAAA and FFF. Until the very end the CDAAA stuck by its position that full participation in the war was "a matter of strategy for the President." Otherwise its views on the necessity of greater American involvement in the war to defeat fascism were the same. Eichelberger's views on the issue were only reinforced following a three-week visit to Britain in which he was convinced that although Britain could not be invaded, it could not fully defeat Germany without the military participation of the United States. A further CDAAA policy statement was being prepared in the days immediately prior to Pearl Harbor. The statement began by recognizing that "America is now at war," with its first point supporting "unrestricted use of American armed forces on land, on the sea, and in the air wherever and whenever they may be needed." By December, the main differences that remained between the committees were the emphasis they placed on the future peace and the tone of their arguments.[27]

The extreme tenor of the FFF rhetoric was noted in Georgetown University's *Foreign Service Log* in October. Issued by the university's School of Foreign Service, the publication contained a piece on FFF entitled "High Pressure Salesmanship." It claimed FFF had determined that "appeal to reason is to be jettisoned for an appeal to the emotions. The animal instinct is to be exploited." In particular, it highlighted lurid propaganda posters portraying a threat to American woman-hood. The piece concluded that such appeals should be rejected and that Americans were too quick to react to "the wheedling of our emotions." Ulric Bell was so enraged by the piece that he asked Cordell Hull to "investigate the background of such an article" so that the author could not join "the already dangerous appeasement-minded minority in our Foreign Service." Although Bell helped lead the fight for freedom, the heat of the debate meant that some freedoms were occasionally more important than others.[28]

One emotive issue that surfaced in internationalist rhetoric only in the final months of 1941 was the extent of Nazi brutality and atrocities in Europe. On November 16, the CDAAA cosponsored an international day of protest that culminated at the Metropolitan Opera House to "denounce barbarism which is at present taking the form of mass murders of innocent civilians." Notable speakers included Jan Masaryk, foreign minister for the Czechoslovakian government in exile, and Federal Security Agency administrator Paul V. McNutt. Eichelberger's request that the president proclaim it an official day of protest was declined on the grounds that it was better for the day to appear as a spontaneous demonstration by citizens than as a protest Roosevelt had requested.[29]

A summary report of verified killings of civilians in Europe (and China) was provided for the use of speakers and for publicity. This included the claim by the Polish ambassador in London that in two years of occupation no fewer than eighty-two thousand Poles had been sentenced to death or tortured by the Gestapo. Others reports were provided from Germany, Czechoslovakia, Belgium, Holland, France, Norway, Greece, and Yugoslavia. Those murdered included labor officials, professors, editors, communists, priests, and otherwise innocent civilians. There were only two specific references to Jewish victims. The first referred to the July arrest of four hundred Dutch Jews, whose parents were informed they would receive their sons' ashes upon payment of seventy-five guilders. A second quoted a press report from Berlin, noting that one thousand "communists, Jews and Saboteurs" had been executed in Yugoslavia. Stories such as these brought a harsh reality to emotional appeals, though it was clear that the extent of the tragedy facing European Jews was not yet fully understood.[30]

Convincing Congress

Of course, internationalists were wary of making strong statements about the treatment of European Jews because of domestic concerns of an anti-Semitic backlash. While internationalist leaders largely sought to avoid controversy here, they did not shy away from it in any other sense as they sought to win the battle for public opinion though 1941. Both the CDAAA and FFF worked to counter non-interventionist influence and attitudes in Congress and in the wider public sphere, where the America First Committee remained their primary opposition. In the absence of major policy debates such as Lend-Lease, the latter half of 1941 saw internationalist leaders—especially those in FFF—seize any issue they could to attack what they saw as the reactionary forces of appeasement.

In attacking congressional non-interventionism, FFF tried to undermine the credibility of the movement's most prominent spokesmen, especially Burton K. Wheeler. One way to do this was to taint non-interventionist leaders with the suggestion they were Nazi sympathizers rather than Americans who genuinely wanted to avoid war. An example of this came in June and July when the FFF leadership led an attack on senators Wheeler, Rush Holt, and Gerald Nye, and congressmen Jacob Thorkelson and George Tinkham for abusing congressional franking privileges. The politicians were accused of supplying large quantities of franked, unaddressed envelopes to the America First Committee and other more extreme fascist organizations. As these envelopes were used to spread reprints of literature including speeches by Charles Lindbergh, it appeared that the United States government was paying to spread America First's message.[31]

To further discredit the non-interventionist congressmen, FFF leaders pointed out that it was unlawful for the congressional frank to be used to benefit any private organization, so not only did it appear that Wheeler and the others were helping to promote fascism, but allowing the use of their frank was illegal. Wheeler fought back against what he called a "vicious libel," threatening to take legal action if the accusations were repeated. Ulric Bell responded with a forceful telegram repeating that "anti-Semitic, pro-Nazi and pro-German outfits have sent out mail on your frank. We note your threat to take action and invite you to do so immediately without hiding under the cloak of Congressional immunity." Wheeler did not take further action.[32]

Later in 1941, FFF led similar attempts to discredit Congressman Hamilton Fish because messages had been sent out from his office referring to Fight for Freedom as "Fight for Jewdom." In this instance, further investigation revealed that Fish's office was being used to disseminate Nazi propaganda, and his second secretary, George Hill, was subsequently convicted of perjury after denying a relationship with Nazi agent George Viereck. While these efforts had some impact on the future credibility of the congressmen in question, they had no dramatic impact on the public debate apart from making it more and more personal and vicious. Yet FFF kept chipping away at the non-interventionists in the hope that numerous small gains would add up to a more substantial whole.[33]

A further example was the support FFF provided to the motion picture industry when it came under investigation in September. In an August 1 address in St. Louis, Senator Nye made an attack on the extreme internationalism of Hollywood, claiming that the silver screen was flooded with pictures—such as *The Great Dictator* and *I Married a Nazi*—designed to "rouse us to a state of war hysteria." On the same day, Nye and fellow senator Bennett Champ Clark introduced a resolution for an inquiry into prowar movies. The resolution was not passed, but the Interstate Commerce Committee, chaired by Wheeler, appointed a subcommittee to begin investigations.[34]

Many Hollywood figures were sympathetic to the internationalist cause, partly because of their British or Jewish heritage. Douglas Fairbanks Jr. was a key CDAAA spokesman, while Burgess Meredith was prominent for FFF. Sympathetic producers included Spyros Skouras, Walter Wanger, Harry Warner, and Darryl Zanuck. Appealing to supporters of his earlier committee on the munitions industry in World War I, Nye referred to the movie industry as a "monopoly" controlled by a small group "all born abroad and animated by the persecutions and hatreds of the Old World." By suggesting that a British defeat would see the end of the movie industry, Nye grouped Jewish filmmakers in with bankers as part of a plan to drag the United States to war.[35]

Recognizing a powerful ally in Hollywood, FFF responded forcefully to the charges and again sought to ally the non-interventionist congressmen with Nazism. FFF minutes refer to the investigation's plan to have "all the appeasers and America First Quislings testify" and its role as "the opening gun in a nation-wide anti-Semitic drive." A letter followed accusing the new subcommittee of exercising censorship, silencing democratic opposition, and leaving the way open for fifth columnists. Senators Wheeler, Nye, and Clark were described as "knowingly or not, playing the role of Hitler's advance guard." The whole campaign was described as an "un-American . . . strategy of terror." The CDAAA also responded, though its message was more measured, asking its supporters to protest directly to the Interstate Commerce Committee, condemning the effort to "destroy the freedom of the movies."[36]

The hearings ran from September 9 until they were adjourned on September 26. Until then, FFF kept up the attacks on Nye and his subcommittee. More important in the subcommittee's failure was its inability to counter the industry's defense—led by Wendell Willkie—that it was producing not propaganda but accurate representations. *Sergeant York*, for example, was described as a factual portrayal of a great American war hero. "If that is propaganda," said Harry Warner, "we plead guilty." Nye, in contrast, came across as ignorant of the very films he claimed were having such lasting and pernicious effect. The hearings never restarted.[37]

One congressional issue that received relatively little attention from the internationalists was the extension of the Selective Service Act. It notably marked one of the few occasions when the CDAAA and FFF managed to agree on a joint statement, but that statement was one of the few actions taken to encourage Congress to keep the nation's fledging conscript army in place. There was clearly a certain amount of complacency on the issue, but there was considerable surprise and relief when the act was extended in the House of Representatives on August 12 by just one vote. F. H. Peter Cusick argued the close vote would serve to arouse supporters who were surprised there had not been a more substantial majority and that a lesson had been learned.[38]

Persuading the Public

Of course, the internationalists were not concerned just with non-interventionist forces in Congress. They were part of a wider debate among the general public. Part of their perceived public role was in countering any efforts to create a fascist fifth column within the United States. Ulric Bell was particularly active in informing Cordell Hull of potentially threatening activity. Bell informed Hull of a number of individuals believed to be promoting Axis thought within the United States. He also urged Hull to investigate Japanese American schoolbooks in California that stressed loyalty to the Japanese emperor. He even went so far as to urge the banning of Axis films altogether, with no acknowledgment of the implications this might have had for freedom of speech.[39]

The main public opponent of the internationalist organizations was of course the America First Committee. Both the CDAAA and FFF fought the battle for public opinion with America First throughout the latter half of 1941. The propaganda battle was fought in meetings, speeches, and the press. The internationalists frequently tried to associate the America First Committee with Nazism, the same tactic they used on non-interventionist congressmen. Not all of the arguments were particularly effective, such as when FFF drew attention to the fact that Hitler had quoted the words of America First chairman General Robert Wood after the German attack on the Soviet Union. Later, responding to America First criticism of the treatment of religion in the Soviet Union, FFF claimed the American people were waiting for the non-interventionists to condemn Nazism in the same manner. After all, FFF argued, Germany practiced the same religious and racial persecution ascribed to the Soviet Union. This was hardly a solid defense of the Soviet Union's stance on religious freedoms.[40]

The internationalists were on stronger ground when asking non-interventionists for responses to acts of German aggression. After the sinking of the *Reuben James*, Henry Hobson sent a telegram to Robert Wood asking him to comment on the sinking of the destroyer. "As leader of an important minority group," Hobson wrote, "we think it is time you tell where you stand on this latest outrage committed against the American people." They were also effective in responding to genuinely muddled logic, as when Charles Lindbergh stated that England might turn against the United States "as she has turned against France and Finland." In emphasizing how Vichy France had in fact turned against Britain, Clark Eichelberger described Lindbergh's speech as "probably the most striking illustration of the perverted and twisted thinking of some of the isolationists." For all of the campaigning and publicity, both sides of the debate were largely preaching to the converted by late 1941. However, neither side was willing to give up, and both continued to push for incremental gains in public support. Internationalists hoped for an incident—foreign or domestic—that could provide a breakthrough.[41]

The most significant incident in the public debate since Lend-Lease was sparked in September 1941 by America First figurehead Charles Lindbergh. Lindbergh had been attacked consistently by the internationalist organizations, particularly FFF, and especially after he joined the America First Committee. He was regularly associated with Nazism, which was easy because he was frequently quoted in the German, Italian, and Japanese press. Yet the biggest attack came after Lindbergh's speech in Des Moines on September 11. In addition to repeating his assertion that Britain was in no position to win the war, he claimed that the three most important groups pushing the United States to war were the British, the Roosevelt administration, and "the Jewish."[42]

With such an explicit statement, Lindbergh opened himself up to accusations of anti-Semitism. Although he understood why Jewish people wanted to see Nazism defeated, he went on to claim that instead of agitating for war, Jewish groups should oppose it "for they will be among the first to feel its consequences." Regarding American Jews who were advocating greater involvement in the war, Lindbergh claimed, "Their greatest danger to this country lies in their large ownership and influence in our motion pictures, our press, our radio and our government." While the internationalists often accused non-interventionists of anti-Semitism, they rarely had such candid evidence to work with. Although Lindbergh rejected the label of anti-Semitism, there was no doubt his speech blurred the line between anti-Semitism and non-interventionism. In the words of historian Wayne Cole, it was "an extremely serious political blunder" that gave the opposition its best opportunity to discredit the America First Committee. It was an opportunity seized with enthusiasm.[43]

In a measured statement, the CDAAA claimed that while it had previously wanted to believe Lindbergh's non-interventionism was sincere, it was "reluctantly forced to conclude that there is some justification for those who feel that he has Fascist sympathies." In response to Lindbergh's comment that "no person with a sense of the dignity of mankind can condone the persecution of the Jewish race in Germany," the statement noted that such persecution "was brought about in Germany by exactly the kind of thing that he said at Des Moines." The CDAAA also deplored the way in which the victim was blamed, describing the "laying of blame for misfortune on the shoulders of the Jewish people" as "one of the cruelest and most used methods of the Nazis." In a separate statement, Lewis Douglas also raised the issue of anti-Semitism in Lindbergh's speech, describing it as "one of the characteristics of Nazism wherever it has stuck up its ugly head."[44]

FFF's official response was not quite so restrained, with Cusick claiming that "Mr. Lindbergh's prestige has descended even more quickly than Hitler's dive-bombers which he talks about so admiringly." Cusick also claimed that Lindbergh had become FFF's "most active recruiting agent" in Iowa, as hundreds had asked to join the FFF branch being formed in the state. Cusick's response to Lindbergh's "barefaced" anti-Semitism was to highlight that interventionist strength was statistically strongest in the South and Southwest, areas with relatively small Jewish or foreign populations. Bishop Hobson telegraphed the America First Committee's Robert Wood to denounce Lindbergh's speech as "foreign to the American character" and to highlight the fundamental issue of anti-Semitism in the non-interventionist group.[45]

Despite the outcry over Lindbergh's remarks, the America First Committee was not mortally wounded. The fact that it had no intention of dissolving was seen in its announcement on December 1 that it intended to actively campaign in the 1942 midterm elections. Its plan was to mobilize support behind politicians who opposed involvement in war. The CDAAA recognized that this represented a significant problem, as the America First Committee had "commanding speakers," a "tenacious" and "embittered" following of millions, and a seemingly "inexhaustible" treasury. Frederick McKee claimed it "may well represent the greatest internal threat the United States has ever known." The CDAAA was steeling itself for its biggest challenge yet when war finally arrived from a surprising direction.[46]

The Looming Threat of "Asiatic Fascism"

The war in Asia had secondary status in the internationalist worldview of 1941, as it had since the outbreak of war in Europe in 1939. Most of the CDAAA's attention and almost all of FFF's was on the battle of the Atlantic and the conflict in Europe. Even then the focus was very much on Germany rather than Italy, which was viewed Germany's junior partner. Calls for the "destruction of Hitlerism" in 1941 placed the focus on Nazi Germany rather than fascism more generally. This approach reflected the nature of the public debate, which was focused on Europe and the greater threat posed by Germany. However, it detracted from the growing threat to American interests in Asia from an increasingly expansionist Japan. These threats had not been completely forgotten in 1941, but they were never a priority.

The continuing sale of oil to Japan was the most significant issue for those concerned with the ongoing war in Asia. From California, John Balderston cabled Bell and Eichelberger in June asking them to take up the issue of oil shipments. It was the CDAAA's Roger Greene, however, who continued to keep Japanese aggression on the group's agenda. This was despite the fact that the CDAAA's Washington representatives (notably Livingstone Hartley, a former Foreign Service officer) believed that the administration's tactic of appeasing Japan would halt Japanese expansion and free up the United States to focus on the Atlantic. A combination of pressure from Greene and further Japanese expansion convinced Clark Eichelberger to keep the war in Asia on the CDAAA's agenda.[47]

In July, while reiterating that the Atlantic was the primary point of concentration, Eichelberger reminded chapters to continue promoting a firm policy on Japan. In particular, he urged all possible aid to China; an increase in economic pressure (particularly on oil); greater cooperation with the British, Chinese, Dutch, and Russians; and a refusal to tolerate the occupation of Singapore or the Dutch East Indies. Interestingly, French Indochina was not on the list, as within a week Japanese forces had moved into naval bases at Saigon and Camranh Bay. The move gave the Japanese a base from which it could attack not only Singapore and the Dutch East Indies but also the Philippines.[48]

It was clear that the policy of appeasement in the Pacific was not working, but as always, the CDAAA refused to openly criticize the Roosevelt administration. Instead, it suggested this was a turning point, arguing that the existing policy "no longer has any valid basis." Instead, the organization urged "immediate adoption of direct embargoes of all shipments of essential war materials to Japan and a freezing of Japanese assets in the United States." By coincidence, the administration announced the freezing of Japanese assets on the same day, having decided to do so two days previously. Yet more broadly, the administration struggled to find a way to contain Japan. While a complete embargo on the sale of oil did not immediately appear, and licenses for the sale of oil could continue in theory, in practice a de facto embargo began as the administration stopped approving licenses through August.[49]

The freezing of Japanese assets marked one of the few occasions when FFF spoke out regarding the war in Asia. F. H. Peter Cusick hoped the move marked the end of a decade of appeasement, remarking that it was no longer possible to send war materials to Japan "even though we were committed to a program of aid to democratic China." The reference to democratic China was very much part of FFF's two-worlds outlook, as was Cusick's view that "it is as futile to attempt to bargain with Asiatic Fascism as it is to try 'negotiating' a peace with the European dictators." More generally, FFF continued to place limited emphasis on the war in Asia, right up until the Pearl Harbor attack.[50]

The CDAAA's continued focus on Asia was largely due to the individual efforts of Roger Greene, but he stood down from his official position in August because of the organization's growing financial difficulties. However, he continued to correspond with the organization and the State Department. His influence was clear in the CDAAA's bold September policy statement that demanded a rejection of "any agreement with Japan which would sacrifice American principles respecting China or our present favorable power position in the Pacific." The statement also called for greater material aid to China and greater economic pressure on Japan, while supporting the limitation of further Japanese expansion in Singapore, the Dutch East Indies, Thailand, and Siberia. In September, Greene revived the ACNPJA name for one last appeal, all but exhausting the committee's scant remaining funds in the process. Following an inside suggestion from the State Department and reports of official negotiations with the Japanese, Greene's last appeal to supporters urged them to write to Roosevelt and Hull to demand a firm stand against Japan and a rejection of appeasement.[51]

As relations between the United States and Japan became increasingly strained through November, CDAAA policy on Asia continued to hold firm. With negotiations ongoing in late November, the CDAAA's Pacific Coast chapters wrote to Hull in support of a positive policy against Japan's continued aggression, appealing for no further appeasement. Despite some calls within the organization to limit its stand against Japan while negotiations took place, Eichelberger ensured that the official policy rejected appeasement. This was seen in the unreleased policy statement being drafted in early December, which called for greater cooperation with China, no agreement with Japan, no tolerance of further Japanese expansion, and action to keep open the Burma Road, described as "China's lifeline."[52]

An appeal to CDAAA chapters on December 5 highlighted the organization's view of the growing importance of events in the Pacific. The conflicts in Europe and Asia were described as "parts of one assault on civilization." Recognizing that the Japanese crisis was "very tense," the CDAAA continued to demand a firm stand from the government to immobilize Japan so that it could not attack Russia or support Germany. Reminding members of the need for the administration to hear from the American public, Eichelberger implored them to "re-double your expressions of opinion for the strongest policy in the Pacific." By that point, the Japanese had already made the decision for war.[53]

The Attack on Pearl Harbor

On the morning of December 7, 1941, Japanese aircraft attacked Pearl Harbor on the Hawaiian island of Oahu. The surprise attack left 2,390 Americans dead, 1,178 wounded, 21 ships sunk or damaged, and 323 aircraft destroyed or damaged. The attack, an example of preventive warfare, intended to destroy the American Pacific fleet, freeing Japan to expand into American, British, and Dutch imperial territories in the southwestern Pacific to secure access to raw materials, including oil and rubber. Despite the devastation, the attack was only a limited success: the harbor remained intact, fuel storage facilities were undamaged, and all aircraft carriers (at sea at the time of attack) remained operational. Significantly, the attack ended the bitter debate within the United States regarding involvement in the war, and a declaration of war against Japan was passed the following day.

The internationalist response was immediate. Both organizations released similar statements that called for national unity, deplored the attack, and—more surprisingly—blamed the attack on Hitler. On the evening of the attack, FFF released a statement claiming "Japan's war on the United States is a last desperate effort of Hitler to turn American attention from the center of war against our world. That center is Berlin." Tokyo and Berlin were linked together, but the attack was seen as part of the "well-known Nazi technique of underhanded aggression. This treachery was masterminded by the thugs and gangsters of Berlin." The message was hammered home in a newspaper advertisement the following day. While a response against Japan was necessary, Americans needed to remember that "Berlin is the meaning of this attack."[54]

The CDAAA's December 8 message dismissed the attack as "treacherous" and "unprovoked," but the fact it was made in the midst of negotiations was described as "the perfect Hitler technique." As Japan was an Axis partner, and as it used "the Hitler methods," the CDAAA recommended that the nation make war upon the Axis as a unit, with a declaration of war against both Germany and Italy. Members were urged to express this view to Washington "with all possible vigor immediately." In a separate statement, Eichelberger declared that "obviously Hitler's grand strategy was back of the Japanese move."[55]

After months of highlighting the threat from Germany, it was perhaps not a great surprise that both FFF and the CDAAA blamed the attack on Hitler. However, it is also clear that Robert Sherwood specifically asked FFF (if not both organizations) to issue such a statement as a favor for the president, as the administration still believed that Europe offered the greater long-term threat to American security. Because Japan had attacked the United States (rather than the other way around), Germany and Italy were under no treaty obligation to declare war against America. There was therefore a significant possibility that American public opinion would turn its full attention to the Pacific, reducing the chance of war with Germany. In the end, internationalist and administration concern was unnecessary. Both Germany and Italy declared war on the United States on December 11.[56]

Those declarations combined with the Pearl Harbor attack to achieve what the internationalists had failed to manage: a united America. Both organizations pledged to end the great debate of the previous two years. Clark Eichelberger volunteered the services of CDAAA to various government departments to assist in the development of public morale. FFF claimed, "It's America First *now*," and that all Americans would unite and "become brothers in the cause of defending the simple decencies of civilization against the men who keep no promises, who know no honor." The fight for freedom had begun, and its battle cry was "Unity!"[57]

Epilogue

War and Beyond

The Pearl Harbor attack and subsequent declaration of war from Germany brought an end to the great public debate of the previous two years. The non-interventionist position all but vanished. The America First Committee was quickly dismantled. Critics of Roosevelt's policies remained, but the nation came together in the face of attack. There were still issues for debate, of course, and not just about how the nation would respond militarily. These included domestic questions regarding national unity and morale, as well as concerns over wartime production and the relationship between business and labor. It was with these questions in mind that the CDAAA and FFF considered their respective futures.

For the CDAAA, there was no real doubt about its future: the organization would continue in some form. Clark Eichelberger, the inveterate organizer, was convinced that the organization had a role to play in wartime, though he was not exactly certain what that role was. Just three days after the Pearl Harbor attack, he asked White House secretary Marvin McIntyre for advice about the place of private citizens' organizations in wartime. While it might be argued that the job of sustaining wartime morale was solely the government's job, it was Eichelberger's firm conviction that "in a democracy, even in wartime, the Government should use the private agencies just as much as possible." His belief was supported by the increase in requests for speakers that had come in since the Hawaiian attack and by his broader sense that the CDAAA's extensive organizational structure had something to contribute "in some form or other."[1]

McIntyre passed the query on to Archibald MacLeish at the Office of Facts and Figures, which had been created in October 1941 to facilitate "the dissemination of factual information to the citizens of the country on the progress of the defense effort and on the defense policies and activities of the Government." MacLeish then met with Eichelberger and Lewis Douglas, along with William Agar of FFF and Ernest Angell of the Council for Democracy, informing them it was the government's opinion there "was most important work to be done" by their committees. They could supplement the government's morale-boosting efforts, and carry "the story of the war effort to the people in ways which could not be available to the government." MacLeish informed the internationalists that the Office of Facts and Figures would provide "a universal joint" for liaison between the government and private organizations. Roosevelt thought that MacLeish had taken "just the right line."[2]

With confirmation that the internationalists could continue to provide constructive support to the government, a new organization—Citizens for Victory— was hastily announced on December 20, 1941. Drawing on the existing resources of the CDAAA, with the smaller Council for Democracy as its research arm, the new organization was dedicated to three key objectives: winning the war, organizing a permanent and lasting peace, and preserving domestic democratic processes in the prosecution of the war and subsequent peace. The CDAAA did not formally evolve into Citizens for Victory, but for all intents and purposes Citizens for Victory replaced it at the end of 1941.[3]

Despite initial efforts, Citizens for Victory never took root in the public imagination for a number of reasons. Its broad, sweeping aims did not easily translate into political action. It was clear from the debate of the previous years that organizations such as the CDAAA worked best with specific objectives to promote, and Citizens for Victory failed to find such objectives. In addition to lacking a clear program, the new organization also lacked a strong opposition to work against. The success of wartime mobilization meant there was little need for a private morale organization. The lack of success in carving a niche for itself led to limited financial contributions, which in turn made it harder to establish itself. It also lacked a significant leader or figurehead. By the end of 1942, it was clear that Citizens for Victory was never going to be a prominent national organization like the CDAAA.[4]

Instead, the efforts of the CDAAA leaders returned to the issues that had drawn them into the great debate in the first place: peace and collective security. After a number of dormant years, the Eichelberger-led League of Nations Association became increasingly active from 1942 in promoting American entry into a new international organization. Building on the CDAAA's latter-day stance of winning the peace as well as the war, the organization fought to ensure the United States did not reject its international obligations as it had in 1919–20. With the

Commission to Study the Organization of Peace as its research arm, it evolved into the American Association for the United Nations in 1945.[5]

FFF also believed that it still had a role to play after Pearl Harbor, but it too was unsure what that role should be. However, it quickly became clear after the declaration of war from Germany that there was little left to achieve. On December 12, Ulric Bell wrote to chapter heads on behalf of Henry Hobson to inform them that FFF was to become inactive. For now, the group was waiting to decide on future policies, which would be determined by future events. This left the organization in limbo. Like Eichelberger and the CDAAA, Bell and FFF were also waiting to see "in what way we can be of most use to the government."[6]

Not wholly convincingly, Bell claimed that "Fight For Freedom has always had a long range program." He continued by making a similar argument to that soon to be proposed by Citizens for Victory, asserting that "we believe we must fight to win a just peace, and to preserve democratic principles in doing so." However, a statement of future policy never came. On December 17, the executive committee agreed to deactivate the organization and to put FFF "on ice." The national organization was reduced to one man, William Agar, who was left to look after remaining affairs and to direct any ongoing interest to the recently established activities of Freedom House.[7]

Freedom House was created on October 31, 1941, after discussions between Ulric Bell, Herbert Agar, columnist Dorothy Thompson, and George Field of the merged New York Fight for Freedom Committee to Defend America. The group was considering the need to bring supporters of a more active foreign policy together, but it knew all too well about the bureaucratic disagreements that arose between existing organizations. At that point, Field suggested simply getting a building, calling it Freedom House, and inviting all interested organizations to move in. While it was not a formal outgrowth of FFF, there were extremely close connections between them, and many of the organization's leaders joined, including Freedom House founders Field, Bell, Ward Cheney, Harold Guinzburg, Wayne Johnson, and Herbert and William Agar.[8]

Rather than acting as a political organization, Freedom House was established as an educational institution to stand as a symbol of the twofold fight for freedom. That fight consisted of the resistance to totalitarianism and the promotion of a world of freedom, peace, and security. Freedom House also promised to promote the principles of freedom and democracy in domestic American life, to act as a clearinghouse "for organizations enlisted in the fight for freedom," and to encourage all democracies around the world to look to Freedom House as "a beacon lighting the struggle for a free world." Freedom House was to act as a counter to Hitler's Braunes Haus in Munich. Given the existence of such an organization, it is easy to see why the FFF leadership chose not to be a part of the not dissimilar Citizens for Victory.[9]

Assessing the Internationalists

Assessing the significance of the organized internationalist movement on the eve of World War II is no easy task. Attempting to assess its influence in Washington is difficult; attempting to assess its impact on the wider American public is even more challenging. It would be going too far to say that the movement was solely responsible for changing the minds of Americans about the need for the nation to play a greater role overseas. That change was primarily due to events overseas, particularly the continuing pattern of fascist aggression culminating in the attack on Pearl Harbor. Yet there is no doubt that the various organizations had an impact both on the popular "great debate" and on activity within the Roosevelt administration.

A private Department of State assessment in 1943 argued that the groups were "of considerable political significance." It claimed that their significance was not that they made many converts but that they clarified and crystallized existing attitudes, mobilizing them and making them more vocal. Existing natural sympathies were converted into specific demands for action. Such demands were all the more effective when applied to particular measures or pieces of legislation, like the Lend-Lease Act. The internationalist groups acted as catalysts, turning "attitudes into action."[10]

The report made particular mention of the work of the individual internationalist organizations. It described the ACNPJA as "a major factor in the crystallization of a steadily advancing popular acceptance of embargoes against Japan" as a result of well-organized popular campaigning and "effective contact work in Washington." The AUCPE played "an important part" in mobilizing public opinion behind neutrality revision. It was noted that the CDAAA attracted much wider support than the collective security movement from which it grew, enabling it to play "a leading role" in the campaigns for the destroyer transfer, Lend-Lease, and selective service. FFF was noted as leading the campaign for an outright declaration of war.[11]

Because of their large public profiles and memberships, the work of the CDAAA and FFF was deemed "more spectacular," and regarding the public debate, their efforts were particularly significant in countering the work of the America First Committee. While America First was of course created after the CDAAA (and the Century Group), the existence of internationalist organizations gave a home and a focus to those who disagreed with the policies or rhetoric of the non-interventionist movement and supported a more active foreign policy for the United States. Their efforts were most effective on specific campaigns such as Lend-Lease, where even if they did not make the difference between success and failure, they helped to speed the process along.[12]

Without a mass membership, the ACNPJA had the least public impact, though it believed that its efforts were important. Looking back from the autumn of 1942, Harry Price believed that the committee had helped to "crack the isolationist front" on the issue of supplying war materials to Japan. Price was informed by one State Department official that the ACNPJA had done the best job of any of the prewar propaganda organizations. He openly conceded that the claim was exaggerated, but it highlighted that the group's efforts had left a mark on the government. That mark was limited, as Congress never passed the full embargo legislation demanded by the committee. Nevertheless, the ACNPJA alerted public opinion to events in Asia and channeled that opinion toward Washington.[13]

The greatest public impact of the internationalist organizations undoubtedly came from the CDAAA. The AUCPE gave the collective security movement a more immediate focus; the NPC then offered a test case of what could be done by mobilizing opinion behind a key legislative issue. The CDAAA built upon that experience, and from its creation in May 1940 through the heated debate over Lend-Lease, it successfully reflected the majority of popular opinion that desired greater aid to Britain short of American involvement in war. Its influence waned once maximum aid to the Allies had been achieved and as war came near, though a decrease in access to the Roosevelt administration did not help. Yet the CDAAA was the main focus for those who opposed the non-interventionist rhetoric of the America First Committee and who believed that the days of isolationism were over.

The CDAAA also suffered from April 1941 with competition from the new and openly hawkish FFF, though the new organization never reached the popular heights of the CDAAA. Its belligerent stance meant its popularity was always likely to be limited to the minority of Americans who believed war was necessary prior to Pearl Harbor. Yet that stance enabled FFF to move boldly ahead of official government policy, which helped in turn to move public opinion slowly forward. This was recognized by the president, who acknowledged the government's appreciation of the organization's efforts. Roosevelt stated that FFF "made a contribution to the national defense and to the national security which is incalculable."[14]

Of course, much of the significant work of the internationalist organizations was undertaken behind the scenes in conjunction with the Roosevelt administration. Almost without exception, the organizations coordinated their efforts with the government and worked to support its policy aims. They also limited all criticism of the administration and passed on concerns in private. The interaction was a two-way street, albeit one to which the government controlled access. The internationalists were able to wield influence within the government, as they most notably did during the destroyer-bases exchange. In return, Roosevelt received an informal propaganda service. As historian Michael Sherry has noted, Roosevelt rejected a more formal propaganda agency in peacetime "in favor of an informal public-private cooperation that would largely prevail for decades after the war." This is where that cooperation began.[15]

Overlooked in assessments of the internationalist movement is its significance in the realm of ideas. The internationalists of 1938–41 defined what internationalism was to the American people. They did so ahead of the administration and with greater detail and force than the White House could. They explained why it was essential for the United States to reject non-interventionism, as the nation's national security was at stake. They also outlined the potential threats to American democratic and religious freedoms in a way that was subsequently echoed by the White House and allies in Congress. They were also able to make an economic argument about the threat to America's standard of living that went completely beyond any position the White House could take in the aftermath of the Nye Committee. By aiming to influence public opinion, they reached a broad audience, broader than that reached by most press commentators, and outlined why the United States had to play a greater role in world affairs. Their significance in this regard would also prevail far beyond the war years.

Legacy

Despite the creation of Freedom House and Citizens for Victory in late 1941, many prominent members of the CDAAA and FFF played no role in either. Many private internationalists of the 1938–41 years decided that the best way to be of use to the government was in fact to join it. Many remained in government roles long after the war was over. As a result, for some of the internationalists, their greatest significance was yet to come. Even before the outbreak of war, William Donovan had left to become Coordinator of Information (which quickly became the Office of Strategic Services in 1942). James Warburg joined him in the summer of 1941 as part of the Foreign Information Service in New York. This propaganda service, initially under Donovan's oversight, evolved into the new Office of War Information's overseas branch in 1942. The Foreign Information Service was headed by Robert Sherwood, and after Pearl Harbor it also briefly included Francis Miller.[16]

The Office of War Information was also the destination for Ulric Bell. He joined the Office of Facts and Figures in December 1941, which became part of the Office of War Information in 1942. Bell was particularly prominent between 1942 and 1944 as the representative in Hollywood of the office's overseas branch. Just as Bell had sought to silence foreign and non-interventionist voices prior to Pearl Harbor, he now took a strong line as a censor in Hollywood, objecting strongly to critical portrayals of the United States that might be used overseas to condemn America. To save freedom, Bell believed that the freedom of filmmakers needed limiting.[17]

Leading internationalists could also be found in other wartime agencies. FFF's Wayne Johnson was in charge of petroleum for the War Production Board. Of the CDAAA principals, only Lewis Douglas went fully into government service, acting as chief adviser to Admiral Emory Land in the War Shipping Administration. After the war, from 1947 to 1950, Douglas was appointed as U.S. ambassador to the United Kingdom. ACNPJA and CDAAA member Roger Greene joined the State Department's Division of Cultural Relations as a consultant on China. In contrast, Harry Price played his part in 1941 by joining China Defense Supplies Inc., which acted as the main agency for securing Lend-Lease aid to China. Part of the Chinese government, it was run by Americans and based in Washington.[18]

Others went into military service, countering the idea that all the internationalists were too old to fight and sending the nation's youth into a war they were unwilling to fight themselves. Ernest Gibson had already left the CDAAA to sign up, and after Pearl Harbor, reservists Robert Allen and Herbert Agar were activated. After a brief period with Bell in the Office of Facts and Figures, F. H. Peter Cusick also enlisted. In contrast, a few returned to their previous lives. Thomas Lamont remained with J.P. Morgan, becoming chairman of the board in 1943. William Allen White returned to the *Emporia Gazette* until his death in January 1944. Carter Glass remained in the Senate until his death in May 1946. Henry Hobson returned to his role as bishop of southern Ohio, a position he held until 1959.[19]

The other CDAAA leaders remained committed to promoting internationalism through private organizations, though they frequently worked with the Roosevelt administration from a position of "constructive support." Clark Eichelberger, Frederick McKee, and Hugh Moore focused their efforts on the League of Nations Association and the promotion of American involvement in the United Nations Organization. However, in 1942 and 1943, Eichelberger (along with the CSOP's James Shotwell) was invited into the State Department's official postwar planning process, an offer too attractive to refuse. In 1944 and 1945 many former members of both the CDAAA and FFF came together again as part of a new organization, Americans United for World Organization. Building on the prestige of both the CDAAA and FFF, the organization was never quite as significant or as necessary, largely because of the overwhelming public support in 1945 for American international engagement.[20]

The fact that Americans had turned their backs on non-interventionism by 1945 suggested that the internationalist movement had been a success, and in many respects it was. Isolationism as it was known before the war was all but dead. Given the strength of non-interventionist sentiment prior to 1941, this was no small victory. Moving ahead, there was unity on most key issues. In the economic realm, the need for free trade and open markets was widely accepted. The political desire for democracy and freedom remained, as did the broader conception of American civilization, along with more specific religious freedoms. However, the different approaches to world affairs proposed before the war foreshadowed divisions that appeared after 1945.

While it was accepted that the United States should play a role in world affairs, there was some debate over exactly what that role should be. The biggest area of debate was how to ensure that the United States remained free from fear. Here, tensions arose between multilateral internationalists and more nationalist or unilateral internationalists. Victory in World War II provided a second chance for American internationalism, but the exact nature of that internationalism was still to be defined. For some, especially those who had led the CDAAA, the true legacy of Woodrow Wilson was international organization. Unsurprisingly, the American Association for the United Nations promoted greater American utilization of the new international organization after 1945. Its multilateral vision for American foreign policy had been reflected in the CDAAA's calls to win the peace, but that vision was often frustrated by an increasingly unilateral foreign policy as the Cold War developed. Even so, such internationalists rarely dissented too fiercely from official U.S. policy.

Ultimately, official U.S. Cold War foreign policy was far more reflective of the two-worlds approach promoted by the Century Group and FFF. Despite a relative lack of concern in 1940 and 1941 with the postwar world order, their approach to Nazi Germany in 1941 offered a template for viewing post-1945 relations with the Soviet Union. It is no coincidence that future Truman administration figures such as Dean Acheson, Will Clayton, and Allen Dulles were FFF members. For many of those internationalists, the primary legacy of Woodrow Wilson was the desire to make the world safe for democracy. But democracy was just one of the four freedoms of internationalism. When confronting the Soviet Union in the postwar world, it was not enough for the United States alone to enjoy the four freedoms. Those freedoms had to be secured for the whole world.[21]

This proactive vision of American foreign policy was promoted in 1941 by another brief and early Century Group member, Henry Luce. In his "American Century" essay, Luce offered a vision for the nation that included "a passionate devotion to American ideals." Those ideals included ones Luce saw as distinctly "American," such as freedom, equality of opportunity, self-reliance, and cooperation. They also included ideals the United States had taken on as inheritor of "the great principles of Western civilization"—justice, truth, and charity. Luce believed it was time for the United States "to be the powerhouse from which the ideals spread throughout the world." No longer was it sufficient for the United States to be simply the city on the hill or simply one nation among many. The time had come to lead the world.[22]

Notes

Introduction

1. Franklin Roosevelt, *The Public Papers and Addresses of Franklin D. Roosevelt*, 1941 (New York: Harper, 1950), 522, 530.

2. Robert Divine, *The Illusion of Neutrality* (Chicago: University of Chicago Press, 1962), 180–181; George Gallup, *The Gallup Poll, 1935–1971* (New York: Random House, 1972), 307. On non-interventionism, see Justus Doenecke, *Storm on the Horizon* (Lanham, MD: Rowman and Littlefield, 2000); Wayne S. Cole, *America First* (Madison: University of Wisconsin Press, 1953); Wayne S. Cole, *Roosevelt and the Isolationists, 1932–1945* (Lincoln: University of Nebraska Press, 1983); and Manfred Jonas, *Isolationism in America* (Ithaca: Cornell University Press, 1966).

3. Roosevelt, *Public Papers and Addresses*, 1941, 63.

4. Though arguably a new bureaucratic history is needed, as the few existing works on these internationalist organizations are dated or limited. The most substantial (though still brief) study of the American Committee for Non-Participation in Japanese Aggression is Donald J. Friedman's *The Road from Isolation: The Campaign of the American Committee for Non-Participation in Japanese Aggression 1938–1941* (Cambridge, MA: Harvard University Press, 1970), which was initially written as a senior honors thesis. Warren Cohen's chapter in Dorothy Borg and Shumpei Okamoto's *Pearl Harbor as History: Japanese-American Relations 1931–1941* (New York: Columbia University Press, 1973) takes a slightly broader perspective. The standard history of the Committee to Defend America by Aiding the Allies remains Walter Johnson's *The Battle against Isolation* (Chicago: University of Chicago Press, 1944), despite its age, limited scope, and overemphasis on the significance of William Allen White (though this is unsurprising, given that the book was a spin-off from a biography of White he was working on). William M. Tuttle Jr.'s "Aid-to-the-Allies Short-of-War versus American Intervention, 1940: A Reappraisal

of William Allen White's Leadership," *Journal of American History* 56 (1970): 840–858, does little to correct this. The standard work on Fight for Freedom, Mark Lincoln Chadwin's *The Hawks of World War II* (Chapel Hill: University of North Carolina Press, 1968), is much better but still treats the organization largely in isolation.

5. ACNPJA, "America's Share in Japan's War Guilt," 1938, 78, box 16, American Committee for Non-Participation in Japanese Aggression Papers, Houghton Library, Harvard University (hereafter ACNPJA Papers).

6. Original statement by William Allen White, May 17, 1940, folder 8, box 10, Committee to Defend America by Aiding the Allies Papers, Mudd Library, Princeton University (hereafter CDAAA Papers).

7. "What Is the Fight for Freedom?" [1941], folder 7, box 132, Freedom House Archives, Mudd Library, Princeton University; Rex Stout interview with Ulric Bell, October 1, 1941, folder 3, box 4, Fight for Freedom Papers, Mudd Library, Princeton University (hereafter FFF Papers).

8. Warren Kuehl and Gary Ostrower, "Internationalism," in *Encyclopedia of American Foreign Policy*, 2nd ed., ed. Alexander DeConde, Richard Dean Burns, and Fredrik Logevall, vol. 2 (New York: Scribner, 2002), 241, 254; Warren Kuehl, "Concepts of Internationalism in History," *Peace and Change* 11 (1986): 1. Also see Andrew Johnstone, "Isolationism and Internationalism in American Foreign Relations," *Journal of Transatlantic Studies* 9 (2011): 7–20.

9. Emily S. Rosenberg, *A Date Which Will Live: Pearl Harbor in American Memory* (Durham, NC: Duke University Press, 2003), 12, 188. Walter Hixson has also commented on how the infamy framework provides a "hegemonic national narrative." See Walter L. Hixson, *The Myth of American Diplomacy* (New Haven: Yale University Press, 2008), 132–162. *War Comes to America* was the title of the final episode in Frank Capra's *Why We Fight* series of wartime propaganda films that examined the origins of World War II. While there have been a few studies in recent years that examine why America fought, they have focused largely on the period after the Pearl Harbor attack when the United States was already at war. See Robert B. Westbrook, *Why We Fought: Forging American Obligations in World War II* (Washington, DC: Smithsonian Books, 2004); Susan Brewer, *Why America Fights: Patriotism and War Propaganda from the Philippines to Iraq* (Oxford: Oxford University Press, 2009); John Bodnar, *The "Good War" in American Memory* (Baltimore: Johns Hopkins University Press, 2010).

10. Franklin Roosevelt, *The Public Papers and Addresses of Franklin D. Roosevelt, 1940* (London: Macmillan, 1941), 663–672. Roosevelt first expanded on the concept of "freedoms" at a press conference the previous July. When addressing long-range peace objectives, he talked of freedom of information, freedom of religion, freedom of expression, freedom from fear, and freedom from want. See ibid., 281–285. Also see Samuel I. Rosenman, *Working with Roosevelt* (New York: Harper, 1952), 262–265.

11. For the argument that an American conception of national security dependent on Eurasian events was easier to sell to the American people than an argument based on more vague notions of democratic principles, see John A. Thompson, "Conceptions of National Security and American Entry into World War II," *Diplomacy and Statecraft* 16 (2005): 671–697.

12. Douglas Miller, *You Can't Do Business with Hitler* (Boston: Little, Brown, 1941).

13. Roland Marchand, *Creating the Corporate Soul: The Rise of Public Relations and Corporate Imagery in American Big Business* (Berkeley: University of California Press, 1998), 317–318. Fears of overproduction—so harmful to business and agriculture during the Great Depression—were still strong on the eve of war.

14. "The Fight for Freedom" by the Rt. Rev. Henry Hobson, undated, folder 2, box 56, FFF Papers.

15. Herbert Agar, "Why We Ought to Go to War," FFF pamphlet, 1941, folder 2, box 133, Freedom House Archives.

16. Doenecke, *Storm on the Horizon*, 43–44.

17. Stout interview, October 1, 1941.

18. Alexis de Tocqueville, *Democracy in America,* trans. George Lawrence (London: Fontana, 1994), 189. There is a vast literature on the relationship between public opinion and American foreign relations. See Melvin Small, "Public Opinion," in *Explaining the History of American Foreign Relations,* ed. Michael Hogan and Thomas Paterson (Cambridge: Cambridge University Press, 1991), 165-176; Thomas A. Bailey, *The Man in the Street: The Impact of American Public Opinion on Foreign Policy* (New York: Macmillan, 1948); Melvin Small, ed., *Public Opinion and Historians: Interdisciplinary Perspectives* (Detroit: Wayne State University Press, 1970); Ralph B. Levering, *The Public and American Foreign Policy 1918–1978* (New York: Morrow, 1978); Melvin Small, *Democracy and Diplomacy: The Impact of Domestic Politics on U.S. Foreign Policy, 1789–1994* (Baltimore: Johns Hopkins University Press, 1996); Andrew Johnstone and Helen Laville, eds. *The US Public and American Foreign Policy* (London: Routledge, 2010). Important perspectives from political science include Gabriel A. Almond, *The American People and Foreign Policy* (New York: Harcourt, Brace, 1950); James N. Rosenau, *Public Opinion and Foreign Policy: An Operational Formulation* (New York: Random House, 1961); Bernard C. Cohen, *The Public's Impact on Foreign Policy* (Boston: Little, Brown, 1973); Ole R. Holsti, *Public Opinion and American Foreign Policy* (Ann Arbor: University of Michigan, 2005).

19. For the suggestion that the ACNPJA was a Chinese front organization, see Tsuchida Akio, "China's 'Public Diplomacy' toward the United States before Pearl Harbor," *Journal of American-East Asian Relations* 17 (2010): 35–55. For the suggestion that FFF was a British front, see Thomas E. Mahl, *Desperate Deception* (London: Brassey's, 1999).

20. The only state the CDAAA failed to establish itself in was North Dakota. Memorandum on chapter organization, October 9, 1941, folder 18, box 5, CDAAA Papers.

21. "What Is the Fight for Freedom?"

22. Policies, Aims, and Accomplishments of the CDAAA, October 9, 1940, folder 15, box 9, CDAAA Papers.

23. Franklin Roosevelt, *The Public Papers and Addresses of Franklin D. Roosevelt,* 1936 (New York: Random House, 1938), 465; Walter Johnson, *William Allen White's America* (New York: Henry Holt, 1947), 529.

24. A number of works on state-private networks in recent years have drawn attention to the blurred line between public and private spheres with respect to American foreign relations. Such works include Michael Wala, *The Council on Foreign Relations and American Foreign Policy in the Early Cold War* (Providence: Berghahn, 1994); Nancy Bernhard, *US Television News and Cold War Propaganda, 1947–1960* (Cambridge: Cambridge University Press, 1999); Steven Casey, "The Campaign to Sell a Harsh Peace for Germany to the American

Public, 1944–48," *History* 90 (2005): 262–292; and Helen Laville and Hugh Wilford, eds., *The US Government, Citizen Groups and the Cold War* (London: Routledge, 2006).

25. Douglas Fairbanks Jr., *The Salad Days* (London: Collins, 1988), 364; Franklin Roosevelt to Ulric Bell, January 1, 1942, PPF 2409, Franklin D. Roosevelt Papers, Franklin D. Roosevelt Library, Hyde Park, New York (hereafter Roosevelt Papers).

1. The Sino-Japanese War and the American Committee for Non-Participation in Japanese Aggression

1. Gallup, *Gallup Poll,* 69, 68, 70.
2. Ibid., 71, 65.
3. Franklin D. Roosevelt, *The Public Papers and Addresses of Franklin D. Roosevelt, 1937* (London: Macmillan, 1941), 410; Cole, *Roosevelt and the Isolationists,* 246–249.
4. Gallup, *Gallup Poll,* 89, 90.
5. Progress and Program of the American Committee for Non-Participation in Japanese Aggression, February 16, 1940, folder: Reports on Progress 1938, box 16, ACNPJA Papers. Janeway and Stimson quoted in "What Japan Is Doing in China—and How," undated, folder: Misc. NPJA—Beginning, box 13, ACNPJA Papers.
6. Friedman, *Road from Isolation,* 1–4; Tentative Proposed Program . . ., May 27, 1938, folder: Misc. NPJA—Beginning, box 13, ACNPJA Papers; Proposed Agenda, June 2, 1938, folder: Misc. NPJA—Beginning, box 13, ACNPJA Papers. Also see Philip West, *Yenching University and Sino-Western Relations, 1916–1952* (Cambridge, MA: Harvard University Press, 1976).
7. Report on trip to Washington, June 6–9, 1938, folder: Misc. NPJA—Beginning, box 13, ACNPJA Papers.
8. Ibid.
9. Perry and Wise Inc. campaign objectives, June 15, 1938, folder: American Committee, box 17, ACNPJA Papers.
10. Report on trip to Washington; also see John W. Masland, "Commercial Influence upon American Far Eastern Policy, 1937–1941," *Pacific Historical Review* 11 (1942): 281–299.
11. Report on trip to Washington; Akio, "China's 'Public Diplomacy,'" 41–42, 46–47. For more on Chinese attempts to change American attitudes, see Youli Sun, *China and the Origins of the Pacific War, 1931–1941* (London: Macmillan, 1993), 136–140.
12. Warren I. Cohen, *The Chinese Connection: Roger S. Greene, Thomas W. Lamont, George E. Sokolsky and American-East Asian Relations* (New York: Columbia University Press, 1978), 278. Also see 7–40 on Greene's early career.
13. Greene to Price, August 17, 1938, folder 686, box 21, Roger S. Greene Papers, Houghton Library, Harvard University (hereafter Greene Papers); Greene to Price, August 26, 1938, folder 687, box 21, Greene Papers; Leaf to Price, September 1, 1938, folder: Leaf Earl H., box 8, ACNPJA Papers.
14. Greene to Price, September 7, 1938, folder 688, box 21, Greene Papers.
15. Price to Mr. Mar, May 21, 1940, folder: Mar–Mars, box 10, ACNPJA Papers; Price to Mr. Beech, November 24, 1939, folder: Irving Trust Company, box 16, ACNPJA Papers;

Price to Mr. M. L. Corey, folder: Irving Trust Company, box 16, ACNPJA Papers; Price to Joseph Green, October 30, 1939, 894.24/726, decimal file, RG 59, Department of State Records, National Archives at College Park, Maryland (hereafter NACP).

16. Price to Dr. T. D. Lee, November 6, 1939, folder: Lee, Dr. T. D., box 8, ACNPJA Papers; Price to Dr. Hu Shih, May 5, 1939, folder: Hu Shih (Dr.), box 7, ACNPJA Papers; Price to Dr. Hu Shih, December 23, 1940, folder: Hu Shih (Dr.), box 7, ACNPJA Papers; contributors of $100 or over from January 1939 to February 13, 1940, folder: Lists Contributions, box 13, ACNPJA Papers; Paul A. Varg, *Missionaries, Chinese, and Diplomats: The American Protestant Missionary Movement in China, 1890–1952* (Princeton: Princeton University Press, 1958), 260; Price to Joseph Green, October 30, 1939.

17. Chiang to Price, February 21, 1939, folder: Chiang Kai-Shek, Madame, box 2, ACNPJA Papers.

18. ACNPJA, "America's Share in Japan's War Guilt," 1938, box 16, ACNPJA Papers; Harry Price to Henry Stimson, December 16, 1938, 0974–0977, reel 96, Henry L. Stimson Papers, Library of Congress, Washington D.C. (hereafter Stimson Papers); Stimson to Price, December 27, 1938, folder 699, box 21, Greene Papers.

19. ACNPJA press release, January 19, 1939, folder: Clippings Misc. & Press Releases Am. Com. for Non P in J Ag, box 17, ACNPJA Papers.

20. Greene to Price, December 30, 1938, folder: Greene Mr Roger S (1) July 38–June 39, box 6, ACNPJA Papers; ACNPJA press release, November 27, 1939, folder: Clippings Misc. & Press Releases Am. Com. for Non P in J Ag, box 17, ACNPJA Papers; Friedman, *Road from Isolation,* 11–12.

21. Price to G. R. Seeley, June 29, 1939, folder: Sea–Sed, box 13, ACNPJA Papers; ACNPJA, "America Supports Japanese Aggression," 1939, folder: Amer Com NPJA Misc Literature, box 19, ACNPJA Papers.

22. Progress and Program of the American Committee for Non-Participation in Japanese Aggression.

23. Ibid.

24. Ibid.

25. Ibid; Partial List of Groups Protesting against Aid to Japan or to Aggressors in General, July 5, 1939, 0880, reel 98, Stimson Papers.

26. Partial List of Groups.

27. ACNPJA brief report on progress, January 14, 1939, folder: American Committee for Non-Participation in Japanese Aggression, box 14, Clark Eichelberger Papers, New York Public Library (hereafter Eichelberger Papers); Warren I. Cohen, "The Role of Private Groups in the United States," in *Pearl Harbor as History: Japanese-American Relations 1931–1941,* ed. Dorothy Borg and Shumpei Okamoto (New York: Columbia University Press, 1973), 437. The American Union for Concerted Peace Efforts was known as the Committee for Concerted Peace Efforts (CCPE) from December 1937 until March 1939; see chapter 2 for more detail.

28. D. Kenneth Rose to Price, January 5, 1939, folder: John Price Jones Corporation, box 15, ACNPJA Papers; Suggested Steps for the American Committee for Non-Participation in Japanese Aggression, January 25, 1939, folder: John Price Jones Corporation, box 15, ACNPJA Papers.

29. Final Report on Publicity for the American Committee for Non-Participation in Japanese Aggression, April 7, 1939, folder: Phoenix News Publicity Bureau, Inc. (Miss Pauline E. Mandigo), box 15, ACNPJA Papers; Dickson Hartwell to Price, February 23, 1939, folder: Hartwell, Jobson and Kibbee, box 15, ACNPJA Papers; Price to Hartwell, April 4, 1940, folder: Hartwell, Jobson and Kibbee, box 15, ACNPJA Papers.

30. Greene to Dr. Mortimer Graves, February 13, 1939, folder: Greene Mr Roger S (1) July 38–June 39, box 6, ACNPJA Papers.

31. Progress and Program of the American Committee for Non-Participation in Japanese Aggression; Greene to Price, June 8, 1939, folder: Greene Mr Roger S (1) July 38–June 39, box 6, ACNPJA Papers; Upton Close to Mrs. Harry Price, February 28, 1940, folder: Close, Mr. Upton, box 3, ACNPJA Papers.

32. Price to Raymond Leslie Buell, July 7, 1938, folder: Buell Raymond L (Dr), box 1, ACNPJA Papers; Friedman, *Road from Isolation,* 18–19.

33. Tae Jin Park, "Guiding Public Opinion on the Far Eastern Crisis: The American State Department and Propaganda on the Sino-Japanese Conflict," *Diplomacy and Statecraft* 22 (2011): 398.

34. Greene to Hull, February 20, 1940, folder: Cordell Hull, box 16, ACNPJA Papers; Greene to Hull, May 14, 1940, folder 743, box 22, Greene Papers; Price to Stimson, April 25, 1940, folder: Cordell Hull, box 16, ACNPJA Papers.

35. Greene to Price, October 18, 1938, folder 693, box 21, Greene Papers; Price to Roosevelt, July 27, 1939, folder: Roosevelt Franklin D. President, box 12, ACNPJA Papers.

36. ACNPJA, "America's Share in Japan's War Guilt," 78.

37. Andrew Preston, *Sword of the Spirit, Shield of Faith: Religion in American War and Diplomacy* (New York: Knopf, 2012), 477. Also see Stephen G. Craft, "Peacemakers in China: American Missionaries and the Sino-Japanese War, 1937–1941," *Journal of Church and State* 41 (1999): 575–591.

38. ACNPJA, "America's Share in Japan's War Guilt," 37.

39. ACNPJA, "Christian Hands of America," 1939, folder: Amer Com NPJA Misc Literature, box 16, ACNPJA Papers; Price to Dr. and Mrs. Thompson, December 9, 1939, folder: Amer Com NPJA Misc Literature, box 19, ACNPJA Papers (this "Special and Urgent Letter to Missionaries from China" was sent to 850 missionary contacts).

40. ACNPJA, "Shall America Stop Arming Japan?," 1940, box 16, ACNPJA Papers, 25; George Kennan, *American Diplomacy, 1900–1950* (London: Secker and Warburg, 1952), 95–101.

41. ACNPJA, "Shall America Stop Arming Japan?," 14–15; ACNPJA, "America's Share in Japan's War Guilt," 17.

42. ACNPJA, "America Supports Japanese Aggression."

43. ACNPJA, "America's Share in Japan's War Guilt," 21–22.

44. ACNPJA, "Shall America Stop Arming Japan?," 5, 9.

45. Report on trip to Washington; Anticipated Public Debate on the Issue, October 5, 1938, folder 692, box 21, Greene Papers.

46. ACNPJA, "Shall America Stop Arming Japan?," 9, 27.

47. Ibid., 27; ACNPJA, "America's Share in Japan's War Guilt," 5.

48. Price to Raymond Leslie Buell, July 7, 1938; Price to Martin Dies, November 2, 1938, folder: Pu–Py, box 11, ACNPJA Papers.

49. Franklin Farrel Jr. to the ACNPJA, January 29, 1940, folder: "Far–Fay," box 5, ACNPJA Papers; Price to Farrel, April 15, 1940, folder: "Far–Fay," box 5, ACNPJA Papers; Thomas Dunbar to Henry Stimson, February 19, 1940, folder: "Du–Dy," box 4, ACNPJA Papers; Mrs. Grover Clark to Dunbar, April 16, 1940, folder: "Du–Dy," box 4, ACNPJA Papers.

50. John Earl Haynes and Harvey Klehr, *Venona: Decoding Soviet Espionage in America* (New Haven: Yale University Press, 1999), 176–178; Frederick V. Field to Harry Price, November 11, 1940, folder: Field Frederick V, box 5, ACNPJA Papers; Harry Price to Frederick V. Field, November 23, 1940, folder: Field Frederick V, box 5, ACNPJA Papers.

51. Price to Farrel, April 15, 1940, folder: "Far–Fay," box 5, ACNPJA Papers; ACNPJA, "Shall America Stop Arming Japan?," 27.

52. Helmuth C. Engelbrecht and Frank C. Hanighen, *Merchants of Death: A Study of the International Armament Industry* (London: Routledge, 1934).

53. ACNPJA, "Shall America Stop Arming Japan?," 29; ACNPJA, "America's Share in Japan's War Guilt," 23.

54. ACNPJA, "Shall America Stop Arming Japan?," 29; ACNPJA, "The Far Eastern Conflict and American Cotton," 1939, box 1, ACNPJA Papers, 18–25.

55. ACNPJA, "The Far Eastern Conflict and American Cotton," 3.

56. Price to Farrel, April 15, 1940.

57. Charles Chatfield, *The American Peace Movement: Ideals and Activism* (New York: Twayne, 1992), 62–73.

58. ACNPJA, "America Supports Japanese Aggression." Correspondents interested in a boycott of Japanese goods were referred to the smaller and unrelated Committee for Boycott against Japanese Aggression, also based in New York City. See Price to Leonard Wilbur, March 14, 1939, folder: "Wia–Wilk," box 15, ACNPJA Papers.

2. The Coming of War and the American Union for Concerted Peace Efforts

1. Gallup, *Gallup Poll*, 121, 125, 141.

2. Divine, *Illusion of Neutrality*, 231–236; Robert Dallek, *Franklin D. Roosevelt and American Foreign Policy, 1932–1945* (Oxford: Oxford University Press, 1979), 180–184.

3. Divine, *Illusion of Neutrality*, 242–243.

4. Cohen, "Role of Private Groups in the United States," 439.

5. Elliot Roosevelt, ed., *FDR: His Personal Letters, 1928–1945*, vol. 2 (New York: Duell, Sloan and Pearce, 1950), 873.

6. Divine, *Illusion of Neutrality*, 239; *New York Times*, February 14, 1939, 4.

7. ACNPJA minutes of the national board, March 15, 1939, folder 2130 (1 of 3), box 54, Greene Papers; ACNPJA minutes of the national board, March 29, 1939, folder 2130 (2 of 3), box 54, Greene Papers.

8. ACNPJA minutes of the national board, April 19, 1939, folder 2130 (2 of 3), box 54, Greene Papers.

9. *New York Times*, March 16, 1939, 11; "A Call to Union for Peace," February 25, 1939, folder 5, box 4, Hugh Moore Fund Papers, Princeton University (hereafter Moore Papers).

10. Memorandum on Origins and Policies of Committee for Concerted Peace Efforts and American Union for Concerted Peace Efforts, July 19, 1948, folder CCPE-AUCPE,

box 53, Eichelberger Papers; Roosevelt, *Public Papers and Addresses of Franklin D. Roosevelt,*
   1937, 408.

11. Press release, December 3, 1938, folder: Press Releases '38, box 12, Eichelberger Papers.

12. Plan of Organization of the American Union for Concerted Peace Efforts, February 8,
   1939, folder: Plans CCPE-AUCPE, box 53, Eichelberger Papers; minutes of the advisory
   group called together by the Committee for Concerted Peace Efforts, February 25, 1939,
   folder: Plans CCPE-AUCPE, box 53, Eichelberger Papers; minutes of the League of
   Nations Association board of directors, February 8, 1939, folder: Board Meeting—Jan.
   24 '39, box 14, Eichelberger Papers; memorandum of tentative agreement reached by
   the AUCPE and LNA, May 22, 1939, folder: Board Meeting—1939—May 22, box 14,
   Eichelberger Papers; minutes of the board of directors of the AUCPE, May 24, 1939,
   folder: American Union for Concerted Peace Efforts 1, box 1, ACNPJA Papers.

13. *New York Times,* March 16, 1939, 11.

14. Clark M. Eichelberger, *Organizing for Peace* (New York: Harper and Row, 1977), 2, 11,
   53–54. On American support for the league in the 1930s, see Warren F. Kuehl and
   Lynne K. Dunn, *Keeping the Covenant: American Internationalists and the League of Nations,
   1920–1939* (Kent, OH: Kent State University Press, 1997), 165–177.

15. Eichelberger to Roosevelt, July 17, 1937, PPF 3833, Roosevelt Papers; memorandum on
   conference with President Roosevelt, July 8, 1937, folder: Interviews with FDR, box 198,
   Eichelberger Papers; Franklin D. Roosevelt, *The Public Papers and Addresses of Franklin D.
   Roosevelt,* 1939 (London: Macmillan, 1941), 3–4.

16. Minutes of the League of Nations Association board of directors, February 8, 1939.

17. "Call to Union for Peace"; Statement of Principles of the AUCPE, undated, folder 6,
   box 4, Moore Papers.

18. "Bring the United States Back to Earth," Committee for Concerted Peace Efforts leaflet,
   undated, folder: LNA Reports, News Summaries, Memos, box 34, James T. Shotwell
   Papers, Columbia University (hereafter Shotwell Papers).

19. Summary of two-day conference, April 26, 1939, folder: American Union for Concerted
   Peace Efforts 1, box 1, ACNPJA Papers.

20. Andrew Johnstone, "Shaping our Post-war Foreign Policy: The Carnegie Endowment
   for International Peace and the Promotion of the United Nations Organisation during
   World War II," *Global Society* 28 (2014): 24–39.

21. Nicholas Murray Butler, "A Brief Review of Thirty-five Years of Service toward Developing International Understanding," *International Conciliation* 417 (1946): 25–28.

22. Eichelberger to branch secretaries of the League of Nations Association, August 31,
   1938, folder: LoN Assoc AAUN 1938–1939, box 247, Carnegie Endowment for International Peace Records, Columbia University (hereafter CEIP Records).

23. "The Stake of Business in Peace," undated, folder: American Union for Concerted Peace
   Efforts 2, box 1, ANCPJA Papers.

24. Statement of Principles of the AUCPE.

25. Minutes of the advisory group.

26. Invitation to the Conference of One Hundred, April 1939, folder: American Union for
   Concerted Peace Efforts 1, box 1, ACNPJA Papers; summary of two-day conference,
   April 26, 1939, folder: American Union for Concerted Peace Efforts 1, box 1, ACNPJA
   Papers; Report on Peace and Security Week, May 1939, OF 394, Roosevelt Papers.

27. Report on Peace and Security Week; AUCPE Manual for Organization, undated, folder 6, box 4, Moore Papers.

28. CCPE statement on President Roosevelt's message to Congress, January 14, 1939, OF 394, Roosevelt Papers.

29. Welles to McIntyre, January 24, 1939, OF 394, Roosevelt Papers.

30. Eichelberger, *Organizing for Peace*, 224–236.

31. Divine, *Illusion of Neutrality*, 246–257.

32. Cordell Hull, *The Memoirs of Cordell Hull*, vol. 1 (New York: Macmillan, 1948), 644–645.

33. *New York Times*, May 29, 1939, 13.

34. Minutes of the meeting of the executive board, May 4, 1939, folder: American Union for Concerted Peace Efforts 1, box 1, ACNPJA Papers.

35. AUCPE statement concerning neutrality policy, June 29, 1939, folder: American Union for Concerted Peace Efforts 2, box 1, ACNPJA Papers.

36. Ibid.

37. Ibid.

38. Ibid.

39. ACNPJA minutes of the national board meeting, June 21, 1939, folder 2130 (3 of 3), box 54, Greene Papers.

40. Dallek, *Franklin D. Roosevelt and American Foreign Policy*, 189–190; ACNPJA minutes of the national board meeting, July 5, 1939, folder 2130 (3 of 3), box 54, Greene Papers.

41. Eichelberger to friends of the AUCPE, July 15, 1939, folder: American Union for Concerted Peace Efforts 2, box 1, ACNPJA Papers; Hull, *Memoirs*, 1:648–653; Dallek, *Franklin D. Roosevelt and American Foreign Policy*, 192.

42. Eichelberger to members of the board and chairmen of committees of the AUCPE, July 22, 1939, folder: American Union for Concerted Peace Efforts 2, box 1, ACNPJA Papers; Gallup, *Gallup Poll*, 178.

43. Eichelberger to Franklin Roosevelt, July 18, 1939, and R. Walton Moore to Eichelberger, July 22, 1939, 811.04418/489, Decimal File, RG 59, NACP.

44. Gallup, *Gallup Poll*, 168.

45. Dallek, *Franklin D. Roosevelt and American Foreign Policy*, 195–196; Cohen, "Role of Private Groups in the United States," 440.

46. Price to Henry Stimson, August 3, 1939, 0014–0016, reel 99, Stimson Papers; national board of the ACNPJA to friends and supporters, July 28, 1939, folder 712, box 22, Greene Papers; *New York Times*, July 27, 1939, 1.

47. National board of the ACNPJA to friends and supporters.

48. Eichelberger to members of the board of the AUCPE, August 1, 1939, folder: American Union for Concerted Peace Efforts 2, box 1, ACNPJA Papers.

49. ACNPJA minutes of the national board meeting, July 5, 1939; ACNPJA minutes of the national board meeting, June 21, 1939.

50. ACNPJA minutes of the national board meeting, June 21, 1939; Roger Greene to Josephine Schain, August 4, 1939, folder: Greene Mr Roger S (2) July–Dec 39, box 6, ACNPJA Papers; Roger Greene to Harry Price, August 16, 1939, folder: Greene Mr Roger S (2) July–Dec 39, box 6, ACNPJA Papers; Cohen, "Role of Private Groups in the United States," 440.

51. Harry Price to Roger Greene, August 15, 1939, folder: Greene Mr Roger S (2) July–Dec 39, box 6, ACNPJA Papers; Harry Price to Hugh Moore, August 21, 1939, folder 2, box 4,

Moore Papers; Price to Chase Kimball, September 7, 1939, folder: Kimball, Mr. Chase, box 8, ACNPJA Papers; Cohen, "Role of Private Groups in the United States," 440.

52. Ibid.

53. Price to Chase Kimball, September 7, 1939, folder: Kimball, Mr. Chase, box 8, ACNPJA Papers.

3. The Phony War and the Non-Partisan Committee for Peace through Revision of the Neutrality Law

1. When asked if the neutrality legislation should be amended so that all nations (not just Britain and France) could purchase war materials in the United States, the primary reason for saying yes was not in fact sympathy for Britain and France but the possibility that it might help the American economy. Gallup, *Gallup Poll*, 180, 186, 181, 183, 185.

2. Ibid. 186.

3. "War in Europe—What about Asia?," September 14, 1939, folder: American Committee for Non-Participation in Japanese Aggression, box 14, Eichelberger Papers; Price to Henry Stimson, September 15, 1939, 0152–0153, reel 99, Stimson Papers; Cohen, "Role of Private Groups in the United States," 440.

4. Roosevelt, *Public Papers and Addresses*, 1939, 479–488, 512–525.

5. Eichelberger to officers, committees and members of the AUCPE, September 4, 1939, folder: American Union for Concerted Peace Efforts 2, box 1, ACNPJA Papers.

6. Clark Eichelberger to Edwin Watson, September 3, 1939, OF 1561, Roosevelt Papers; Edwin Watson to Franklin Roosevelt, September 5, 1939, OF 1561, Roosevelt Papers; confidential notes on interview with the president, September 10, 1939, folder 1938, box 14, Eichelberger Papers (notes taken three days after the meeting).

7. Confidential notes on interview with the president.

8. Ibid; Gallup, *Gallup Poll*, 181.

9. Memorandum from Joseph Green, September 19, 1939, R. Walton Moore Papers, Franklin D. Roosevelt Library, Hyde Park, New York; AUCPE minutes of the meeting of the board of directors, September 20, 1939, folder: American Union for Concerted Peace Efforts 2, box 1, ACNPJA Papers.

10. AUCPE Statement on Neutrality Revision, September 22, 1939, folder: American Union for Concerted Peace Efforts 2, box 1, ACNPJA Papers.

11. Ibid. For an analysis of the exaggerated nature of the direct threat to the United States, see John A. Thompson, "Another Look at the Downfall of 'Fortress America,'" *Journal of American Studies* 26 (1992): 393–408.

12. Eichelberger, *Organizing for Peace*, 106–107.

13. Roosevelt, *Public Papers and Addresses*, 1936, 465; Johnson, *William Allen White's America*, 516–517; memorandum for Henry Stimson, September 28, 1939, 0243, reel 99, Stimson Papers.

14. Eichelberger, *Organizing for Peace*, 107–108; William Allen White to Franklin Roosevelt, December 22, 1939, folder: Roosevelt, Franklin D., box 320, series C, William Allen White Papers, Library of Congress (hereafter White Papers). For accounts that emphasize White's personal role and leadership during the whole 1939–41 period, see Johnson, *The Battle against Isolation,* and Tuttle, "Aid-to-the-Allies Short-of-War," 840–858.

15. AUCPE press release, Supplementary Information to Statement Issued by William Allen White at Emporia, Kansas, October 3, 1939, folder: AUCPE Releases, box 45, Eichelberger Papers.

16. Pertinent Facts about the Non-Partisan Committee for Peace through Revision of the Neutrality Law, October 1939, folder: Eichelberger, Clark M., box 317, series C, White Papers; AUCPE minutes of the meeting of the board of directors, October 16, 1939, folder: Minutes 1939–40 AUCPE, box 53, Eichelberger Papers.

17. Draft of suggested direct mail appeal letter, October 4, 1939, folder: Eichelberger, Clark M., box 317, series C, White Papers. For a detailed analysis of non-interventionist arguments, see Doenecke, *Storm on the Horizon*, 59–68.

18. Pertinent Facts about the Non-Partisan Committee for Peace Through Revision of the Neutrality Law, October 1939.

19. "The Hour is Striking," October 15, 1939, OF 1561, Roosevelt Papers. White, like many Americans, used Russia as a synonym for the Soviet Union.

20. Ibid.

21. NPC progress bulletin, October 12, 1939, folder: American Union for Concerted Peace Efforts 2, box 1, ACNPJA Papers; Dallek, *Franklin D. Roosevelt and American Foreign Policy*, 204–205.

22. White to the NPC, November 14, 1939, folder: Eichelberger, Clark M., box 317, series C, White Papers; White to Eichelberger, November 18, 1939, folder: W. A. White 1939, box 50, Eichelberger Papers; Eichelberger to White, December 8, 1939, folder: Eichelberger, Clark M., box 317, series C, White Papers.

23. Roosevelt to White, November 8, 1939, folder: Roosevelt, Franklin D., box 320, series C, White Papers; Roosevelt to White, December 14, 1939, folder: Roosevelt, Franklin D., box 320, series C, White Papers; White to Roosevelt, December 22, 1939, folder: Roosevelt, Franklin D., box 320, series C, White Papers.

24. Eichelberger, *Organizing for Peace*, 111. On the Winter War, see Dallek, *Franklin D. Roosevelt and American Foreign Policy*, 208–212; also see Robert Sobel, *The Origins of Interventionism: The United States and the Russo-Finnish War* (New York: Bookman, 1960).

25. Eichelberger to Nicholas Murray Butler, August 31, 1939, folder: LoN Assoc/AAUN 1938–39, box 247, CEIP Records.

26. CEIP board of trustees semiannual meeting minutes, December 13, 1943, folder: Board of Trustees Meetings 1943, box 15, CEIP Records, 79.

27. Members of the Commission to Study the Organization of Peace, December 4, 1939, folder: Eichelberger, Clark M., box 317, series C, White Papers.

28. Confidential notes on interview with the president, September 10, 1939, folder 1938, box 14, Eichelberger Papers; Eleanor Roosevelt to Eichelberger, October 12, 1939, folder 1939, box 16, Eichelberger Papers

29. CSOP General Outline of Studies, December 4, 1939, folder: Eichelberger, Clark M., box 317, series C, White Papers.

30. Eichelberger to Eleanor Roosevelt, December 21, 1939, folder 1939, box 16, Eichelberger Papers.

31. CSOP minutes, November 5, 1939, folder 15, box 5, Moore Papers; Commission to Study the Organisation of Peace, *Building Peace: Reports of the Commission to Study the Organisation of Peace 1939–1972* (Metuchen, NJ: Scarecrow Press, Inc., 1973), 1–10.

32. AUCPE minutes of the meeting of the board of directors, November 30, 1939, folder: American Union for Concerted Peace Efforts 2, box 1, ACNPJA Papers; statement of the AUCPE, December 7, 1939, folder: American Union for Concerted Peace Efforts 2, box 1, ACNPJA Papers.

33. Statement of the AUCPE, December 7, 1939.

34. AUCPE Newsletter, January 12, 1940, folder 2132 (4 of 5), box 54, Greene Papers.

35. Harry Price to Roger Greene, October 24, 1939, folder 719, box 22, Greene Papers; Greene to Price, January 6, 1940, folder 732, box 22, Greene Papers; Price to William Allen White, November 25, 1939, folder 724, box 22, Greene Papers.

36. Confidential notes on luncheon given by the Hon. Henry L. Stimson, November 9, 1939, folder: Stimson Luncheon, box 12, ACNPJA Papers.

37. Roger Greene to Harry Price, December 4, 1939, folder: Greene Mr Roger S (2) July–Dec 39, box 6, ACNPJA Papers; Harry Price to Henry Stimson, December 30, 1939, 0981–0983, reel 99, Stimson Papers.

38. *Changing World*, December 1939, 5; Jonathan Utley, *Going to War with Japan, 1937–1941* (New York: Fordham University Press, 2005), 76–81.

39. Greene to Price, December 18, 1939, folder 727, box 22, Greene Papers; Harry Price to Henry Stimson, December 30, 1939, 0981–0983, reel 99, Stimson Papers; *New York Times*, January 11, 1940, 1, 4.

40. Roger Greene to Clark Eichelberger, January 21, 1940, folder "E," box 16, ACNPJA Papers; Roger Greene to Clark Eichelberger, February 17, 1940, folder "E," box 16, ACNPJA Papers; Harry Price to Henry Stimson, February 2, 1940, 0302–0303, reel 100, Stimson Papers.

41. Roger Greene to Clark Eichelberger, January 21, 1940, folder "E," box 16, ACNPJA Papers; Roger Greene to Clark Eichelberger, February 17, 1940, folder "E," box 16, ACNPJA Papers.

42. Roger Greene to Harry Price, February 6, 1940, folder: Greene Mr Roger S (3) Jan–Mar 40, box 6, ACNPJA Papers.

43. Roger Greene to Harry Price, February 16, 1940, folder: Greene Mr Roger S (3) Jan–Mar 40, box 6, ACNPJA Papers; Roger Greene to Franklin Roosevelt, February 10, 1940, PPF 5826, Roosevelt Papers (underlining in original); Harry Price to Henry Stimson, March 7, 1940, 0533, reel 100, Stimson Papers.

44. Harry Price to Henry Stimson, April 25, 1940, 0898–0901, reel 100, Stimson Papers.

45. A Gallup Poll in January 1940 suggested that only one in ten Americans had an understanding of the term "reciprocal trade." Gallup, *Gallup Poll*, 206.

46. AUCPE Press Release, March 27, 1940, folder: AUCPE Statement, box 53, Eichelberger Papers; Roger Greene to Clark Eichelberger, February 17, 1940, folder "E," box 16, ACNPJA Papers; Hull, *Memoirs*, 1:749–750.

47. AUCPE minutes of the meeting of the board of directors, March 16, 1940, folder: American Union for Concerted Peace Efforts 3, box 1, ACNPJA Papers.

48. Clarence Streit, *Union Now* [shorter version] (New York: Harper, 1940), 4, 9. The democracies were the United States, the United Kingdom, Canada, Australia, New Zealand, South Africa, Ireland, France, Belgium, the Netherlands, Switzerland, Denmark, Norway, Sweden, and Finland.

49. LNA minutes of the meeting of the board of directors, November 30, 1939, folder: LNA Minutes 1924–1939, box 34, Shotwell Papers; Eichelberger memorandum, March 25, 1940, folder: Office Memos and Correspondence, box 48, Eichelberger Papers.

50. Clark Eichelberger to LNA branch secretaries, April 30, 1940, folder: CME Memos and rough drafts, box 17, Eichelberger Papers.

51. Clarence Streit to Clark Eichelberger, May 3, 1940, folder: 1940, box 5, part 1, Clarence Streit Papers, Library of Congress (hereafter Streit Papers).

52. Clark Eichelberger to LNA branch secretaries, April 30, 1940; William P. Blake to the Union Now executive committee, November 7, 1940, folder: 1940, box 5, part 1, Streit Papers.

53. Clark Eichelberger to LNA branch secretaries, April 30, 1940, folder: CME Memos and Rough Drafts, box 17, Eichelberger Papers.

54. Eichelberger memorandum, March 25, 1940.

4. Blitzkrieg and the Committee to Defend America by Aiding the Allies

1. Roosevelt, *Public Papers and Addresses,* 1940, 198–205, 230–240, 261.

2. Gallup, *Gallup Poll*, 220, 226, 231, 224.

3. Ibid. 222, 230.

4. Breakdown of chapter organization, April 28, 1941, folder 7, box 11, CDAAA Papers.

5. Minutes of the meeting of the AUCPE board of directors, May 28, 1940, folder: W. A. White Correspondence Jan–Jun 1940, box 50, Eichelberger Papers; minutes of the meeting of the AUCPE national board, December 13, 1940, folder 7, box 4, Moore Papers; Memorandum on Origins and Policies of Committee for Concerted Peace Efforts and American Union for Concerted Peace Efforts, July 19, 1948, folder: CCPE-AUCPE, box 53, Eichelberger Papers.

6. Minutes of the meeting of the AUCPE board of directors, April 23, 1940, folder: American Union for Concerted Peace Efforts 3, box 1, ACNPJA Papers; Margaret Olsen to William Allen White, December 9, 1940, folder: CDA-White Correspondence July–August 1940, box 50, Eichelberger Papers.

7. Original statement by William Allen White, May 17, 1940, folder 8, box 10, CDAAA Papers.

8. Press release, May 20, 1940, folder 9, box 36, CDAAA Papers.

9. Thomas Lamont to Franklin Roosevelt, May 15, 1940, PPF 70, Roosevelt Papers.

10. Johnson, *Battle against Isolation*, 64, 84. The Johnson Act forbade loans to nations that had previously defaulted on their debts.

11. Ibid., 86–87. The advertisement is reprinted on page 86 in full.

12. *Washington Evening Star*, July 11, 1940, clipping in 811.43, Committee to Defend America by Aiding the Allies/91, decimal file, RG 59, NACP; Clark Eichelberger to John Blank, July 26, 1940, 811.43, Committee to Defend America by Aiding the Allies/119, decimal file, RG 59, NACP.

13. Johnson, *Battle against Isolation*, 67; Thomas Lamont to John Price Jones, June 5, 1940, folder 3: Jones, John Price, 1920–1948, box 101, Thomas W. Lamont Papers, Baker

Library Historical Collections, Harvard Business School (hereafter Lamont Papers). Conant, scientist and president of Harvard University, was also a CDAAA member. On Conant, see James Hershberg, *James B. Conant: Harvard to Hiroshima and the Making of the Nuclear Age* (Stanford: Stanford University Press, 1993), 119, 130–133.

14. Lothian cited in Nicholas John Cull, *Selling War: The British Propaganda Campaign against American "Neutrality" in World War II* (Oxford: Oxford University Press, 1995), 122.

15. Carl Beck to Thomas Lamont, May 20, 1940, folder: W. A. White correspondence Jan–Jun 1940, box 50, Eichelberger Papers; American Defenders of Freedom press release, May 21, 1940, folder: W. A. White correspondence Jan–Jun 1940, box 50, Eichelberger Papers; memorandum from Robert Duncan to John Price Jones, July 2, 1940, "Decisions," vol. 1, CDAAA files, John Price Jones Company Records, Baker Library Historical Collections, Harvard Business School (hereafter JPJ Records). Burton K. Wheeler, a Democratic senator from Montana, was one of the most prominent non-interventionist politicians of the era.

16. Policies, Aims and Accomplishments of the CDAAA, October 9, 1940, folder 15, box 9, CDAAA Papers; memorandum on chapter organization, October 9, 1941, folder 18, box 5, CDAAA papers; Johnson, *Battle against Isolation*, 74–75; *Changing World*, July 1940, 15.

17. Breakdown of chapter organization, April 28, 1941.

18. Policies, Aims and Accomplishments of the CDAAA, October 9, 1940.

19. Memorandum from Robert Duncan to John Price Jones, July 2, 1940.

20. Memorandum on chapter organization, October 9, 1941; Policies, Aims and Accomplishments of the CDAAA, October 9, 1940; report on college division, June 1941, folder 25, box 28, CDAAA Papers.

21. "The Answers to Your Questions: The Women's Division Primer," October 7, 1940, folder 2, box 24, FFF Papers; Clark Eichelberger to Mrs. Rushmore Patterson, July 26, 1940, folder 4, box 29, CDAAA Papers.

22. Memorandum from Robert Duncan to John Price Jones, July 2, 1940; memorandum from Irwin Jaffe, May 1, 1941, folder 4, box 24, FFF Papers; Policies, Aims and Accomplishments of the CDAAA, October 9, 1940; Margaret Paton-Walsh, *Our War Too: American Women against the Axis* (Lawrence: University Press of Kansas, 2002), 93–96.

23. Policies, Aims and Accomplishments of the CDAAA, October 9, 1940; "Organized Labor's Stake in the War," undated, folder 2, box 29, CDAAA Papers; William Loeb to William Allen White, September 13, 1940, box 14, series D, White Papers; Alfred Baker Lewis to Clark Eichelberger, Report on the Activities of the Labor Movement, May 16, 1941, folder 3, box 29, CDAAA Papers.

24. William Allen White to Lowell Mellett, August 19, 1941, folder: White, Wm A & Wm L, box 18, Lowell Mellett Papers, Franklin D. Roosevelt Library (hereafter Mellett Papers).

25. Inderjeet Parmar, "'. . . Another Important Group That Needs More Cultivation': The Council on Foreign Relations and the Mobilization of Black Americans for Interventionism, 1939–1941," *Ethnic and Racial Studies* 27 (2004): 717; Harold J. Seymour to John Price Jones and Robert Duncan, June 14, 1940, "'Fifth Column' Activities," vol. 1, CDAAA files, JPJ Records.

26. Roger Greene to Margaret Olson, October 7, 1940, folder 43, box 8, CDAAA Papers; "Colored People Have a Stake in the War," undated, folder 44, box 8, CDAAA Papers.

27. Policies, Aims and Accomplishments of the CDAAA, October 9, 1940.

28. Ibid.

29. Brief for a Survey and Plan, October 2, 1940, "Brief," vol. 1, CDAAA files, JPJ Records; CDAAA Review of Finances, December 20, 1940, vol. 11, CDAAA files, JPJ Records.

30. Objectives of the Committee to Defend America by Aiding the Allies, July 1940, folder 16, box 35, CDAAA Papers.

31. "Battle of America," June 1940, vol. 5, CDAAA files, JPJ Records; "Ten Billion Dollars Is Not Enough," July 1940, folder 15, box 35, CDAAA Papers (italics in original); "Suppose Britain Loses," August 1940, vol. 5, CDAAA files, JPJ Records.

32. "Suppose Britain Loses"; "Ten Billion Dollars Is Not Enough."

33. Johnson, *Battle against Isolation*, 86.

34. Ibid; "Battle of America."

35. "Battle of America."

36. "Ten Billion Dollars Is Not Enough"; "Suppose Britain Loses."

37. "80,000,000 Americans Can't Be Wrong! An Outline of Some of the Reasons Why the Majority Favor Aid to the Allies," July 12, 1940, box 13, series D, White Papers.

38. Ibid; Objectives of the Committee to Defend America by Aiding the Allies, July 1940.

39. Alfred Baker Lewis to Clark Eichelberger, Report on the Activities of the Labor Movement, May 16, 1941, folder 3, box 29, CDAAA Papers.

40. Objectives of the Committee to Defend America by Aiding the Allies; "Trade War—Or War of Freedom? Primer Number Three," undated, folder 5, box 356, Adlai Stevenson Papers, Princeton University (hereafter Stevenson Papers).

41. "Trade War—Or War of Freedom?"; "The Answers to Your Questions: The Women's Division Primer."

42. "Suppose Britain Loses."

43. Ibid; Albert Lord to William Allen White, June 26, 1940, folder 20, box 5, Moore Papers; Hugh Moore to Albert Lord, August 8, 1940, folder 20, box 5, Moore Papers.

44. Roger Greene to Franklin Roosevelt, May 17, 1940, 894.24/944, decimal file, RG 59, NACP; ACNPJA letter to All Friends and Cooperating Groups, June 17, 1940, 894.24/960, decimal file, RG 59, NACP.

45. Roger Greene to Clark Eichelberger, June 12, 1940, folder 761, box 23, Greene Papers; Harry Price to Roger Greene, June 15, 1940, folder: Greene Mr Roger S (4) Apr–Jun 40, box 6, ACNPJA Papers; Roger Greene to Harry Price, June 16, 1940, folder: Greene Mr Roger S (4) Apr–Jun 40, box 6, ACNPJA Papers.

46. Policies, Aims and Accomplishments of the CDAAA, October 9, 1940.

47. William Allen White to members of the national committee and local chairmen, July 23, 1940, folder 14, box 33, CDAAA Papers.

5. The Destroyer-Bases Agreement and the Century Group

1. Warren Kimball, ed., *Churchill and Roosevelt: The Complete Correspondence*, vol. 1 (Princeton: Princeton University Press, 1984), 37–38, 51; Dallek, *Franklin D. Roosevelt and American Foreign Policy*, 243–244.

2. Gallup, *Gallup Poll*, 220.

3. Johnson, *Battle against Isolation*, 114.

4. Francis Pickens Miller, *Man from the Valley: Memoirs of a 20th-Century Virginian* (Chapel Hill: University of North Carolina Press, 1971), 87, 89–90; "The National Policy Committee: Its story, Its technique; Cross Country Comment on Labor-Management Relations," 1947, folder: Corres., Papers, and Book re: National Policy Committee, box 24, Francis Pickens Miller Papers, Albert and Shirley Small Special Collections Library, University of Virginia (hereafter Miller Papers), 7–11, 16–17. Attending the meeting were Francis Miller, his wife, Helen Hill Miller, Richard Cleveland, Stacy May, Winfield Riefler, Mr. and Mrs. Whitney Shepardson, Edward Warner, and M. L. Wilson. Miller, Riefler, Warner, and Wilson had all been present at the founding of the National Policy Committee in 1935. Unlike the other seven attendees, Warner and Wilson did not sign the subsequent "Summons" because of their governmental roles.

5. Miller, *Man from the Valley*, 90; *New York Times*, June 10, 1940, 10.

6. Signatories to "A Summons to Speak Out," undated, folder: Reply Corres. and Papers re: "A Summons to Speak Out" re: Entrance of U.S. into World War II, box 26, Miller Papers; memorandum to those invited to sign "A Summons to Speak Out," June 20, 1940, folder: Subsequent Corres. and Papers re: "A Summons to Speak Out" re: Entrance of U.S. into World War II, box 26, Miller Papers; Chadwin, *Hawks of World War II*, 38–40; *New York Times*, June 10, 1940, 10.

7. Will Clayton to Francis Miller, June 6, 1940; William Allen White to Francis Miller, June 7, 1940; Lewis Douglas to Francis Miller, June 6, 1940; Francis Miller to Lewis Douglas, June 12, 1940—all in folder: Reply Corres. and Papers re: "A Summons to Speak Out" re: Entrance of U.S. into World War II, box 26, Miller Papers.

8. Miller, *Man from the Valley*, 93.

9. Meeting at Columbia Club, July 11, 1940, folder 22, box 50, FFF Papers; Henry Luce, "The American Century," *Life*, February 17, 1941, 61–65. For brief biographical descriptions of the key Century group internationalists, see Chadwin, *Hawks of World War II*, 43–73.

10. Meeting at Columbia Club, July 11, 1940.

11. Tentative draft, July 12, 1940, folder: 1940 May–Aug. Articles and Addresses (some by FPM), Corres. and Papers re: the Century Group, box 25, Miller Papers.

12. Ibid. Underlining in original.

13. Memorandum of meeting, July 25, 1940, folder 22, box 50, FFF Papers.

14. Ibid.

15. Ibid; William Allen White to Francis Miller, July 25, 1940, folder 6, box 20, FFF Papers.

16. The CDAAA members attending on July 25 were Eichelberger, Ward Cheney, Henry Sloane Coffin, Henry Hobson, Ernest Hopkins, Robert Sherwood, Henry Van Dusen, former undersecretary of State Frank L. Polk, Washington columnist Robert Allen, and publisher Barry Bingham. Johnson, *Battle against Isolation*, 249.

17. Francis Miller to J. R. M. Butler, September 21, 1956, folder: Misc. Late Corres. re: the Century Group, box 26, Miller Papers; memorandum on British defense quoted in Miller, *Man from the Valley*, 97–98.

18. *New York Times*, August 2, 1940, 3; Walter L. Langer and S. Everett Gleason, *The Challenge to Isolation 1937–1940* (New York: Harper, 1952), 749; CDAAA Progress Bulletin, August 3, 1940, box 13, series D, White Papers.

19. *New York Times*, August 5, 1940, 1; Herbert Agar, *Britain Alone: June 1940–June 1941* (London: Bodley Head, 1972), 151–152; Miller, *Man from the Valley*, 98–101.

20. Eichelberger, *Organizing for Peace*, 132–134.

21. *New York Times*, August 2, 1940, 3; Philip Goodhart, *Fifty Ships That Saved the World* (London: Heinemann, 1965), 163.

22. FDR memorandum, August 2, 1940, PSF Navy: Destroyers and Naval Bases 1940: Part 1, Roosevelt Papers. The importance of the meeting is reflected in the fact that the president took and subsequently dictated his own notes.

23. Ibid.

24. Johnson, *Battle against Isolation*, 128; Langer and Gleason, *Challenge to Isolation*, 754.

25. Henry L. Stimson Diaries, diary entry, August 13, 1940, Library of Congress, Washington, D.C. (hereafter Stimson Diaries); Langer and Gleason, *Challenge to Isolation*, 754; Steve Neal, *Dark Horse: A Biography of Wendell Willkie* (Garden City: Doubleday, 1984), 140.

26. Roosevelt, *Public Papers and Addresses,* 1940, 391–407; *New York Times,* September 4, 1940, 1, 16.

27. CDAAA press release, September 4, 1940, folder 14, box 36, CDAAA Papers.

28. Franklin Roosevelt to Stephen Early, September 5, 1940, PPF 1196, Roosevelt Papers; Stephen Early to William Allen White, September 6, 1940, PPF 1196, Roosevelt Papers; Clark Eichelberger memorandum on conversation with the president, September 5, 1940, folder: Interviews with FDR, box 198, Eichelberger Papers.

29. John Balderston to William Allen White, August 16, 1940, box 15, series D, White Papers; Chadwin, *Hawks of World War II*, 101–102.

30. Ibid.; Johnson, *Battle against Isolation*, 118–119.

31. William Allen White News Service wire letter, September 4, 1940, folder: Correspondence, Telegrams and Press Releases, 1940, box 1, John Balderston Papers, Library of Congress (hereafter Balderston Papers).

32. Johnson, *Battle against Isolation*, 119–121; *New York Herald Tribune*, September 6, 1940, clipping copied in folder: Correspondence, Telegrams and Press Releases, 1940, box 1, Balderston Papers.

33. John Balderston to Raymond Gram Swing, September 22, 1940, folder: Correspondence, Telegrams and Press Releases, 1940, box 1, Balderston Papers; Johnson, *Battle against Isolation*, 121.

34. Editorial Section, *St. Louis Post-Dispatch*, September 22, 1940, 1, 3, 6, copy in box 26, Miller Papers; Chadwin, *Hawks of World War II*, 115; Will Clayton to Francis Miller, August 12, 1940, folder: Miller, Francis P., box 202, Henry Morgenthau Papers, Franklin Roosevelt Library.

35. Editorial Section, *St. Louis Post-Dispatch*, September 22 1940, 6; Chadwin, *Hawks of World War II*, 116.

36. Congressional Record—Senate, September 26, 1940, 19130–19143, copies in folder: 1940 Sept.–Nov. Articles and Addresses (some by FPM), Corres. and Papers re: the Century Group, box 25, Miller Papers.

37. John Balderston, "The William Allen White Committee News Service and a Little 'Smear Campaign' in the Senate," folder: Corres. and Papers re: the William Allen White News Service of the Committee to Defend America by Aiding the Allies, box 27, Miller Papers.

38. Cole, *America First*, 11–12.

39. Ibid., 15–16.

40. Doenecke, *Storm on the Horizon*, 165.

41. Ibid., 117; memorandum to all chapter chairmen on "Peace or War Ad" of the America First Committee, October 4, 1940, folder 17, box 33, CDAAA Papers.

42. Memorandum to all chapter chairmen on "Peace or War Ad," October 4, 1940; on the Selective Training and Service Act, see J. Garry Clifford and Samuel R. Spencer Jr., *The First Peacetime Draft* (Lawrence: University Press of Kansas, 1986).

43. Memorandum to all chapter chairmen on "Peace or War Ad," October 4, 1940; Johnson, *Battle against Isolation*, 163–167.

44. Clark Eichelberger memorandum on conversation with the president, September 5, 1940; diary entry, September 9, 1940, Stimson Diaries; William Allen White to members of the national committee, officers and chairmen of chapters, September 12, 1940, folder 16, box 33, CDAAA Papers.

45. Thomas Lamont to William Allen White, October 4, 1940, folder 9: Committee to Defend America by Aiding the Allies, 1940, box 21, Lamont Papers; Clark Eichelberger to chapter chairmen of the CDAAA, October 11, 1940, folder 17, box 33, CDAAA Papers.

46. Memorandum "For Consideration," September 5, 1940, folder 22, box 50, FFF Papers; Francis Miller notice, September 6, 1940, folder 22, box 50, FFF Papers.

47. Subcommittee report to meeting at Century Club, September 13, 1940, folder 22, box 50, FFF Papers; Herbert Agar to Helen Everitt, September 15, 1940, folder 4, box 1, FFF Papers.

48. Memorandum of telephone conversation between C. W. Gray and U. Bell, October 3, 1940, folder 7, box 12, FFF Papers.

49. Herbert Agar to Helen Everitt, September 15, 1940, folder 4, box 1, FFF Papers.

50. Memorandum on Far Eastern policy, October 7, 1940, box 14, series D, White Papers; Clark Eichelberger to chapter chairmen, October 15, 1940, folder 17, box 33, CDAAA Papers; Roger Greene to Harry Price, August 22, 1940, folder: Greene Mr Roger S (5) July 40–Feb 41, box 6, ACNPJA Papers.

51. "Proposals to Feed Peoples of Occupied Areas Are Dangerous Both to England and to Us," October 28, 1940, folder 6, box 20, FFF Papers; Chadwin, *Hawks of World War II*, 134–141.

52. Dallek, *Franklin D. Roosevelt and American Foreign Policy*, 250; Roosevelt, *Public Papers and Addresses*, 1940, 517.

53. William Allen White to members of the national committee, officers and chairmen of chapters, September 12, 1940, folder 16, box 33, CDAAA Papers; Johnson, *Battle against Isolation*, 137.

54. Frank Kingdon to Thomas Lamont, October 16, 1940, folder 10: Committee to Defend America by Aiding the Allies, 1940, box 21, Lamont Papers.

55. Johnson, *Battle against Isolation*, 138–142.

56. Ibid.; William Allen White to Fredric Coudert, October 22, 1940, folder 10: Committee to Defend America by Aiding the Allies, 1940, box 21, Lamont Papers.

57. Draft mail appeal enclosure, October 26, 1940, folder 31, box 30, CDAAA Papers; Memorandum on Some Aspects of Policy, October 31, 1940, box 14, series D, White Papers; Clark Eichelberger to William Allen White, October 30, 1940, box 14, series D, White Papers; Johnson, *Battle against Isolation*, 142–143.

58. Chadwin, *Hawks of World War II*, 66, 129–131.

6. Maximum Aid and the Battle for Lend-Lease

1. Dallek, *Franklin D. Roosevelt and American Foreign Policy*, 253.

2. Gallup, *Gallup Poll*, 259.

3. *New York Times*, November 6, 1940, 3; William Allen White to Marguerite LeHand, November 6, 1940, box 1, OF 4230, Roosevelt Papers; Harry Price to Franklin Roosevelt, November 6, 1940, folder: Roosevelt Franklin D. President, box 12, ACNPJA Papers; "How a Strong American Policy in the Far East Could Help Britain," folder 746, box 22, Greene Papers.

4. Weak and Strong Points, October 30, 1940, vol. 1, CDAAA files, JPJ Records.

5. Ibid.

6. Commission to Study the Organisation of Peace, *Building Peace*, 1–10; Frank Boudreau to LNA members, November 11, 1940, folder 22, box 48, Lamont Papers.

7. Official Statement of Policy, November 26, 1940, folder 15, box 38, CDAAA Papers.

8. Ibid.

9. Ibid.

10. Further Clarification of Policy, December 7, 1940, box 13, series D, White Papers.

11. Ibid.

12. Livingston Hartley to William Allen White, December 4, 1940, folder: White, William Allen, box 50, Eichelberger Papers.

13. *New York Times*, November 28, 1940, 8; *New York Times*, November 29, 1940, 18.

14. *New York Times*, December 6, 1940, 21; Johnson, *Battle against Isolation*, 175; Arthur Hays Sulzberger to William Allen White, December 6, 1940, box 14, series D, White Papers.

15. Arthur Hays Sulzberger to William Allen White, December 6, 1940; draft letter from Ulric Bell to Franklin Roosevelt, November 29, 1940, folder 6, box 11, FFF Papers.

16. Small dinner meeting minutes, November 20, 1940 (notes written November 25), folder 22, box 50, FFF Papers. Others at the dinner included Herbert and William Agar, Ulric Bell, Ward Cheney, Henry Hobson, Robert Allen, Robert Millikan, and Harold Guinzburg.

17. William Allen White to Clark Eichelberger, December 3, 1940, folder: CDA VIII, box 51, Eichelberger Papers; William Allen White to Thomas Lamont, December 10, 1940, folder 12, box 21, Lamont Papers.

18. Herbert Bayard Swope to William Allen White, December 17, 1940, box 14, series D, White Papers.

19. Fairbanks, *Salad Days*, 364.

20. Roosevelt, *Public Papers and Addresses,* 1940, 604–615; William Allen White to Franklin Roosevelt, December 18, 1940, folder: Roosevelt, Franklin Delano, box 347, series C, White Papers. On the development of the Lend-Lease bill, see Warren Kimball, *The Most Unsordid Act: Lend-Lease 1939–1941* (Baltimore: Johns Hopkins University Press, 1969).

21. Johnson, *Battle against Isolation*, 181–183.

22. *New York Times*, December 25, 1940, 14.

23. Johnson, *Battle against Isolation*, 186–187; Herbert Bayard Swope to Franklin Roosevelt, December 24, 1940, box 1, OF 4230, Roosevelt Papers.

24. Johnson, *Battle against Isolation*, 188–189; William Allen White to Lewis Douglas. December 28, 1940, box 14, series D, White Papers.

25. Fiorello LaGuardia to William Allen White, December 26, 1940, folder 20, box 4, CDAAA Papers; *New York Herald Tribune*, December 29, 1940, copy in folder 13, box 21, Lamont Papers.

26. Herbert Bayard Swope to Franklin Roosevelt, December 24, 1940; James Conant and Lewis Douglas to William Agar, December 24, 1940, folder 7, box 17, FFF Papers; *New York Times*, December 26, 1940, 4; Clark Eichelberger to local chapters, December 28, 1940, folder 2, box 34, CDAAA Papers.

27. Reprint of Stephen Early telegram, December 27, 1940, folder 7, box 17, FFF Papers; Roosevelt, *Public Papers and Addresses,* 1940, 633–644.

28. Statement adopted by the advisory policy committee of the CDAAA, December 30, 1940, folder 2, box 34, CDAAAA Papers; Clark Eichelberger to chapter representatives and members of the national committee, December 31, 1940, folder 2, box 34, CDAAA Papers; William Allen White to Franklin Roosevelt, December 28, 1940, folder: Roosevelt, Franklin Delano, box 347, series C, White Papers; Franklin Roosevelt to William Allen White, December 31, 1940, folder: Roosevelt, Franklin Delano, box 347, series C, White Papers.

29. Reprint of telegram from William Allen White to the executive committee of the CDAAA, undated; Hugh Moore to William Allen White, undated; Thomas Lamont to William Allen White, January 2, 1941—all in folder 14: Committee to Defend America by Aiding the Allies, 1941, box 21, Lamont Papers.

30. Memorandum, undated, folder 30: State, Department of, 1939–1940, box 209, Lamont Papers; Thomas Lamont to Franklin Roosevelt, January 3, 1941, box 1, OF 4230, Roosevelt Papers; William Allen White to Franklin Roosevelt, January 11, 1941, OF 1196, Roosevelt Papers; Franklin Roosevelt to William Allen White, January 16, 1941, OF 1196, Roosevelt Papers.

31. Roosevelt, *Public Papers and Addresses,* 1940, 663–672.

32. Clark Eichelberger to chapter representatives and members of the national committee, December 31, 1940; Clark Eichelberger to Henry Haskell, January 6, 1940, folder C-1941, box 18, Eichelberger Papers; CDAAA minutes of the executive committee, January 9, 1941, folder 17, box 10, CDAAA Papers.

33. Kenneth Colegrove to Clark Eichelberger, January 2, 1940, folder: Election—Suggestions etc., box 46, Eichelberger Papers; press release, January 9, 1941, folder 3, box 37, CDAAA Papers; memorandum for the president, January 8, 1941, OF 4193, Roosevelt Papers.

34. Robert Paul Browder and Thomas G. Smith, *Independent: A Biography of Lewis W. Douglas* (New York: Knopf, 1986), 146–147.

35. Reprinted extract from *Uncensored,* January 11, 1941, folder: Goldsmith, box 47, Eichelberger Papers.

36. CDAAA minutes of the executive committee, January 9, 1941; William Allen White to Hugh Moore, January 6, 1941, folder 20, box 5, Moore Papers.

37. Transcript of address by Ernest W. Gibson, January 18, 1941, folder 3, box 37, CDAAA Papers.

38. Ibid.

39. *New York Times,* January 12, 1941, 2; *New York Herald Tribune,* January 13, 1941, 6.

40. James C. Schneider, *Should America Go to War? The Battle over Foreign Policy in Chicago, 1939–1941* (Chapel Hill: University of North Carolina Press, 1989), 58; *Washington Post,* January 13, 1941, 7; Roosevelt, *Public Papers and Addresses,* 1940, 711–712.

41. *Washington Post*, January 13, 1941, 7; outline of dinner meeting, January 9, 1941, folder 1, box 51, FFF Papers.

42. *New York Times*, January 19, 1941, 36.

43. William L. Langer and S. Everett Gleason, *The Undeclared War, 1940–1941* (New York: Harper, 1953), 270; *New York Times*, February 2, 1941, 30; Thomas Lamont to Wendell Willkie, February 2, 1941, folder 24, box 137, Lamont Papers.

44. *Washington Post*, February 4, 1941, 9.

45. Press conference, February 4, 1941, folder: Gibson Correspondence, box 50, Eichelberger Papers; *New York Herald Tribune*, January 24, 1941, 10.

46. Outline of dinner meeting, February 6, 1941, folder 1, box 51, FFF Papers; telegram to the president, February 15, 1941, folder 13, box 22, FFF Papers.

47. Paton-Walsh, *Our War Too*, 125–126, 138–139; Chadwin, *Hawks of World War II*, 114–115; *Chicago Daily News*, January 17, 1941, 8; *New York Herald Tribune*, December 29, 1940, 6; *Washington Post*, February 9, 1941, 5

48. *New York Times*, February 10, 1941, 10; press conference, February 26, 1941, folder 4, box 37, CDAAA Papers; outline of dinner meeting, February 13, 1941, folder 1, box 51, FFF Papers.

49. Johnson, *Battle against Isolation*, 185; *New York Times*, March 12, 1941, 15; Chadwin, *Hawks of World War II*, 157; Council for Democracy: A Brief Statement of Aims and Activities, undated, folder 8, box 26, FFF Papers.

50. Ernest Gibson and Clark Eichelberger to Franklin Roosevelt, February 21, 1941, box 1, OF 4230, Roosevelt Papers; Stephen Early to Clark Eichelberger, February 25, 1941, box 1, OF 4230, Roosevelt Papers; Clark Eichelberger to Henry Morgenthau, February 20, 1941, folder M-1941, box 19, Eichelberger Papers; Henry Morgenthau to Clark Eichelberger, February 26, 1941, folder M-1941, box 19, Eichelberger Papers.

51. Press release and press conference transcription, February 26, 1941, folder 4, box 37, CDAAA Papers.

52. *New York Herald Tribune*, February 28, 1941, 4; *New York Times*, March 4, 1941, 9; *New York Herald Tribune*, March 1, 1941, 3.

53. Kimball, *Most Unsordid Act*, 216, 220, 244; Roosevelt, *Public Papers and Addresses,* 1941, 63.

54. Schneider, *Should America Go to War?*, 86–87; message from William Allen White, March 12, 1941, folder 3, box 24, FFF Papers; Clark Eichelberger to all chapters, March 10, 1941, folder 5, box 34, CDAAA Papers.

55. Clark Eichelberger to all chapters; Ernest Gibson to fellow workers, March 3, 1941, folder 5, box 34, CDAAA Papers.

56. *New York Times*, March 11, 1941, 10; *New York Herald Tribune*, March 11, 1941, 1, 12.

57. Chadwin, *Hawks of World War II*, 159–163.

58. Outline of dinner meeting, January 9, 1941.

7. Deliver the Goods and Fight for Freedom

1. Gallup, *Gallup Poll*, 270, 276.

2. Ibid. 275, 280, 276–277.

3. Gibson quoted by Clark Eichelberger in letter to CDAAA chapters, April 6, 1941, folder 4, box 24, FFF Papers; CDAAA Official Statement of Policy, March 17, 1941, folder 3, box 2, CDAAA Papers.

4. Ibid.

5. Ernest Gibson to "Friends," March 28, 1941, folder 3, box 24, FFF Papers; Clark Eichelberger to all chapters, April 21, 1941, folder 4, box 24, FFF Papers; "Speed Production," 1941, folder 4, box 24, FFF Papers.

6. Clark Eichelberger to Franklin Roosevelt, April 6, 1941, OF 394, Roosevelt Papers; Franklin Roosevelt to Clark Eichelberger, May 12, 1941, OF 394, Roosevelt Papers; Harley Notter, *Postwar Foreign Policy Preparation 1939–1945* (Washington, DC: Department of State, 1949), 44–45.

7. "A Statement of American Proposals for a New World Order," June 6, 1941, folder 24, box 34, CDAAA Papers.

8. Ernest Gibson to Cordell Hull, March 14, 1941, 851.48/252, decimal file, RG 59, NACP; Ernest Gibson to Franklin Roosevelt, 851.48/295, decimal file, RG 59, NACP; Ulric Bell to Cordell Hull, March 11, 1941, 840.48/4832, decimal file, RG 59, NACP; "Shall We Feed Europe?," undated, folder 4, box 24, FFF Papers; Doenecke, *Storm on the Horizon*, 96–97.

9. Clark Eichelberger to CDAAA chapters, April 6, 1941, folder 4, box 24, FFF Papers.

10. Dallek, *Franklin D. Roosevelt and American Foreign Policy*, 260–261.

11. Thomas Lamont to Clark Eichelberger, April 8, 1941, folder: Lamont, Thomas W., box 141, PSF, Roosevelt Papers.

12. William Allen White to Roger Greene, April 11, 1941, folder 20, box 4, CDAAA Papers; William Allen White to Clark Eichelberger, April 23, 1941, folder: WA White 1941 & 1942, box 50, Eichelberger Papers; Clark Eichelberger to William Allen White, May 7, 1941, folder: WA White 1941 & 1942, box 50, Eichelberger Papers.

13. Mrs. Harriman File (memorandum, "Facts about Finances," and suggestions), April 15, 1941, OF 4230, Roosevelt Papers.

14. Ibid.; situation reports, April–June 1941, vol. 1, CDAAA files, JPJ Papers; Roger Greene to Hugh Moore, June 23, 1941, folder 20, box 5, Moore Papers.

15. Statement of Policy, May 7, 1941, folder 3, box 2, CDAAA Papers; *New York Times*, May 8, 1941, 1, 11.

16. Minutes of the executive committee, May 28, 1941, folder 20, box 10, CDAAA Papers; minutes of the executive committee, June 13, 1941, folder 21, box 10, CDAAA Papers; Clark Eichelberger to chapter representatives, May 31, 1941, folder 7, box 34, CDAAA Papers; press release, July 3, 1941, folder 9, box 37, CDAAA Papers.

17. Mrs. Kermit Roosevelt memorandum, May 1, 1941, OF 4230, Roosevelt Papers; Harold Ickes to Marguerite LeHand, May 13, 1941, folder: Interior Harold Ickes 1941, box 55, PSF, Roosevelt Papers; Ernest Gibson to William Hassett, May 20, 1941, box 1, OF 4230, Roosevelt Papers; CDAAA draft statement, May 21, 1941, folder: Statement to President Roosevelt, box 49, Eichelberger Papers; Stephen Early to Lewis Douglas and Mrs. J. Borden Harriman, May 27, 1941, folder: Statement to President Roosevelt, box 49, Eichelberger Papers; Clark Eichelberger to Franklin Roosevelt, June 25, 1941, folder: R-1941, box 19, Eichelberger Papers.

18. Hugh Moore to Roger Greene, May 13, 1941, folder 17, box 3, CDAAA Papers; progress bulletin, May 15, 1941, folder 32, box 34, CDAAA Papers; minutes of the executive committee, June 26, 1941, folder 21, box 10, CDAAA Papers; talk with Wendell Willkie, June 30, 1941, folder 4, box 3, Moore Papers; press release, October 19, 1941, folder 12, box 37, CDAAA Papers.

19. Outline of dinner meeting, January 9, 1941, folder 1, box 51, FFF Papers; proposed manifesto as revised at dinner group meeting, January 30, 1941, folder 1, box 51, FFF Papers.
20. Chadwin, *Hawks of World War II*, 51–52, 170; Francis Miller to Henry Hobson, April 30, 1941, folder 7, box 11, FFF Papers. The group's other vice chairman was Mrs. Calvin Coolidge.
21. Chadwin, *Hawks of World War II*, 164–166; Fight for Freedom address, April 19, 1941, folder 7, box 11, FFF Papers.
22. Chadwin, *Hawks of World War II*, 31.
23. Fight for Freedom address, April 19, 1941.
24. Ibid.
25. *New York Times*, April 20, 1941, 21; Ulric Bell to Hugh Moore, April 7, 1941, folder 20, box 5, Moore Papers; memorandum for Mr. Eichelberger, undated, folder: Memos and Office Correspondence, box 19, Eichelberger Papers; Eichelberger, *Organizing for Peace*, 131.
26. Dinner meeting, Century Club, April 22, 1941, folder 1, box 51, FFF Papers.
27. Wayne S. Cole, *Charles A. Lindbergh and the Battle against American Intervention in World War II* (New York: Harcourt Brace Jovanovich, 1974), 123; *New York Times*, April 24, 1941, 12; "America First?" by James Warburg, April 24, 1941, folder 15, box 19, FFF Papers.
28. "America First?" by James Warburg; Henry Hobson to Peter Cusick, April 26, 1941, folder 15, box 19, FFF Papers.
29. Cull, *Selling War*, 119–120.
30. Harold L. Ickes, *The Secret Diary of Harold L. Ickes: The Lowering Clouds 1939–1941* (New York: Simon and Schuster, 1955), 497–500, 507; Chadwin, *Hawks of World War II*, 201–203; Francis Miller to Henry Wallace, April 11, 1941, folder: Corres. and Papers re: Meeting Held by V. Pres. Henry Wallace to Discuss Aims of National Efforts, May 3, 1941, box 27, Miller Papers; Ulric Bell to Henry A. Wallace, April 11, 1941, folder: Corres. and Papers re: Meeting Held by V. Pres. Henry A. Wallace to Discuss American Aims and Future Policies, June 23, 1941, box 27, Miller Papers; press release, May 28, 1941, folder 9, box 45, Robert G. Spivack Papers, Library of Congress (hereafter Spivack Papers).
31. Chadwin, *Hawks of World War II*, 234–236; Eichelberger notes on correspondence with Roosevelt, June 12, 1941, folder: Roosevelt FD, box 49, Eichelberger Papers; James P. Warburg, *The Long Road Home: The Autobiography of a Maverick* (Garden City, NY: Doubleday, 1964), 187.
32. Franklin Roosevelt to Lowell Mellett, May 19, 1941, OF 4422, Roosevelt Papers; Ickes, *Secret Diary of Harold L. Ickes,* 519.
33. Adlai Stevenson to Ulric Bell, August 1, 1941, folder 11, box 18, FFF Papers.
34. Rex Stout interviewing Ulric Bell, October 1, 1941, folder 3, box 4, FFF Papers; Chadwin, *Hawks of World War II*, 190.
35. Fight for Freedom address, April 19, 1941; "What Is the Fight for Freedom?" [1941], folder 7, box 132, Freedom House Archives, Princeton University; memorandum from A. Liddon Graham to Ulric Bell, July 10, 1941, folder 4, box 51, FFF Papers.
36. Chadwin, *Hawks of World War II*, 180–184, 190; "Labor Unions Are Ridiculous!" print ad, undated, folder: Clippings, Pics re: Fight for Freedom Inc., box OV2, Spivack Papers;

Ickes, *Secret Diary of Harold L. Ickes,* 507; executive committee meeting notes, May 8, 1941, folder 1, box 51, FFF Papers.

37. Landon Thomas to Carter Glass (with enclosed letter and *New York Herald-Tribune* clipping), May 28, 1941, folder: Fight for Freedom Com, box 403, Carter Glass Papers, University of Virginia (hereafter Glass Papers); Carter Glass to Landon Thomas, June 9, 1941, folder: Fight for Freedom Com, box 403, Glass Papers.

38. Letter to FFF members, December 1, 1941, folder: Clippings, Pics re: Fight for Freedom Inc., box OV2, Spivack Papers; Walsh, *Our War Too,* 126, 150–151, 186.

39. "What Is the Fight for Freedom?"; *New York Times,* October 20, 1941, 8; *New York Times,* November 12, 1941, 9.

40. Parmar, "'. . . Another Important Group That Needs More Cultivation,'" 717; Chadwin, *Hawks of World War II,* 184–186.

41. Fight for Freedom address, April 19, 1941.

42. Ibid.; "America First?" by James Warburg.

43. Rex Stout, "The New Order and Who Will Run It," April 24, 1941, reprinted in "Our Enemy Is Hitler," FFF pamphlet, folder 1, box 57, FFF Papers.

44. "What Hitlerism Means to the American Businessman," FFF pamphlet, undated, vertical file: Fight for Freedom Inc., Roosevelt Papers.

45. Douglas Miller, "You Can't Do Business with Hitler (A Condensed Version)" (New York: Fight for Freedom, 1941), 13–15 (available in folder 2, box 133, Freedom House Archives); Herbert Agar, "Why We Ought to Go to War," FFF pamphlet, undated, folder 2, box 133, Freedom House Archives.

46. "Business with Hitler?" print ad, undated, box OV1, Spivack Papers. Emphasis in original.

47. "Fourteen Questions and Answers about the Fight for Freedom," undated, folder 6, box 57, FFF Papers.

48. Ibid.

49. Rex Stout interview with Ulric Bell, October 1, 1941, folder 3, box 4, FFF Papers.

50. Agar, "Why We Ought to Go to War."

51. "Fourteen Questions and Answers."

52. Ibid.; "The Fight for Freedom" by the Rt. Rev. Henry Hobson, undated, folder 2, box 56, FFF Papers; Agar, "Why We Ought to Go to War."

53. *New York Times,* November 3, 1941, 40; Fight for Freedom pamphlet, undated, folder 2, box 56, FFF Papers.

54. "America First?" by James Warburg.

55. Agar, "Why We Ought to Go to War."

56. Ibid.; notes on the conversation of May 3rd, folder: Corres. and Papers re: Meeting Held by V. Pres. Henry Wallace to Discuss Aims of National Efforts, May 3, 1941, box 27, Miller Papers.

57. Roger Greene to Ulric Bell, December 2, 1941, folder 8, box 10, FFF Papers. By this point Greene had left the CDAAA and was working for his local FFF chapter in Worcester, Massachusetts.

58. CDAAA minutes of the executive committee, April 25, 1941, folder 19, box 10, CDAAA Papers; Clark Eichelberger to local chapters, May 2, 1941, folder 7, box 34, CDAAA Papers.

59. Clark Eichelberger to local chapters, May 2, 1941; memorandum from Irwin Jaffe, May 1, 1941, folder 4, box 24, FFF Papers; Henry Hobson to Peter Cusick, May 13, 1941, folder 7, box 11, FFF Papers.

60. Clark Eichelberger to Ulric Bell, May 22, 1941, folder 4, box 24, FFF Papers; Hugh Moore to Clark Eichelberger, June 6, 1941, folder: Fight for Freedom, box 46, Eichelberger Papers; memorandum on cooperation between the CDAAA and FFF, June 13, 1941, folder: Fight for Freedom, box 46, Eichelberger Papers; Frederick McKee to Hugh Moore, June 11, 1941, folder 20, box 5, Moore Papers.

61. Memorandum re: Meeting with Fight for Freedom, October 13, 1941, folder 18, box 5, CDAAA Papers; Hugh Moore to Clark Eichelberger, June 6, 1941, folder: Fight for Freedom, box 46, Eichelberger Papers; FFF executive committee luncheon, August 25, 1941, folder 1, box 51, FFF Papers.

62. Press release, June 2, 1941, folder 12, box 8, CDAAA Papers; Christopher Emmet to Ulric Bell, July 31, 1941, folder 4, box 24, FFF Papers; Ulric Bell to FFF members, August 15, 1941, folder 5, box 24, FFF Papers.

63. Memorandum from A. Liddon Graham to Ulric Bell, July 2, 1941, folder 2, box 4, FFF Papers; Clark Eichelberger to Ulric Bell, July 9, 1941, folder 4, box 24, FFF Papers.

64. Memorandum from A. Liddon Graham to Ulric Bell, July 10, 1941, folder 4, box 51, FFF Papers; Herbert Agar memorandum, July 10, 1941, folder 6, box 57, FFF Papers; Hugh Moore to Clark Eichelberger, June 6, 1941, folder: Fight for Freedom, box 46, Eichelberger Papers.

65. Memorandum from Ulric Bell to the executive committee, November 7, 1941, folder 4, box 4, FFF Papers; Clark Eichelberger to Tom Finletter, November 26, 1941, folder 24, box 2, CDAAA Papers; Clark Eichelberger to Ulric Bell, August 18, 1941, folder 5, box 24, FFF Papers; Clark Eichelberger to Ulric Bell, December 3, 1941, folder 5, box 24, FFF Papers; Ulric Bell to James Gould, December 3, 1941, folder 5, box 24, FFF Papers.

8. The Battle of the Atlantic from Barbarossa to Pearl Harbor

1. Gallup, *Gallup Poll*, 288, 307, 300, 311.
2. Ibid., 306, 311.
3. Press release, June 23, 1941, folder 3, box 56, FFF Papers.
4. Robert G. Spivack, letter to the city editor, *New York Times,* June 25, 1941, folder 21, box 15, FFF Papers.
5. Press release, June 23, 1941; Clark Eichelberger to "Friends," June 24, 1941, folder 8, box 34, CDAAA Papers.
6. Clark Eichelberger to CDAAA chapters, August 9, 1941, folder 10, box 34, CDAAA Papers.
7. Chadwin, *Hawks of World War II*, 247; Ulric Bell to Clifford T. McAvoy, July 26, 1941, folder: Fight for Freedom, box 382, Glass Papers; memorandum to chapter heads, October 30, 1941, folder 5, box 24, FFF Papers; memorandum on communists in America, undated, folder 6, box 25, FFF Papers.
8. Press release, July 3, 1941, folder 9, box 37, CDAAA Papers; *New York Times*, July 3, 1941, 10.
9. Ibid.

10. Press release, July 7, 1941, folder 4, box 56, FFF Papers.
11. Executive committee minutes, July 22, 1941, folder 1, box 51, FFF Papers; *New York Times*, July 20, 1941, 30.
12. Executive committee minutes, July 22, 1941.
13. Dallek, *Franklin D. Roosevelt and American Foreign Policy*, 281–285; Roosevelt, *Public Papers and Addresses*, 1941, 314–315. Also see Theodore Wilson, *The First Summit: Roosevelt and Churchill at Placentia Bay 1941* (London: Macdonald, 1969).
14. Headquarters letter (including headquarters statement), August 16, 1941, folder 29, box 34, CDAAA Papers.
15. Ibid.
16. *New York Times*, August 15, 1941, 4; Langer and Gleason, *Undeclared War, 1940–1941*, 690.
17. Roosevelt, *Public Papers and Addresses*, 1941, 384–392.
18. Headquarters letter, September 6, 1941, folder 29, box 34, CDAAA Papers; press release, September 5, 1941, folder 5, box 56, FFF Papers; *New York Times*, September 13, 1941, 3.
19. Statement of policy, September 16, 1941, folder 11, box 34, CDAAA Papers.
20. Ibid.
21. Clark Eichelberger to Lewis Mumford, July 27, 1941, folder: Mumford Urging Declaration of War, box 48, Eichelberger Papers.
22. Roosevelt, *Public Papers and Addresses*, 1941, 392–397; press release, September 27, 1941, folder 11, box 37, CDAAA Papers.
23. Roosevelt, *Public Papers and Addresses*, 1941, 406–413; *Changing World*, October 1941, 1.
24. *New York Times*, November 14, 1941, 3; Dallek, *Franklin D. Roosevelt and American Foreign Policy*, 292.
25. Henry Hobson, Ulric Bell, and Francis Miller to Carter Glass, August 13, 1941, folder: Fight for Freedom Com, box 403, Glass Papers. In coming out for a declaration of war, Fight for Freedom was in fact beaten to the punch by another citizens' organization, the Associated Leagues for a Declared War. Formed in Westport, Connecticut, in June 1941, the organization issued a few pamphlets and newspaper advertisements but failed to break through on a national scale before the Pearl Harbor attack. See "History and Program of the Leagues for a Declared War," September 15, 1941, folder 11, box 2, FFF Papers.
26. Chadwin, *Hawks of World War II*, 259–260; *New York Times*, October 11, 1941, 22.
27. Clark Eichelberger to Edwin Embree, November 10, 1941, unnamed folder, box 51, Eichelberger Papers; headquarters letter, October 18, 1941, folder 29, box 34, CDAAA Papers; Thomas Power to members of the National Policy Board (and attached statement), November 24, 1941, folder 13, box 34, CDAAA Papers; provisional statement of policy, December 5, 1941, folder 14, box 34, CDAAA Papers. The other five points in the provisional December statement were better team work for domestic defense production; unlimited cooperation with Britain, China, Russia, and governments-in-exile; no agreement with Japan at the expense of China; severance of diplomatic relations with Germany, Italy, and Vichy France; and preparation for future peace on the basis of the Atlantic Charter.
28. Ulric Bell to Cordell Hull (including extract), November 5, 1941, 811.911/299-1/2, decimal file, RG 59, NACP.

29. Clark Eichelberger to chapter representatives, October 28, 1941, folder: Stop Mass Murders, box 49, Eichelberger Papers; memorandum to the president from Lowell Mellett, October 30, 1941, OF 4230, FDR Papers; *New York Times*, November 17, 1941, 7.

30. "Arsenal of Facts on Mass Murders Abroad," November 1941, folder: Stop Mass Murders, box 49, Eichelberger Papers.

31. Christian Gauss et al. to Henry Wallace, June 12, 1941, folder 12, box 19, FFF Papers.

32. Ibid.; Chadwin, *Hawks of World War II*, 213–214.

33. *New York Times*, November 1, 1941, 6; Chadwin, *Hawks of World War II*, 214–215.

34. *New York Times*, September 14, 1941, E2.

35. Ibid; Chadwin, *Hawks of World War II*, 215–217.

36. Executive committee luncheon minutes, August 25, 1941, folder 1, box 51, FFF Papers; Stringfellow Barr et al. to Carter Glass, September 8, 1941, folder: Fight for Freedom, box 382, Glass Papers; headquarters letter, September 6, 1941.

37. Clayton R. Koppes and Gregory D. Black, *Hollywood Goes to War: How Politics, Profits and Propaganda Shaped World War II Movies* (London: I. B. Tauris, 1987), 41–45.

38. Joint press release, August 11, 1941, folder 1, box 25, FFF Papers; executive committee luncheon minutes, August 25, 1941, folder 1, box 51, FFF Papers.

39. Ulric Bell to Cordell Hull, November 3, 1941; Ulric Bell to Cordell Hull, November 10, 1941; Ulric Bell to Cordell Hull, July 21, 1941—all in folder 7, box 12, FFF Papers.

40. *New York Times*, June 27, 1941, 13; *New York Times*, October 4, 1941, 11.

41. *New York Times*, November 1, 1941, 2; *New York Times*, August 31, 1941, 18.

42. Rex Stout, "The New Order and Who Will Run It," April 24, 1941, reprinted in "Our Enemy Is Hitler," FFF pamphlet, folder 1, box 57, FFF Papers; *New York Times*, September 12, 1941, 2.

43. *New York Times*, September 12, 1941, 2; Cole, *America First*, 154.

44. Press release, September 13, 1941, folder 11, box 37, CDAAA Papers; *New York Times*, September 14, 1941, 25.

45. *New York Times*, September 13, 1941, 1; Chadwin, *Hawks of World War II*, 211.

46. Cole, *America First*, 181–187; Frederick McKee to Mrs. Thomas Lamont, December 6, 1941, folder 17: Committee to Defend America by Aiding the Allies 1941, box 21, Lamont Papers.

47. John Balderston to Ulric Bell, June 16, 1941, folder: Correspondence 1941–42, box 1, Balderston Papers; Roger Greene to John Balderston, June 16, 1941, folder: Correspondence 1941–42, box 1, Balderston Papers; Cohen, "Role of Private Groups in the United States," 450.

48. Clark Eichelberger to chapter representatives, July 18, 1941, folder 4, box 24, FFF Papers.

49. Press release, July 26, 1941, folder 9, box 37, CDAAA Papers; Waldo Heinrichs, *Threshold of War: Franklin D. Roosevelt and American Entry into World War II* (Oxford: Oxford University Press, 1988), 133–136; Dallek, *Franklin D. Roosevelt and American Foreign Policy*, 275.

50. Chadwin, *Hawks of World War II*, 255–256.

51. Statement of policy, September 16, 1941, folder 11, box 34, CDAAA Papers; Roger Greene to Stanley Hornbeck, September 23, 1941, folder 774, box 23, Greene Papers; Henry Hobson to Roger Greene, September 27, 1941, folder 1149, box 30, Greene

Papers; Roger Greene to Henry Hobson, October 1, 1941, folder 1150, box 30, Greene Papers.

52. E. Guy Talbott to Cordell Hull, November 27, 1941, 711.94/2499, decimal file, RG 59, NACP; Cohen, "The Role of Private Groups in the United States," 454; provisional statement of policy, December 5, 1941, folder 14, box 34, CDAAA Papers.

53. Headquarters letter, December 5, 1941, folder 29, box 34, CDAAA Papers.

54. *New York Times*, December 8, 1941, 6, 19.

55. Clark Eichelberger to chapter representatives, December 8, 1941, folder 14, box 34, CDAAA Papers; Clark Eichelberger statement, December 8, 1941, folder 14, box 37, CDAAA Papers.

56. Chadwin, *Hawks of World War II*, 264–266.

57. Clark Eichelberger to chapter representatives, December 8, 1941; *New York Times*, December 8, 1941, 19.

Epilogue

1. Clark Eichelberger to Marvin McIntyre, December 10, 1941, box 2, OF 4230, Roosevelt Papers.

2. Roosevelt, *Public Papers and Addresses,* 1941, 425–429; Archibald MacLeish to Marvin McIntyre, December 22, 1941, box 2, OF 4230, Roosevelt Papers. On the Office of Facts and Figures, see Allan M. Winkler, *The Politics of Propaganda: The Office of War Information 1942–1945* (New Haven: Yale University Press, 1978), 22–24.

3. Citizens for Victory press release, December 20, 1941, box 10, Mellett Papers.

4. On Citizens for Victory see Andrew Johnstone, *Dilemmas of Internationalism: The American Association for the United Nations and US Foreign Policy 1941–1948* (Farnham, UK: Ashgate, 2009), 13–28.

5. Also see ibid.

6. Ulric Bell to chapter heads, December 12, 1941, folder 7, box 55, FFF Papers.

7. Ibid.; Chadwin, *Hawks of World War II*, 268; Memorandum Regarding Present Status of Fight for Freedom Committee, December 17, 1941, folder: Fight for Freedom, box 46, Eichelberger Papers.

8. Aaron Levenstein (in collaboration with William Agar), *Freedom's Advocate: A Twenty-Five Year Chronicle* (New York: Viking, 1965), 20–22; Ulric Bell to William Agar (plus enclosed papers), October 23, 1941, folder 2, box 28, FFF Papers.

9. Levenstein, *Freedom's Advocate*, 21. Freedom House still exists as an "independent watchdog organization dedicated to the expansion of freedom around the world." See http://www.freedomhouse.org.

10. John W. Masland, "Attitudes and Activities of the Organized 'Peace' Pressure Groups, 1920–1941," March 29, 1943, 32, folder 286: Foreign Policy, Public Opinion On, 1931–43, box 65, Cordell Hull Papers, Library of Congress, Washington, DC. Masland, a professor of political science at Stanford University, worked for the Department of State in 1942 and 1943.

11. Ibid., 22–26.

12. Ibid., 29.

13. Harry Price to E. Snell Hall, September 1, 1942, folder: ACNPJA Ending, box 16, ACNPJA Papers; Harry Price to Sidney Gamble, September 1, 1942, folder: ACNPJA Ending, box 16, ACNPJA Papers.

14. Franklin Roosevelt to Ulric Bell, January 1, 1942, PPF 2409, Roosevelt Papers.

15. Michael S. Sherry, *In the Shadow of War: The United States since the 1930s* (New Haven: Yale University Press, 1995), 54.

16. Chadwin, *Hawks of World War II*, 267; Winkler, *Politics of Propaganda*, 27; Warburg, *Long Road Home* 189–192; Miller, *Man from the Valley*, 105–107.

17. *New York Times*, January 18, 1960, 27. For detail on Bell's wartime experience in Hollywood, see Koppes and Black, *Hollywood Goes to War*.

18. Chadwin, *Hawks of World War II*, 267; Browder and Smith, *Independent*, 163–174; *New York Times*, March 29, 1947, 15; Cohen, *Chinese Connection* 243, 300.

19. Chadwin, *Hawks of World War II*, 267; Cohen, *Chinese Connection,* 243; Johnson, *William Allen White's America*, 558–576; *New York Times*, February 11, 1983, B5.

20. Harley Notter, *Postwar Foreign Policy Preparation 1939–1945* (Washington, DC: Department of State, 1949), 108–114; Andrew Johnstone, "Americans Disunited: Americans United for World Organization and the Triumph of Internationalism," *Journal of American Studies* 44 (2010): 1–18.

21. On the subsequent Cold War implications of this outlook, see John Fousek, *To Lead the Free World: American Cultural Nationalism and the Cultural Roots of the Cold War* (Chapel Hill: University of North Carolina Press, 2000).

22. Luce, "American Century," 65.

Bibliography

Manuscripts

Baker Library Historical Collections, Harvard Business School
  John Price Jones Company
  Thomas W. Lamont
Butler Library, Columbia University
  Carnegie Endowment for International Peace
  James T. Shotwell
Houghton Library, Harvard University
  American Committee for Non-Participation in Japanese Aggression
  Roger S. Greene
Library of Congress, Washington, DC.
  John Balderston
  Cordell Hull
  Robert G. Spivack
  Henry L. Stimson Diaries
  Henry L. Stimson Papers
  Clarence Streit
  William Allen White
Seeley G. Mudd Manuscript Library, Princeton University
  Committee to Defend America by Aiding the Allies
  Fight for Freedom
  Freedom House
  Hugh Moore Fund
  Adlai Stevenson
National Archives, College Park, Maryland
  U.S. State Department Records (RG 59)
New York Public Library, New York
  Clark Eichelberger

Franklin D. Roosevelt Library, Hyde Park, New York
  Lowell Mellett
  R. Walton Moore
  Henry Morgenthau
  Franklin D. Roosevelt
Albert and Shirley Small Special Collections Library, University of Virginia
  Carter Glass
  Francis Pickens Miller

Published Primary Sources

Cantril, Hadley, ed. *Public Opinion 1935–1946*. Princeton: Princeton University Press, 1951.
Gallup, George. *The Gallup Poll, 1935–1971*. New York: Random House, 1972.
Kimball, Warren, ed. *Churchill and Roosevelt: The Complete Correspondence*. Vol. 1. Princeton: Princeton University Press, 1984.
Lindbergh, Charles A. *The Wartime Journals of Charles A. Lindbergh*. New York: Harcourt Brace Jovanovich, 1970.
Notter, Harley. *Postwar Foreign Policy Preparation 1939–1945*. Washington, DC: Department of State, 1949.
Roosevelt, Elliott, ed. FDR. *His Personal Letters, 1928–1945*. Vol. 2. London: Duell, Sloan and Pearce, 1950.
Roosevelt, Franklin D. *The Public Papers and Addresses of Franklin D. Roosevelt*. 1928–1936, 5 Vols. Edited by Samuel I. Rosenman. New York: Random House, 1938.
——. *The Public Papers and Addresses of Franklin D. Roosevelt*. 1937–1940, 4 Vols. Edited by Samuel I. Rosenman. London: Macmillan: 1941.
——. *The Public Papers and Addresses of Franklin D. Roosevelt*. 1941–1945, 4 Vols. Edited by Samuel I. Rosenman. New York: Harper, 1950.
United States Department of State. *Peace and War: United States Foreign Policy, 1931–1941*. Washington, DC: U.S. Department of State, 1943.

Secondary Sources

Accinelli, Robert D. "Militant Internationalists: The League of Nations Association, the Peace Movement, and U.S. Foreign Policy 1934–1938." *Diplomatic History* 4 (1980): 19–38.
Acheson, Dean. *Present at the Creation*. London: Hamish Hamilton, 1969.
Adler, Selig. *The Isolationist Impulse*. New York: Abelard-Schuman, 1957.
Agar, Herbert. *Britain Alone*. London: Bodley Head, 1972.
Akami, Tomoko. *Internationalizing the Pacific: the United States, Japan and the Institute of Pacific Relations in War and Peace, 1919–1945*. London: Routledge, 2002.
Akio, Tsuchida. "China's 'Public Diplomacy' toward the United States before Pearl Harbor." *Journal of American-East Asian Relations* 17 (2010): 35–55.
Alexander, Charles. *Nationalism in American Thought 1930–1945*. Chicago: Rand McNally, 1969.
Almond, Gabriel A. *The American People and Foreign Policy*. New York: Harcourt, Brace, 1950.
Alonso, Harriet Hyman. "The Transformation of Robert E. Sherwood from Pacifist to Interventionist." *Peace and Change* 32 (2007): 467–498.

Bailey, Thomas A. *The Man in the Street: The Impact of American Public Opinion on Foreign Policy.* New York: Macmillan, 1948.

Bennett, M. Todd. *One World, Big Screen: Hollywood, the Allies and World War II.* Chapel Hill: University of North Carolina Press, 2012.

Bernhard, Nancy. *U.S. Television News and Cold War Propaganda, 1947–1960.* Cambridge: Cambridge University Press, 1999.

Blum, John Morton. *Years of Urgency 1938–1941: From the Morgenthau Diaries.* Boston: Houghton Mifflin, 1965.

Bodnar, John. *The "Good War" in American Memory.* Baltimore: Johns Hopkins University Press, 2010.

Borg, Dorothy, and Shumpei Okamoto, eds. *Pearl Harbor as History: Japanese American Relations 1931–1941.* New York: Columbia University Press, 1973.

Brewer, Susan A. *Why America Fights: Patriotism and War Propaganda from the Philippines to Iraq.* Oxford: Oxford University Press, 2009.

Browder, Robert P., and Thomas C. Smith. *Independent: A Biography of Lewis W. Douglas.* New York: Knopf, 1986.

Buell, Raymond Leslie. *Isolated America.* New York: Knopf, 1940.

Burns, James MacGregor. *Roosevelt: The Soldier of Freedom.* New York: Harcourt Brace Jovanovich, 1970.

Butler, Nicholas Murray. "A Brief Review of Thirty-five Years of Service Toward Developing International Understanding." *International Conciliation* 417 (1946): 17–39.

Casey, Steven. "The Campaign to Sell a Harsh Peace for Germany to the American Public, 1944–48," *History* 90 (2005): 262–292.

———. *Cautious Crusade: Franklin D. Roosevelt, American Public Opinion, and the War against Nazi Germany.* Oxford: Oxford University Press, 2001.

Carew, Michael G., *The Power to Persuade: FDR, the Newsmagazines, and Going to War, 1939–1941.* Lanham, MD: University Press of America, 2005.

Chadwin, Mark L. *The Hawks of World War II.* Chapel Hill: University of North Carolina Press, 1968.

Chatfield, Charles. *The American Peace Movement: Ideals and Activism.* New York: Twayne, 1992.

Clavadetscher, Carl Julius. "An Analysis of the Rhetoric of the Committee to Defend America by Aiding the Allies." PhD diss., University of Oregon, 1973.

Clifford, J. Garry, and Samuel R. Spencer, Jr. *The First Peacetime Draft.* Lawrence: University Press of Kansas, 1986.

Cohen, Bernard C. *The Public's Impact on Foreign Policy.* Boston: Little, Brown, 1973.

Cohen, Warren I., *The Chinese Connection: Roger S. Greene, Thomas W. Lamont, George S. Sokolsky, and American-East Asian Relations.* New York: Columbia University Press, 1978.

Cole, Wayne S. *America First.* Madison: University of Wisconsin Press, 1953.

———. *Charles A. Lindbergh and the Battle against American Intervention in World War II.* New York: Harcourt Brace Jovanovich, 1974.

———. *Roosevelt and the Isolationists.* Lincoln: University of Nebraska Press, 1983.

Commission to Study the Organisation of Peace. *Building Peace: Reports of the Commission to Study the Organisation of Peace 1939–1972.* Metuchen, NJ: Scarecrow Press, 1973.

Craft, Stephen G. "Peacemakers in China: American Missionaries and the Sino-Japanese War, 1937–1941." *Journal of Church and State* 41 (1999): 575–591.

Cull, Nicholas J. *Selling War: The British Propaganda Campaign against American "Neutrality" in World War II*. Oxford: Oxford University Press, 1996.

Dallek, Robert. *Franklin D Roosevelt and American Foreign Policy, 1932–1945*. Oxford: Oxford University Press, 1995.

Davenport, Marcia. *Too Strong for Fantasy*. London: Collins, 1968.

DeConde, Alexander, Richard Dean Burns, and Fredrik Logevall, eds. *Encyclopedia of American Foreign Policy*. Vol. 2. New York: Scribner, 2002.

Divine, Robert A. *The Illusion of Neutrality*. Chicago: University of Chicago Press, 1962.

———. *The Reluctant Belligerent*. New York: Wiley, 1965.

———. *Second Chance: The Triumph of Internationalism in America during World War II*. New York: Atheneum, 1967.

Doenecke, Justus D. *Storm on the Horizon: The Challenge to American Intervention, 1939–1941*. Lanham, MD: Rowman and Littlefield, 2000.

Donahoe, Bernard F. *Private Plans and Public Dangers*. Notre Dame: University of Notre Dame, 1965.

Dunn, Susan. *1940: FDR, Willkie, Lindbergh, Hitler—The Election amid the Storm*. New Haven: Yale University Press, 2013.

Edwards, Mark. "'God Has Chosen Us': Re-Membering Christian Realism, Rescuing Christendom, and the Contest of Responsibilities during the Cold War." *Diplomatic History* 33 (2009): 67–94.

Eichelberger, Clark M. *Organizing for Peace*. New York: Harper and Row, 1977.

Engelbrecht, Helmuth Carol, and Frank Cleary Hanighen, *Merchants of Death: A Study of the International Armament Industry*. London: Routledge, 1934.

Fairbanks, Douglas Jr. *The Salad Days*. London: Collins, 1988.

Feis, Herbert. *The Road to Pearl Harbor*. New York: Atheneum, 1965.

Fousek, John. *To Lead the Free World: American Cultural Nationalism and the Cultural Roots of the Cold War*. Chapel Hill: University of North Carolina Press, 2000.

Friedman, Donald J. *The Road from Isolation: The Campaign of the American Committee for Non-Participation in Japan Aggression, 1938–1941*. Cambridge, MA: Harvard University Press, 1970.

Fullilove, Michael. *Rendezvous with Destiny: How Franklin D. Roosevelt and Five Extraordinary Men Took America into the War and into the World*. New York: Penguin, 2013.

Garlid, George. "Minneapolis Unit of the Committee to Defend America by Aiding the Allies." *Minnesota History* 41 (1969): 267–283.

Goodhart, Philip. *Fifty Ships That Saved the World: The Foundation of the Anglo-American Alliance*. London: Heinemann, 1965.

Haynes, John Earl, and Harvey Klehr. *Venona: Decoding Soviet Espionage in America*. New Haven: Yale University Press, 1999.

Hearden, Patrick J. *Roosevelt Confronts Hitler: America's Entry into World War II*. DeKalb: Northern Illinois University Press, 1987.

Heinrichs, Waldo. *Threshold of War: Franklin D. Roosevelt and American Entry into World War II*. Oxford: Oxford University Press, 1988.

Heinrichs, Waldo. "Waldo H. Heinrichs, George D. Aiken, and the Lend Lease Debate of 1941." *Vermont History* 69 (2001): 267–283.

Hershberg, James. *James B. Conant: Harvard to Hiroshima and the Making of the Nuclear Age*. Stanford: Stanford University Press, 1993.

Herzstein, Robert E. *Henry R. Luce, Time, and the American Crusade in China.* Cambridge: Cambridge University Press, 2005.

——. *Roosevelt and Hitler: Prelude to War.* New York: Paragon House, 1989.

Hillmann, Robert P. "Quincy Wright and the Commission to Study the Organization of Peace." *Global Governance* 4 (1998): 485–499.

Hixson, Walter L. *The Myth of American Diplomacy: National Identity and U.S. Foreign Policy.* New Haven: Yale University Press, 2008.

Hoenicke Moore, Michaela. *Know Your Enemy: The American Debate on Nazism, 1933–1945.* Cambridge: Cambridge University Press, 2010.

Hogan, Michael, and Thomas Paterson, eds. *Explaining the History of American Foreign Relations.* Cambridge: Cambridge University Press, 1991.

Holsti, Ole R. *Public Opinion and American Foreign Policy.* Ann Arbor: University of Michigan, 2005.

Hoover, Herbert. *Freedom Betrayed: Herbert Hoover's Secret History of the Second World War and Its Aftermath.* Edited with an introduction by George H. Nash. Stanford: Hoover Institution Press, 2011.

Hull, Cordell. *The Memoirs of Cordell Hull.* Vol. 1. New York: Macmillan, 1948.

Ickes, Harold L. *The Secret Diary of Harold L. Ickes: The Lowering Clouds 1939–1941.* New York: Simon and Schuster, 1955.

Johnson, Walter. *The Battle against Isolation.* Chicago: Chicago University Press, 1944.

——, ed. *Selected Letters of William Allen White* New York: Henry Holt, 1947.

——. *William Allen White's America.* New York: Henry Holt, 1947.

Johnstone, Andrew. "Americans Disunited: Americans United for World Organization and the Triumph of Internationalism." *Journal of American Studies* 44 (2010): 1–18.

——. *Dilemmas of Internationalism: The American Association for the United Nations and U.S. Foreign Policy 1941–1948.* Farnham, UK: Ashgate, 2009.

——. "Isolationism and Internationalism in American Foreign Relations." *Journal of Transatlantic Studies* 9 (2011): 7–20.

——. "Shaping our Post-war Foreign Policy: The Carnegie Endowment for International Peace and the Promotion of the United Nations Organisation during World War II." *Global Society* 28 (2014): 24–39.

Johnstone, Andrew, and Helen Laville, eds. *The U.S. Public and American Foreign Policy.* London: Routledge, 2010.

Jonas, Manfred. *Isolationism in America, 1935–1941.* Ithaca: Cornell University Press, 1966.

Josephson, Harold. *James T. Shotwell and the Rise of Internationalism in America.* Rutherford, NJ: Fairleigh Dickinson Press, 1975.

Kennan, George. *American Diplomacy, 1900–1950.* London: Secker and Warburg, 1952.

Ketchum, Richard M. *The Borrowed Years, 1938–1941: America on the Way to War.* New York: Random House, 1989.

Kimball, Warren F. "Franklin D. Roosevelt and World War II." *Presidential Studies Quarterly* 34 (2004): 83–99.

——. *The Juggler: Franklin Roosevelt as Wartime Statesman.* Princeton: Princeton University Press, 1991.

——. *The Most Unsordid Act: Lend-Lease 1939–1941.* Baltimore: Johns Hopkins University Press, 1969.

Koppes, Clayton R., and Gregory D. Black. *Hollywood Goes to War: How Politics, Profits and Propaganda Shaped World War II Movies.* London: I.B. Tauris, 1987.

Kuehl, Warren, F., ed. *Biographical Dictionary of Internationalists.* Westport, CT: Greenwood Press, 1983.

———. "Concepts of Internationalism in History." *Peace and Change* 11 (1986): 1–10.

Kuehl, Warren F., and Lynne K. Dunn. *Keeping the Covenant: American Internationalists and the League of Nations, 1920–1939.* Kent, OH: Kent State University Press, 1997.

Langer, William L., and S. Everett Gleason. *The Challenge to Isolation.* New York: Harper, 1952.

———. *The Undeclared War: 1940–1941.* New York: Harper, 1953.

Laurie, Clayton D. *The Propaganda Warriors: America's Crusade against Nazi Germany.* Lawrence: University Press of Kansas, 1996.

Laville, Helen, and Hugh Wilford, eds. *The U.S. Government, Citizen Groups and the Cold War.* London: Routledge, 2006.

Leigh, Michael. *Mobilizing Consent: Public Opinion and American Foreign Policy, 1937–1947.* Westport. CT: Greenwood Press, 1976.

Levenstein, Aaron (in collaboration with William Agar). *Freedom's Advocate: A Twenty-Five Year Chronicle.* New York: Viking Press, 1965.

Levering, Ralph B. *The Public and American Foreign Policy 1918–1978.* New York: Morrow, 1978.

Lowenthal, Mark M. "Roosevelt and the Coming of the War: The Search for United States Policy 1937–42." *Journal of Contemporary History* 16 (1981): 413–440.

Mahl, Thomas E. *Desperate Deception: British Covert Operations in the United States, 1939–44.* Washington, DC: Brassey's, 1998.

Marchand, Roland. *Creating the Corporate Soul: The Rise of Public Relations and Corporate Imagery in American Big Business.* Berkeley: University of California Press, 1998.

Marks, Frederick W. III. *Wind over Sand: The Diplomacy of Franklin Roosevelt.* Athens: University of Georgia Press, 1988.

Masland, John W. "Commercial Influence upon American Far Eastern Policy, 1937–1941." *Pacific Historical Review* 11 (1942): 281–299.

———. "Missionary Influence upon American Far Eastern Policy." *Pacific Historical Review* 10 (1941): 279–296.

———. "The 'Peace' Groups Join Battle." *Public Opinion Quarterly* 4 (1940): 664–673.

———. "Pressure Groups and American Foreign Policy." *Public Opinion Quarterly* 6 (1942): 115–122.

McBane, Richard L. "The Crisis in the White Committee." *Midcontinent American Studies Journal* 4 (1963): 28–38.

Miller, Douglas. *You Can't Do Business with Hitler.* Boston: Little, Brown, 1941.

Miller, Francis P. *Man from the Valley: Memoirs of a 20th-Century Virginian.* Chapel Hill: University of North Carolina Press, 1971

Moe, Richard. *Roosevelt's Second Act: The Election of 1940 and the Politics of War.* Oxford: Oxford University Press, 2013.

Moser, John E. "'Gigantic Engines of Propaganda': The 1941 Senate Investigation of Hollywood." *Historian* 63 (2001): 731–752.

Muresianu, John M. *War of Ideas: American Intellectuals and the World Crisis, 1938–1945.* New York: Garland, 1988.

Namikas, Lise. "The Committee to Defend America and the Debate between Internationalists and Interventionists, 1939–1941." *Historian* 61 (1999): 843–863.

Neal, Steve. *Dark Horse: A Biography of Wendell Willkie.* Garden City, NY: Doubleday, 1984.

Olsen, Lynne. *Those Angry Days: Roosevelt, Lindbergh, and America's Fight over World War II, 1939–1941.* New York: Random House, 2013.

Osgood, Kenneth, and Andrew K. Frank, eds. *Selling War in a Media Age: The Presidency and Public Opinion in the American Century.* Gainesville: University Press of Florida, 2010.

Park, Tae Jin. "Guiding Public Opinion on the Far Eastern Crisis: The American State Department and Propaganda on the Sino-Japanese Conflict." *Diplomacy and Statecraft* 22 (2011): 388–407.

Parmar, Inderjeet. "'. . . Another Important Group That Needs More Cultivation': The Council on Foreign Relations and the Mobilization of Black Americans for Interventionism, 1939–1941." *Ethnic and Racial Studies* 27 (2004): 710–731.

Paton-Walsh, Margaret. *Our War Too: American Women against the Axis.* Lawrence: University Press of Kansas, 2002.

———. "Women's Organizations, U.S. Foreign Policy, and the Far Eastern Crisis, 1937–1941." *Pacific Historical Review* 70 (2001): 601–626.

Perkins, Frances. *The Roosevelt I Knew.* London: Hammond, 1948.

Peters, Charles. *Five Days in Philadelphia: 1940, Wendell Willkie, and the Political Convention That Freed FDR to Win World War II.* New York: PublicAffairs, 2005.

Platt, Rorin M. *Virginia in Foreign Affairs, 1933–1941.* Lanham, MD: University Press of America, 1991.

Preston, Andrew. *Sword of the Spirit, Shield of Faith: Religion in American War and Diplomacy.* New York: Knopf, 2012.

Rauch, Basil. *Roosevelt: From Munich to Pearl Harbor.* New York: Creative Age Press, 1950.

Reynolds, David. *The Creation of the Anglo-American Alliance 1937–41: A Study in Competitive Co-operation.* London: Europa, 1981.

———. *From Munich to Pearl Harbor: Roosevelt's America and the Origins of the Second World War.* Chicago: Ivan R. Dee, 2001.

Rofe, J. Simon. *Franklin Roosevelt's Foreign Policy and the Welles Mission.* New York: Palgrave, 2007.

Rosenau, James N. *Public Opinion and Foreign Policy: An Operational Formulation.* New York: Random House, 1961.

Rosenberg, Emily S. *A Date Which Will Live: Pearl Harbor in American Memory.* Durham, NC: Duke University Press, 2003.

Rosenman, Samuel I. *Working with Roosevelt.* London: Harper, 1952.

Sarles, Ruth. *A Story of America First: The Men and Women Who Opposed U.S. Intervention in World War II.* Westport, CT: Praeger, 2003.

Schmitz, David F. *The Triumph of Internationalism: Franklin D. Roosevelt and a World in Crisis, 1933–1941.* Washington, DC: Potomac, 2007.

Schneider, James C. *Should America Go to War?* Chapel Hill: University of North Carolina Press, 1989.

Schwar, Jane Harriet Dashiell. "Interventionist Propaganda and Pressure Groups in the United States, 1937–1941." PhD diss., Ohio State University, 1973.

Sherry, Michael S. *In the Shadow of War.* New Haven: Yale University Press, 1995.

Sherwood, Robert E. *Roosevelt and Hopkins.* New York: Harper, 1948.

Shogan, Robert. *Hard Bargain: How FDR Twisted Churchill's Arm, Evaded the Law, and Changed the Role of the American Presidency.* New York: Scribner, 1995.

Shotwell, James T. *The Autobiography of James T. Shotwell.* Indianapolis: Bobbs-Merrill, 1961.

Small, Melvin. *Democracy and Diplomacy: The Impact of Domestic Politics on U.S. Foreign Policy, 1789–1994.* Baltimore: Johns Hopkins University Press, 1996.

——, ed. *Public Opinion and Historians: Interdisciplinary Perspectives.* Detroit: Wayne State University Press, 1970.

Sniegoski, Stephen John. "The Intellectual Wellsprings of American World War II Interventionism, 1939–1941." PhD diss., University of Maryland, 1977.

Sobel, Robert. *The Origins of Interventionism: The United States and the Russo-Finnish War.* New York: Bookman, 1960.

Steele, Richard W. "The Great Debate: Roosevelt, the Media and the Coming of the War, 1940–41." *Journal of American History* 71 (1984): 69–92.

——. "Preparing the Public for War: Efforts to Establish a National Propaganda Agency, 1940–1941." *American Historical Review* 75 (1970): 1640–1653.

——. *Propaganda in an Open Society: The Roosevelt Administration and the Media, 1933–1941.* Westport, CT: Greenwood Press, 1985.

Stettinius, Edward R. *Lend-Lease: Weapon for Victory.* New York: Macmillan, 1944.

Stimson, Henry L., and McGeorge Bundy. *On Active Service in Peace and War.* New York: Harper, 1948.

Streit, Clarence, K., *Union Now: The Proposal for Inter-Democracy Federal Union* [shorter version]. New York: Harper, 1940.

Sun, Youli. *China and the Origins of the Pacific War, 1931–1941.* London: Macmillan, 1993.

Tansill, Charles C. *Back Door to War.* Chicago: Regnery, 1952.

Tierney, Dominic. *FDR and the Spanish Civil War: Neutrality and Commitment in the Struggle That Divided America.* Durham, NC: Duke University Press, 2007.

Thompson. John A. "Another Look at the Downfall of 'Fortress America.'" *Journal of American Studies* 26 (1992): 393–408.

——. "Conceptions of National Security and American Entry into World War II." *Diplomacy and Statecraft* 16 (2005): 671–697.

——. "The Exaggeration of American Vulnerability: The Anatomy of a Tradition." *Diplomatic History* 16 (1992): 23–43.

Thompson, Robert Smith. *A Time for War: Franklin D. Roosevelt and the Path to Pearl Harbor.* New York: Prentice Hall, 1991.

Throntveit, Trygve. "A Strange Fate: Quincy Wright and the Trans-war Trajectory of Wilsonian Internationalism." *White House Studies* 10 (2011): 361–377.

De Tocqueville, Alexis. *Democracy in America.* Translated by George Lawrence. London: Fontana, 1994.

Tuttle Jr., William M. "Aid-to-the-Allies Short-of-War versus American Intervention, 1940: A Reappraisal of William Allen White's Leadership." *Journal of American History* 56 (1970): 840–858.

Utley, Jonathan G. "Diplomacy in a Democracy: The United States and Japan, 1937–1941." *World Affairs* 139 (1976): 130–140.

——. *Going to War with Japan, 1937–1941.* New York: Fordham University Press, 2005.

Varg, Paul A. *Missionaries, Chinese, and Diplomats: The American Protestant Missionary Movement in China, 1890–1952.* Princeton: Princeton University Press, 1958.

Wala, Michael. "Advocating Belligerency: Organized Interventionism 1939–1941." *Amerikastudien—American Studies* 38 (1993): 49–59.

———. *The Council on Foreign Relations and American Foreign Policy in the Early Cold War.* Providence, RI: Berghahn Books, 1994.

———. "Selling War and Selling Peace: The Non-Partisan Committee for Peace, the Committee to Defend America, and the Committee for the Marshall Plan." *Amerikastudien—American Studies* 30 (1985): 91–105.

Warburg, James P. *Foreign Policy Begins at Home.* New York: Harcourt, Brace, 1944.

———. *The Long Road Home.* Garden City, NY: Doubleday, 1964.

———. *Our War and Our Peace.* New York: Farrar and Rinehart, 1941.

Warren, Frank A. *Noble Abstractions: American Liberal Intellectuals and World War II.* Columbus: Ohio State University Press, 1999.

West, Philip. *Yenching University and Sino-Western Relations, 1916–1952.* Cambridge, MA: Harvard University Press, 1976.

Westbrook, Robert B., *Why We Fought: Forging American Obligations in World War II.* Washington, DC: Smithsonian, 2004.

White, William A. *The Autobiography of William Allen White.* New York: Macmillan, 1946.

Wilson, Theodore. *The First Summit: Roosevelt and Churchill at Placentia Bay 1941.* London: Macdonald, 1969.

Winkler, Allan M. *The Politics of Propaganda: The Office of War Information 1942–1945.* New Haven: Yale University Press, 1978.

Index

Acheson, Dean, 96–97, 180
Agar, Herbert, 116, 124, 127, 143, 146–50, 152, 158–59, 175, 179; and the Century Group, 92–93, 105–6; and the destroyer-bases exchange, 96–97; origins of FFF, 137–38
Agar, William, 106, 174, 175
Allen, Robert, 139, 159, 179
Alsop, Joseph, 93
America First Committee, 12, 91, 109, 111, 118, 128–29, 131, 139, 141, 142, 149, 151–53, 173, 176, 177; and Congress, 164–66; and Lend-Lease, 124, 125, 126; origins, 102–4; and public debate (fall 1941), 166–69
American Association for the United Nations, 175, 180
American Association of University Women, 25, 40, 62
American Committee for Non-Participation in Japanese Aggression, 3–4; assessment of, 176–78; becomes largely dormant, 88; and Chinese communism, 32–33; and connections to China, 20–22; and economic security, 34; on the ending of the Treaty of Commerce and Navigation, 51, 66–69; final appeal, 170; and the National Defense Act, 88; and national security, 31–32; on neutrality revision, 37–39; origins, 19–23; and political freedoms, 32–33; proposed ACNPJA-AUCPE merger, 52–53; and the public, 20, 24–26; and religion, 28–30;

response to war in Europe, 55–56; and the U.S government, 14, 19–20, 26–28
American Defenders of Freedom, 78
American Federation of Labor, 81
American Legion, 82
American Peace Mobilization, 33, 81, 157
American Student Union, 25, 80
Americans United for World Organization, 179
American Union for Concerted Peace Efforts, 4, 36; and the ACNPJA, 25; and economic security, 43–44; on the ending of the Treaty of Commerce and Navigation, 51–52; and national security, 42–43; and neutrality revision (1939), 56–58; origins, 39–41; and political freedoms, 43; proposed ACNPJA-AUCPE merger, 52–53; and relations with government, 45–47; and the Union Now movement, 70–72; winding down with the creation of the CDAAA, 75
American Youth Congress, 40
Angell, Ernest, 174
Astor, Vincent, 134
Atkinson, Henry, 40, 59
Atlantic Charter, 159–60

Balderston, John, 92, 93, 104, 138, 169; newsletter controversy, 99–102, 109
Barkley, Alben W., 127
Baruch, Bernard, 134